Explore th

NELLES

G000153545

PRAGUE

CZECH REPUBLIC

Authors:
Hana Černá, Bernd F. Gruschwitz, Marton Radkai,
Hans-Horst Skupy, Zdeněk Zofka

An Up-to-date travel guide with 162 color photos
and 17 maps

Second Revised Edition
1999

Dear Reader,

Being up-to-date is the main goal of the Nelles series. To achieve it, we have a net-work of far-flung correspondents who keep us abreast of the latest developments in the travel scene, and our cartographers always make sure that maps and texts are adjusted to each other.

Each travel chapter ends with its own list of useful tips, accommodations, restaur-ants, tourist offices, sights. At the end of the book you will find practical information from A to Z. But the travel world is fast moving, and we cannot guarantee that all the contents are always valid. Should you come across a discrepancy, please write us at: Nelles Verlag GmbH, Schleissheimer Str. 371 b, D-80935 München, Germany, Tel: (089) 3571940, Fax: (089) 35719430.

LEGEND

■	Public or Significant Building	Prag	Place Mentioned in Text		National Border
■	Hotel	✳	Place of Interest		Expressway
✝	Church	✈	International Airport		Principal Highway
✡	Synagogue	● 10 ●	Distance in Kilometres		Main Road
	Pedestrian Zone	6 E 94	Route Number		Other Road
M	Metro	P	Parking		Railway

PRAGUE –
Czech Republic
© Nelles Verlag GmbH, 80935 München
   All rights reserved

Second Revised Edition 1999
ISBN 3-88618-907-4
Printed in Slovenia

Publisher:	Günter Nelles	**Color Separation:**	Priegnitz, Munich
Project Editor:	Bernd F. Gruschwitz	**Maps:**	Nelles Verlag GmbH, Munich
Editor-in-Chief:	Berthold Schwarz		with the kind permission of
Photo Editor:	Kirsten Bärmann-Thümmel		Freytag & Berndt, Vienna and RV-Verlag, Munich
English Editor:	Anne Midgette	**Printed by:**	Gorenjski Tisk
Translations:	Ginger Henry-Künzel Mariana Schroeder		

TABLE OF CONTENTS

GUIDELINES

MAP LIST

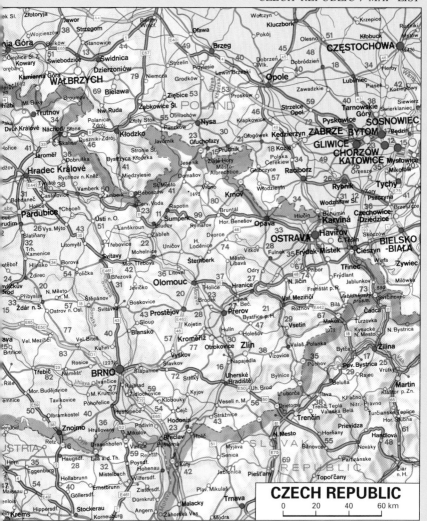

CZECH REPUBLIC
0   20   40   60 km

THE COUNTRY OF THE CZECHS

Prague is "in," Czech is "out;" so, at least, runs conventional wisdom these days. Since the historic changes of 1989, which Czechs tend to refer to time and again as the dawning of a new age, between 40 and 60 million people a year have visited the new republic. More than 90% of these have concentrated mainly or exclusively on Prague.

To whet your appetite for the unique character of this region, take just a few of the distinctive characteristics of Prague and the Czech Republic. One of the first things you notice in every city here, especially in Prague, is that the medieval city plan is still in evidence. Although Czechoslovakia was involved in both of the World Wars in this century, most of its cities remained undamaged; and even Socialism tended to leave the old city centers – though only the city centers! – alone. As a result, these centers still have a certain museum-like quality, preserving something that's long since been lost almost everywhere else. This, together with the (still) reasonable prices of goods and services, is one main reason to visit this country.

While other European metropolises commanded whole kingdoms or empires, Prague has had to fight for its independence against imperial Vienna and politically turbulent Budapest until well into this century. Because of this, the city lacks – with a very few exceptions – the often pompous public architecture of many other European cities. The city, moreover, is small in size, which gives it a familiar, comfortable feeling, even to visitors. Located on a riverbank, and incorporating the river into the cityscape (epitomized by the quintessential Prague landmark, Charles Bridge), the city achieves a romantic quality virtually unparalleled by any other city in Europe. The same can't be said, certainly, for the outskirts where visitors seldom venture: what you find here are the concrete blocks of unrelievedly modern apartment buildings, wholly devoid of charm.

Hardly another country, hardly another city in Europe managed to maintain a multicultural society, which evolved out of a feudal system, as long as this Central European republic. People say that Prague had three cultures: Czech, German and Jewish. Because of the wide territorial range of the Habsburg Empire and the universalism of the Middle Ages, however, three is a modest estimate. The influence of Italy, for example, is present everywhere; and there's ample testimony to a number of other cultures throughout the area, as well, even if it's more in the nature of memorials than of a living present. And this kind of multiculturalism remains a thing of the past; for the stream of international visitors to the city over the last few years is something quite different, even if it's clearly bringing about profound changes here, the extent of which we can't begin to estimate.

Still, these visitors may be providing the impetus for a new cultural flowering. Hardly any other city uses its historic architectural gems for contemporary art events as much as Prague does; and because of the number of visitors, there's always an eager audience. Ultimately, public taste will determine which of many possibilities will become the reality of Prague's future.

GEOGRAPHY

The Czech Republic lies at the heart of Europe, surrounded by Austria (Lower and Upper Austria) to the south, Germany (Bavaria and Saxony) to the west

Preceding pages: On the banks of the Moldau. Street musicians. The unique basalt cliffs near Česká Kamenice. Left: Crossing Charles Bridge toward the Lesser City.

and northwest, Poland (Silesia) to the northeast, and Slovakia to the southeast. It consists of the three historic regions of Bohemia (Čechy) and Moravia (Morava), linked by a central chain of hills called the Bohemian-Moravian Mountains, and a section of what was formerly Silesia. Although the Czech Republic has only been an autonomous Czech national state since 1993, the Czech people can look back on a changing, volatile history going back some 13 centuries. Linguistically, the Czechs belong to the West Slovakian peoples; but culturally they've been influenced at least as strongly by Central Europe (especially the former Austro-Hungarian Empire) and Western Europe as by Eastern Europe.

At certain periods of history the Czechs, particularly residents of Prague, have been at the forefront of events which made their effects felt around the

Above: Prague honors two great astronomers. Right: Church holidays are again observed with due festivities (Ascension Day).

world. Take, for example, the two masters of Czech music, Smetana and Dvořák; Jan Hus or Comenius, Brahe or the astronomer Kepler; literati such as Rilke or Kafka, Jan Neruda or Mucha. And because time behind the impenetrable "Iron Curtain" seemed to stand still, you can still sense here, far better than anywhere else in Europe, the melancholy flavor of past ages and bygone splendors.

Facts and Figures

Measuring 30,757 square miles (78,864 sq. km), the Czech Republic is about as large as Scotland, or almost twice as large as Switzerland. The young country has a population of 10.3 million, about the same as its neighbor, Hungary, although Hungary is larger in area. This means that there are an average of 131 people living on every square kilometer, making the Czech Republic more densely populated than any of its neighbors except Germany. 94.5% of its population is Czech, and 3.1 % Slovak; the rest is made up of a number of minorities including Poles, Germans, Hungarians, Ukrainians, and Russians, as well as some 300,000 Gypsies living on Czech territory. Some three-quarters of the population lives in the cities. Prague (Praha), with 1.2 million inhabitants, is the largest city in the country; it's also, appropriately enough, the capital of the Czech Republic and Bohemia. Moravia's capital, Brno, is the second-largest city, with 388,000 inhabitants.

The Roman Catholic Church has the largest following of any religion, amounting to 46% of the country's population; in addition to this, there are 85,000 Protestants, 54,000 Orthodox, and 3,000 Jews. More than 50% of the citizens are not officially members of any faith. The country's official language is Czech. Many older people, and a number of younger ones, also understand or even

speak a little German. In Prague and other tourist centers, you can easily get by with English.

Bohemia

The western part of the country, Bohemia, is 20,368 square miles (52,764 sq. km). In effect, it's a land basin sloping gradually down to the Elbe, surrounded by a ring of forested hills. On the German side, these are the Bohemian Woods (Šumava), the Upper Palatinate Woods (Český les) the Spruce Mountains and the Ore Mountains (Krušné hory); on the Polish side, the highlands of Jeseník and Beskydy. In the Giant Mountains (Krkonoše) is the 5,239-foot (1,602 m) Sněška, or "Snow Peak," the highest point in the Czech Republic.

Bohemia's major rivers, the Moldau (Vitava), Beraun (Berounka) and Eger (Ohře), flow from the mountains around the edge of the plateau toward the Elbe Basin (Polabí) in the northeast, ultimately flowing into the Elbe (Labe) itself. The Elbe's source is in the Krkonoše; the river flows from here in broad curves through the Elbe basin, finally leaving Bohemia territory at the eastern edge of the Erz Mountains and passing onto Saxon soil to flow through Dresden.

At the bottom of the Elbe basin, a layer of chalk underlies fertile loess soil, where farmers cultivate wheat, barley, sugarbeets, corn, hops, fodder plants, vegetables and fruit. Beneath the so-called Bohemian Massif south of the Elbe, as well as beneath the ring of mountains around Bohemia, is a layer of underground crystal. At higher altitudes, where the soil is poorer, the main crops are rye, oats, and potatoes. Beyond this, Bohemia is known for its beer (Plzeň, Budweis and Prague) and for its heavy industry (in Plzeň, Prague and Kladno). The region's wealth of natural resources have historically proved something of a mixed blessing; extracting them has often meant destroying the "natural" element altogether. South of the Ore Mountains are mines for uranium and silver ore; the Eger mines

17

extract brown coal; Kladno and Plzeň, pit coal. In the northwest, natural mineral springs led to the establishment of a number of world-renowned thermal baths. In the highlands, timbering is a source of revenue; although, according to a 1991 UNO report, some 75% of the woods of what was then Czechoslovakia were ill or dying.

Prague

At the southeastern edge of the Bohemian basin, but centrally located in relation to Bohemia overall, is the city of Prague, the political, economic and cultural center of the whole country. The streets and buildings of Prague's city center are one of the few places in Europe where you can still get a look at medieval urban planning. The city gets its special flair from its narrow, crooked streets, its

Above: The basics of beer: hops then and now. Right: the atomic power plant Kadaň in Northern Bohemia.

towers, gables and bridges, the slightly decaying wood and stone of its buildings and its location beneath the old castle high over the Moldau. Even under socialism, Prague was a powerful magnet for visitors; today, the tourist season lasts virtually year-round. The breathtakingly fast development of the city's market economy has reclothed entire city streets with new façades and display windows, at least up to the second story. Where once there was an atmosphere of pleasant, stagnant melancholy is today dominated by plastic, neon, and advertising.

Moravia

The eastern part of the country, Moravia (with a part of former Silesia), has some 4 million inhabitants, measures 10,177 square miles (26,095 sq. km) in area, and lies between the Bohemia-Moravian Highlands to the west, Jeseník and Beskydy to the north, and the western Beskides and the White Carpathians to the east. To the south, the valley of

March (Morava) extends towards Austria. Moravia is divided into the regions of Northern and Southern Moravia. Its main city, Brno, is at once Moravia's capital and the provincial capital of Southern Moravia. The capital of Northern Moravia, Ostrava, is the third-largest city in the whole Republic with 328,000 inhabitants. Highest elevation here is the mountain of Hrubý Jeseník, measuring 4,875 feet (1,491 m).

The so-called Moravian Gate (Moravská brána), through which the Oder flows northward, helped Moravia develop into a thoroughfare for foreign trade. The "Amber Road," which led through here, linked the Baltic with the Adriatic. The March Valley is particularly fertile, and has made Moravia a wine-growing region.

Politics

The Czech Republic, independent since January 1, 1993, is a parliamentary democracy with an economy that is still in the process of transforming itself from a state-controlled socialist system to a system of privatized market capitalism. Parliament, elected by the people, has 200 members; and there are 81 members in the second chamber of the House of Representatives, the Senate. Both houses together elect the head of state for a five-year term; and according to the new constitution, ratified on December 16, 1993, this head can serve a second term. The president can veto laws passed by the Parliament, and international treaties can only be drawn up with his participation. The constitution expressly provides for referendums as a means for the population to express its political views. Human rights, furthermore, are set forth in the constitution; one of the few relics of the former socialist system is the fact that one of these rights is the right to work.

On January 26, 1993, Václav Havel, the writer who was severely persecuted under the former regime for his battle for human rights, was elected the first President of the Czech Republic, an office he still holds in Spring 1998.

HISTORY

The Beginnings

Some one and a half thousand years ago, Slavic tribes, the ancestors of today's Czechs, penetrated into the territory of Bohemia and Moravia – a nearly uninhabited region. The Marcomanni, a Germanic tribe which had migrated here around 100 AD and fought under their leader Marbod against the Roman Empire, had long since quit the territory. Before them, the area's residents were the Celtic Boi tribe who gave the territory its name: Bohemia derives from Bojohaemum, home of the Boi.

The Romans never managed to conquer Bohemia; the Roman walls only briefly touch the borders of southern Moravia. Its independence of the Roman Empire was to have long-range effects on the country's cultural development: Bohemia and Moravia had none of the developed urban centers or extensive transportation networks which the Romans left behind in other of their territories.

The Slavic tribes were followed by the Avars, a nomadic Turkic people who quickly subdued whole sections of the agricultural Slavic population. This led, in around AD 620, to a Slavic uprising against their oppressors. The Slavs only managed to succeed after they had united under the leadership of the Frankish merchant Samo. The result was a tribal alliance on Bohemian soil. Samo's empire held up for about 30 years and managed to withstand not only the Avars, but also attacks from the Frankish king Dagobert.

Some 150 years later, the Great Moravian Empire developed; this extended into Hungary and present-day Slovakia.

Left: Memorial to Jan Hus, the Bohemian national hero, in Prague.

During the reign of Mojmír I, the first Christian missionaries arrived on the scene from Bavaria and the Salzburg region; they had some success converting a portion of the aristocratic classes. Mojmír's successor, Rostislav, attempting to make his realm strong enough to withstand the influence of the mighty East Frankish Empire, turned to Byzantium; and the missionaries Kyrillos (Cyril) and Methodios arrived from there in 863. These "Slavic apostles" developed "Old Church Slavic" as well as two forms of a new Slavic alphabet: Glagolithic and Cyrillic. The Cyrillic alphabet is, of course, still used in Russia, the Ukraine, Serbia, and Bulgaria.

Methodios baptized the Bohemian prince Bořivoj, who was still regarded as a vassal of the Moravian Empire. As the Hungarians began to move westwards at the turn of the 10th century, however, the Bohemian princes took advantage of the situation to free themselves from their subordination to the Moravian Empire altogether. Seeking aid from the Franks, they swore allegiance to the East Frankish king Arnulf in 895. The move Westward went hand in hand with a religious shift toward Rome. Followers of the "Slavic Apostles" were persecuted, while new missionaries arrived from Bavaria.

In 907, the Hungarians attacked the Great Moravian Empire and wiped it out. In the wars for power which ensued, the Přemyslid family gained the upper hand. Their first historically documented leader was the above-mentioned Prince Bořivoj.

One of his descendants, Prince Wenceslas (Václav), was murdered in battle by his brother Boleslav. Wenceslas, who was later canonized, is the patron saint of Bohemia, something commemorated by the statue of him in Prague's Wenceslas Square. But the horrible conflicts, which wiped out entire families of aristocrats, continued.

In order to come out on top in all these bitter battles, the Přemyslids turned to the

the spiritual authority of the Pope and the secular authority of the Emperor.

Because the Holy Roman Emperors were trying to cover their backs, the Přemyslids were able to secure their power over their Slavic rivals; in return, the Bohemian lords stood by the German rulers when they were in need. But the Germans were not ungrateful: in 1086, Emperor Henry IV named Vratislav II King of Bohemia as a gesture of thanks for having supported him against the Pope. Similarly, in 1158 Emperor Frederick Barbarossa named Duke Vladislav II King in thanks for his having taken part in a campaign against Italy. And Otakar I also received this title in 1189 for helping the Emperor out of financial difficulties.

In the Golden Bull of Sicily of 1212, Frederick II finally established that the kingdom of Bohemia was to be hereditary. A few decades later, the King of Bohemia was made an Elector, with the right to take part in the election of the Holy Roman Emperor. In the meantime, the Přemyslids had become firmly integrated into the European nobility, and, as a result of tactical marriages, had achieved considerable territorial gains and hereditary rights.

Holy Roman Empire to secure their might: Prince Vladivoj had Emperor Henry II confirm his position in the year 1002. From then on, Bohemia was regarded as a part of the Germanic kingdom of the Holy Roman Empire.

In the Holy Roman Empire

While Bohemia was seen as a part of the Empire after 1002, it certainly wasn't regarded as more than a marginal possession. The king never performed the traditional ceremony of riding around the land before taking possession; there were still tributes to be paid, and the Přemyslids were still obliged to muster armies. Bohemia did not, in short, become "part of Germany"; rather, it was a part of an empire which, based on medieval concepts of universality, was supposed to embrace all of the Christian world, under

The Přemyslid Otakar II, for example, married Margarete of Babenberg and thereby received the duchy of Austria. Otakar, known as the "King of Iron and Gold" because of his great wealth and power, even dared to aspire to the crown of the Holy Roman Empire itself. Here, however, he ran up against the joint resistance of the rest of the Empire's aristocracy, and was finally defeated in the 1278 Battle on the March Field by Rudolph of Habsburg. Rudolph had already grabbed the Duchy of Austria for himself two years earlier, but he guaranteed Otakar's heirs the right to continue in the position of Electors; Otakar himself had fallen on the field of battle.

Under Otakar II, the "expansion of the country," the systematic colonization of

Above: Boleslav murders his brother Wenceslas. Right: Rudolph of Hapsburg before the corpse of Otokar II. Far right: Charles IV.

border territories by German settlers summoned to the country by the Bohemian king because of their sophisticated agricultural techniques, had reached its height. To make resettlement a more attractive proposition, the new arrivals were granted greater freedoms, which were soon enough also extended to Bohemian peasants. A number of cities were founded during this period, all according to German law and with German settlers.

In 1306, the male line of the Přemyslids died out. In the resulting fight for succession, Johann of Luxemburg, the husband of the Přemyslid Elizabeth, emerged the victor. Their son Charles IV ultimately became German King and Holy Roman Emperor; under him, Bohemia saw one of its greatest flowerings, and Prague became the capital of the Holy Roman Empire. Charles (1316-1378) supported the rebuilding of the city (under the supervision of Peter Parler) and founded the first university of the German Empire. The Bishopric of Prague became an archdiocese. The

"lands of the Bohemian Crown," established by law in a constitutional document of 1348, included not only Bohemia and the margravate of Moravia, but also the Silesian duchies as well as Upper and Lower Lusatia.

As early as the beginning of the 15th century, long before the days of Martin Luther, Bohemia saw the dawning of a movement that demanded that the church reform and completely renounce all secular authority. Spiritual leader of this movement was the preacher and university professor Jan Hus. In 1414, after King Sigismund had assured him a safe-conduct, he accepted an invitation to the Council of Constance, where he was to defend his beliefs. Instead of this, however, he was subjected to an inquisition, condemned as a heretic, and burned at the stake on July 6, 1415.

The death of the leader, however, did not diminish the ardor of his followers, the Hussites; soon enough, they had won over a majority of Bohemia's Czech-speaking population. The movement was

23

supported by the dawning of a national consciousness or identity; and attempts to suppress the Hussites went awry.

The church and the Emperor therefore had no choice but to negotiate with the Hussites, which they did at the Council of Basel, beginning in 1431. They were only able to reach an accord after the Hussites had defeated the radicals in their own ranks, the Taborites, at the Battle of Lipany. In the "Compacts of Iglau" of July 5, 1436, King and Council officially recognized the Hussite confession as an autonomous branch of the Roman faith.

The Pope, however, was loath to accept this new situation, and "heretical" Bohemia therefore remained hotly disputed, particularly after the Hussite nobility dared to crown as King their close ally Jiří of Podiebrad. After his death, the Bohemian crown went to the Polish line of the Jagiellos. In 1485, the Catholic and Hussite rulers concluded the Religious Peace of Kuttenberg (today Kutná Hora), and Bohemia became an island of religious tolerance.

Soon enough, however, new conflicts broke out, this time between the urban and rural classes; these were set to rest in the St. Wenceslas Treaty of 1517. The cities renounced a part of their privileges; but the nobility had to accept the presence of city representatives in the country's parliaments. Thus Bohemia came to have a form of representational government, similar to those in the surrounding countries, in which the King had to share his power with the aristocracy and the patrician city residents in the state parliament.

Under the Habsburgs

In the summer of 1526, the Bohemian and Polish King Ludwik, who was also King of Hungary under the name Lajos I,

Above: Jan Hus at the stake (woodcut of 1558). Above right: Ferdinand I (mosaic after a painting by Titian). Right: The Prague Defenestration as painted by Vaclav Brozik, 1889.

24

fell in the Battle of Mohács against the Turks. The Ottoman advance forced the Bohemian aristocracy to rethink their position vis-à-vis the kingdom: a strong king should be able to repulse the Turkish advance through the Danube plains and Moravia. The Bohemian Parliament therefore elected the Austrian Habsburg Archduke Ferdinand to be the new King of Bohemia.

Ferdinand I, also King of Hungary, consolidated his power by building up a strong bureaucracy and holding the cities' influence in check. He also set the Counter-Reformation into motion: court and administrative positions were generally filled by Catholics; members of the radical Hussite movement "Bohemian Brothers" were persecuted; and Jesuits were brought into the country.

In the meantime, the Reformation was in full swing throughout the Empire, and when Ferdinand and his brother, Emperor Charles V, took to the field against the Schmalkaldian Alliance of Protestant nobles, the Bohemian aristocrats refused their assistance. After their victory over the Protestants in 1547, Ferdinand moved on to Prague to punish his recalcitrant Bohemians. After a huge trial, high members of the aristocracy were made examples of and punished, while insubordinate patricians lost their privileges and saw the confiscation of their goods and revenues.

Under Ferdinand's successors, the nobility was able to regain its authority. Power clashes within the house of Habsburg, as well as rebellions within the Protestant Hungarian aristocracy, encouraged the Bohemians to step up their claims for more power vis-à-vis the King. Protestant nobles in Germany egged the Bohemians on to open rebellion against the House of Habsburg. A relatively harmless dispute about the building of Protestant houses of worship on Church property led in 1618 to the "Prague Defenstration" which sparked off the Thirty Years' War: outraged representatives of the non-Catholic nobility forced their way into Prague Castle and

25

threw the King's representatives out of the window.

In the wake of this rather symbolic act came real rebellion. The Bohemian nobility declared Ferdinand II deposed, and elected Frederick of the Palatinate their new King. They hoped for support from Protestants from the Holy Roman Empire and the rest of Europe, but in vain. Their armies were defeated in the Battle of the White Mountain near Prague in 1620; and the "winter king" Frederick fled after a reign of only six months. Unable to deny themselves the pleasure of a merciless war trial, the Habsburgs had 27 leaders of the rebellion executed on Prague's Old City Ring on June 21, 1621. This defeat marked the end of the autonomy of Bohemia. With the "New State Order" of 1627, which granted (Catholic)

Above: Execution of Protestant rebels in 1621, from a contemporary flyer. Right: František Palacký. Far right: Rioting in Prague, June, 1848.

spiritual authorities places in Parliament by taking some seats away from the cities, the kingdom became the property of the House of Habsburg. Tens of thousands of Czechs who weren't prepared to convert left the country. The hopes of these "exiles" centered briefly on the Bohemian general Albrecht von Waldstein; at Ferdinand II's command, however, he was murdered in Eger in 1634.

Czech historians describe the next few decades as *temno*, the time of darkness. The population had shrunk by one-third, the economy was in awful shape, and the peasants, above all, suffered terribly from ever-increasing hardship. They expressed their rage in a series of heartfelt but ineffective revolts.

Economic improvement didn't begin to dawn until the 18th century. Tangible improvements in the quality of life came from a number of sources: the reforms of the "enlightened" monarchs Maria Theresa (1740-1780) and Joseph II (1780-1790); the development of the school system and institution of mandatory schooling (1774), the abolition of serfdom (1781), and the judicial reforms of 1787, which eliminated torture and the death penalty. And, while it didn't quite bring about equality of the various religious confessions, the Tolerance Edict of 1781 did legally put a stop to the thereto common practices of religious persecution.

And yet Czech historians have criticized the rule of the two above-mentioned reformers on the Imperial throne. Maria Theresa abolished the Bohemian Court Chancellery, thereby eradicating the last shreds of Bohemian autonomy. And Joseph II, more on rational than nationalistic grounds, instituted German, instead of Latin, as the official language. This meant that while Czech was taught in elementary schools, admission to any higher institution of learning depended on one's mastery of the German language.

The dispute about language led to a development which Czech history books term the "National Renaissance of the Czech Nation." Spokesman of the Czech revival was the historian František Palacký, who published the first volume of his *History of Bohemia* in 1836. In the revolution of 1848, which also swept the Habsburg Empire, the Czechs called for a Federalistic restructuring of the country. Palacký turned down an invitation to take part in the Parliament at St. Paul's Church in Frankfurt, which was the first attempt to form a democratic German state. Instead, as a kind of counterweight to this German national convention, a "Slavic Congress" was held in Prague. During this phase, pan-Slavic thinking became an important element of the Czech national consciousness.

At the congress, however, there was already disagreement within the Czech national movement, which divided into a moderate, conservative faction of "Old Czechs," led by Panacký, who weren't overly opposed to remaining within the Habsburg Empire, and a radical, more liberal party of "Young Czechs." In the elections to the Bohemian Parliament after 1861, which were legally restricted, both parties were able to take seats in Parliament.

The Czechs' growing self-confidence was supported by the success of industrialism in the country. This was true above all of heavy industry: the Škoda plant in Plzeň became the most important armaments industry in the monarchy. Economic and social changes were reflected in the range of political parties. When the first general elections to Parliament were held in 1907, Social Democrats and Agrarians were the strongest Czech parties.

Yet social conflicts were overshadowed by national ones: the Czech Social Democrats refused to integrate with the Austrian mother party. Too late, efforts were made to bring about negotiations between the countries. The "Moravian Settlement" of 1905, which served to ensure that no single ethnic group could outvote a local minority, was a model piece of legislation; yet it could not prevent the collapse of the multi-ethnic country.

The First Czech Republic

With the beginning of World War I, pressure on the Czech national opposition increased: it was under surveillance from the secret police, something that led to imprisonments and sentences of death. Many members of the opposition left the country, including the leader of the small "Realist party," Tomáš G. Masaryk. It was during this exile that the idea formed of creating a joint country together with the neighboring land of Slovakia, which had been under Hungarian rule for centuries.

Masaryk pulled diplomatic strings and sought support from the Allies. In this, he had considerable success, in part because he was able to point to Czech and Slovak combat against the Central Powers in the war. As early as 1915, whole Czech regiments went over to the Serbs, who were allies of the French; and in Russian prisoner of war camps, Czechs and Slovaks formed a "Czechoslovakian Legion" which was sent in to fight German and Austro-Hungarian troops.

In May, 1918, representatives of the associations of Czechs and Slovaks abroad signed the Treaty of Pittsburgh, agreeing on a united country in which Slovakia was to have its own administration, parliament, and courts. In anticipation of the impending defeat of German and Austro-Hungarian troops, the Czecho-Slovakian Republic was declared on October 28, 1918. A few weeks later, Tomáš G. Masaryk was elected the country's first President.

Thus was born a new, multi-ethnic country which encompassed not only Bohemia, Moravia and Slovakia, but also

Right: Tomáš G. Masaryk, President of the first Czech Republic.

the Těšín regions and the Carpathian territory of the Ukraine. In addition to 6.8 million Czechs and 2 million Slovaks, there were 3.2 million Germans as well as large Hungarian, Polish, and Ruthenian minorities in the country's territory. Both Germans and Hungarians protested vehemently against being thus incorporated, so that the Republic's boundaries weren't definitively set until the 1919 Treaty of Versailles. While the American President Wilson proclaimed a new European order based on the self-government of peoples and nations, the Germans in northern Bohemia, northern Moravia, and Austrian Silesia, who had declared themselves "Provinces of the German-Austrian State," were bitter at the fact that no referendums were held in an area that had been a German-speaking territory of the Austrian Empire for so long, and their own wishes were not taken into account. This sowed the seeds of a long-term conflict between the main body of Czechs and the country's German population, the Sudeten Germans, which was to ignite later in the century.

In spite of its rough beginning, the new republic developed very well. A constitution was passed in 1920 based on the democratic system of France, with the difference that the President was not elected by the people, but rather by the two houses of Parliament. After the Constitution was passed, the German parties, too, ran for Parliamentary office. The Germans had abandoned their opposition to the idea of the new country, and the "Negativists," who continued to be against the Czechoslovakian nation, were outweighed by the "Activists," who stood for cooperation on a limited basis.

In the 1925 elections, the "Activist" parties (Christian Socialists, Alliance of Farmers and Social Democrats) won three-fourths of the German vote, and thus took part in the government. From 1926 to 1938, the Germans consistently represented in the government. In the

1929 elections, the Activists won 51 of the 65 German parliamentary seats; and it seemed that the German minority was reconciled with the new country. When the Slovakian People's Party entered the government, as well, it even seemed that problems of nationality might be on their way to being solved. This development was doubtless related to the country's flourishing economy: the Republic of Czechoslovakia was among the ten leading industrial nations in the world. The country had modern heavy and consumer goods industries, and its farmers used the very latest agricultural methods. Domestic peace and the playing down of social opposition served the cause of an advanced social policy and a land reform program that provided middle-class farmers with larger acreage.

But minority issues continued to be a nagging problem. The German population was incensed when, in the course of the land reform, the government settled Czech farmers in territories that had previously been purely German. Another move which the Sudeten Germans regarded askance was a Czech language law, another effort to further unify the country, which required that all officials, even in the post office or railway, be conversant in Czech as well as German; they saw this as harsh in light of the fact that the country's administration had for years been entirely in German.

The Slovaks, whose illiteracy rate was nearly 50% in 1918, profited greatly from the quick development of the education system; but they were also at certain disadvantages in the Czech-dominated state. The independent Parliament which they had been promised was denied them, and the Slovakian administration was largely staffed with Czech officials, who, furthermore, earned three times more than their Slovak colleagues.

The conflict over nationality broke out anew when the world economic crisis of 1929 made itself felt in the Czechoslova-

kian Republic. This was particularly divisive because the Slovaks and Germans were the hardest hit: of the 800,000 people who were now unemployed, more than 500,000 were German, as many of the most susceptible industries were in the German-speaking territories. The crisis in Czechoslovakia lasted considerably longer than it did in Germany: in 1936 more than half a million Czechoslovakian Germans were still unemployed. The government contributed to their dissatisfaction by sending Czechs in to work provisionally in German territories.

In this situation, the autonomy movements in Slovakia and the Sudeten German regions found tremendous resonance. In 1933, the German gym teacher Konrad Henlein founded the "Sudeten German Home Front" (called the Sudeten German Party after 1935), which demanded first autonomy, then annexation to the German Empire. In the local elections of 1938, this party received nearly 90% of the German vote; the "activist" parties were routed.

In 1938, Hitler, who had been in power in Germany since 1933, came into the picture. After the *Anschluss*, or annexation, of Austria, he demanded "self-government" for the Sudeten Germans. Czechoslovakia came increasingly under international pressure. Because of its alliance with France and the "little entente" with Yugoslavia, the Czechs has lulled themselves into a false sense of security. And yet Edvard Beneš, who had replaced Masaryk as President in 1935, had cemented a military alliance with the Soviet Union, which had encountered vehement resistance in Czechoslovakia's military circles.

Egged on by Hitler, the Sudeten Germans provoked conflicts with Czech security forces, which led to the Czechs' imposing a state of emergency. The Sudeten German Party was proscribed;

Above: Chamberlain, Daladier, Hitler, Mussolini and Count Ciano in Munich, September 1938. Right: Reichs Protector von Neurath and Emil Hácha.

Henlein fled to the German Reich. In light of Hitler's threats of war, the English Prime Minister, Neville Chamberlain, tried to bring about some kind of reconciliation. Shortly before the expiration of an ultimatum from Hitler, Mussolini entered the game. On September 29, 1938, the English, French, Italian and German heads of state met in Munich and negotiated a dubious solution: to turn Czechoslovakia's German border territories over to the Nazi-governed German Reich. The Czechs themselves were not invited to this Munich Pact.

The Czechoslovakian army, which had prepared for war, retreated. In addition to the Sudeten territories, the Republic had to turn the Těšín region over to Poland, and – after the Vienna Arbitration of November 2, 1938 – the southern Slovakian regions to Hungary. The Czechs, understandably, felt that Europe had betrayed them. President Beneš resigned and emigrated to England. His flight became a symbol of the end of the first Czechoslovakian Republic.

The German Occupation

With President Emil Hácha, a conservative, right-wing government, obedient to Germany, came into power in Czechoslovakia. But this still wasn't enough for Hitler. He urged the Slovaks, who had been promised autonomy by the Czechslovakian Parliament of November 19, 1938, to secede altogether from the nation, which they accordingly did on March 14, 1939. The ensuing crisis and confusion was, for Hitler, a perfect excuse to send German troops in to occupy the rest of Bohemia and Moravia.

The Western powers, who had seen the Munich Accord as a guarantee for the continued existence of the Czechoslovakian Republic, didn't lift a finger against the liquidation of their ally. Slovakia became a German "protected nation" which, governed by the bureaucratic Fascist president Jozef Tiso, achieved some measure of autonomy.

Hitler forced the rest of Bohemia and Moravia into a German "protectorate" which, although it formally had its own government, was *de facto* under the control of the "Imperial Protector" appointed by Hitler. First holder of this office was former Foreign Minister Konstantin Baron von Neurath. Under him, as Secretary of State, was the ambitious and unscrupulous Karl Hermann Frank, a leading member of the Sudeten German Party and a hater of all things Czech.

The Nazis immediately set upon the Czech intelligentsia, subjecting them to a merciless policy of oppression. Hitler saw a harmless student protest in Prague in November, 1939 as an excuse to close the universities. Nine students, the alleged ringleaders, were shot without trial; over a thousand others were deported to the concentration camp in Oranienburg.

The protectorate became a key provider of armaments to the Germans: while the disarmament of regular Czechoslovakian troops provided enough

weapons for 22 German divisions. In addition, the protectorate produced large amounts of coal, iron, and steel, while its resources of manganese were also of strategic significance as raw materials for the Third Reich. The highly-developed armaments industries, notably the Skoda plants in Plzeň and the weapons manufacturers in Brno, was able to fulfill a great portion of the German Army's needs. In 1944, the Czechs delivered 30,000 guns, 11,000 pistols, 3,000 machine guns and hundreds of cannons, trucks, and airplane engines – and all this every month.

The Reich Protector wanted to get the maximum use out of the Czech workers. Wages were raised, unemployment insurance introduced, retirement benefits improved and other social and political improvements made in quick succession. In order to keep the Czech protectorate officials from taking such improvements as a sign of their own success, the department of wages policy was staffed with German officials.

Yet an underground resistance movement did begin to form. In the autumn of 1941, it became known that even the acting Minister President of the protectorate government, General Eliáš, was maintaining contact with the exile government in London. Hitler took this as a reason to send Imperial Protector von Neurath, whom he regarded as too lax, on extended leave. His substitute was the Head of the Reich's Central Security Office, Reinhard Heydrich. The first official action of Hitler's new governor was to arrest the accused Minister President Eliáš in Prague and sentence him to death. He proceeded to impose a state of emergency, and within a few days some 200 people had been sentenced by provisional courts and immediately executed.

On May 27, 1942, parachute troops of the Czech army in exile made an assassination attempt on Heydrich; he died

shortly thereafter. Germany's revenge was swift and ruthless. Not only were hundreds of prisoners immediately shot; the village of Lidice, north of Prague, was razed to the ground, its male residents killed, and the women and children shipped off to concentration camps. All in all, about 30,000 Czechs were victims of political persecution or died in the resistance. Some 200,000 Jews were collected in the "model" concentration camp Theresienstadt and subsequently shipped off to be murdered in Nazi death camps.

The Czech army in exile was on the side of the Allies. On May 5, 1945, shortly after there'd been yet another uprising in Prague against the German occupiers, Czechoslovakia was liberated by the Americans; Russian troops moved in four days later.

Socialist Days

Above: German troops march into Brno, March, 1939. Right: Statue of Gottwald in the Socialist Realist style.

Even before the liberation, the exiled president Beneš had returned to power. After April 5, 1945, the new government met in Košice, in Slovakia, before moving back to Prague on May 10. This government was formed by the parties of the "National Front," i.e. the Popular Socialists, People's and Christian Democrats, and the Communists, who immediately assumed a position of considerable power. Parties that stood farther to the right were forbidden on the grounds of their actual or alleged collaboration with the Germans.

At the end of the war, there were a great many instances of spontaneous Czech revenge on the country's German population. Now, the new government began systematically to expel every German, even those who had remained loyal to Czechoslovakia in 1938, from the country. An estimated 2.5 to 3 million Germans were shipped out, sometimes under conditions that cost many lives. This population "transfer" was approved by a decision at the conference of Potsdam. Even today, the exiles and their descendants, settled in Germany, declare their outrage at the event and angle to have their lands returned to them; their powerful lobby has had unfortunate effects on German-Czech relations, even in the last few years.

Although the bourgeois President Beneš was among the most energetic proponents of the German expulsion, it was the Communists who profited from it the most. The distribution of lands that had become free helped them to cement their support among the general population. And the confiscated factories and plants became government property, something that accelerated the program, introduced in 1945, of nationalizing the economy.

In the still largely free elections of 1946, the Communists were the strongest party in Bohemia and Moravia, with 40% of the vote; from then on, led by Klement Gottwald, they represented the loudest voice in the government. In Slovakia, on the other hand, the newly-founded Democratic Party, which had national

and Catholic leanings, won an absolute majority and took over the government there. In the Government Program of Košice in April, 1945, Gottwald had yielded, due to tactical considerations, to Slovakia's demands for an autonomous parliament and government.

The next goal of the Communists in Prague, therefore, was to get Slovakia over onto their own political track. President Beneš helped them in this by gradually reining in the authority of the Slovakian state government ("Board of Representatives"), so that it was in effect under the control of the Prague Ministry. On November 18, 1947, the Slovakian "Board of Representatives" was reformed by Prague in such a way that the Democratic Party was in the minority.

The last stage in the Communist ascent to power in Czechoslovakia started in February, 1948. It all began with a dispute about the illegal promotion of Communist police officers, a promotion opposed by legal government means by the Popular Socialist Minister of Justice,

Drtina, with the support of the other non-Communist ministers. In response, the Communists mobilized their mass organizations, which put pressure on Beneš with mass demonstrations and warning strikes. When twelve ministers of the governing coalition resigned in protest on February 20, 1948, Beneš, rather than calling new elections as expected, filled the vacant positions with Communist candidates. Beneš resigned shortly thereafter; his successor was Gottwald, who also happened to be Secretary of Czechoslovakia's Communist Party.

The Communists now took every conceivable precaution to secure their power. From then on, at elections, there was only a single ballot with a tremendous Communist majority. Parliament became merely a formal entity, supposedly symbolizing the unity of people and state. Newspapers which were too

Above: Alexander Dubček in the "Prague Spring." Right: Warsaw Pact troops march into Prague, August 21, 1968.

critical of the party were simply forbidden, and opponents of the regime (particularly in military circles, the Catholic Church, and other parties of the "National Front") were persecuted on a large scale, sent off to work camps or sentenced to death.

In 1950 Rudolf Slánský, General Secretary of the Communist Party, initiated a campaign against "nationalistic-bourgeois" dissenters within the party: these included the chairman of the "Council of Representatives," Gustav Husák. In this, Slánský didn't do himself any favors: he later became himself a victim of party "purges" carried out on the Stalinist model.

In restructuring the economy, as well, the Czechoslovakian Communists followed the Soviet model: the agricultural sector was forcibly pressed into collectives, industry nationalized, and heavy industry built up on a massive scale, often at the cost of other sectors. In 1949, the Czechoslovakian Republic entered the Soviet-dominated "Council for Mutual Economic Assistance." In 1955, this was followed by the country's entry into the Warsaw Pact.

When Soviet Party leader Khrushchev revealed the extent of Stalin's crimes in 1956, ushering in the "thaw" in the Soviet Union, Czechoslovakia's Communists hesitated for a long time before turning to move in this new political direction. Not until their Party Convention in 1962 did they approve this change of tactics. The national and Party leader Antonín Novotný, who had come to power in 1957 and thereto been ever faithful to the party line, suddenly changed his tune and became the veritable personification of a convinced anti-Stalinist.

One effect of this new kind of party "cleansing" was the election of Alexander Dubček to the leadership of the Slovakian Communist Party. And when the USSR's course changed yet again two

years later, when Khrushchev was replaced by the faithful Stalinist Brezhnev, the heads of the Czechoslovakian Communist Party were again somewhat slower to change their tack. Novotný, always so loyal to strict Party discipline, protested against Khrushchev's fall from power; he thus managed to lose Brezhnev's sympathy from the start, isolating the country. Meanwhile, calls for reform from those within the party who saw a "Socialist market economy" as the answer to the country's problems grew louder in light of the steady downward trend of the Czechoslovakian economy.

From the Prague Spring to the Velvet Revolution

After the police brutally put down a student demonstration on October 31, 1967, the conflict intensified between loyal Stalinists and reformers in the Czechoslovakian Communist Party. Under increasing pressure, Novotný finally gave up on January 4, 1968. Elected as

his successor in a compromise measure was the head of the Slovakian Communist Party, Alexander Dubček; while his office as State President, which he resigned on March 30, 1968, was filled by General Ludvík Svoboda.

On April 5, the new Party leaders issued an active program which provided for a step-by-step overhaul of the government and economy; Dubček characterized his plan as "Communism with a human face." Press censorship had already been lifted on March 5, making free public discussion possible for the first time. A mood of change came over the entire country. Soon, a few people even ventured to raise their voices to question the overall validity of the Communist Party.

In the Soviet Union and its neighboring "brother countries," leaders feared that this reform movement might burst its banks. After a few threatening gestures and some negotiations which led to nothing, troops from the USSR, Poland, Bulgaria, Hungary, and the German Demo-

cratic Republic marched in and occupied Czechoslovakia on the night of August 21, 1968. The Czechs and Slovaks saw the arrival of the Russian tanks with shock and outrage, and gave passive resistance. The leading reform politicians were arrested and shipped to the USSR.

President Svoboda, who had appealed to the population to keep calm, resisted the attempt to form a new government led by officials more loyal to Moscow. On August 22, the Czechoslovakian Communist Party met in secret and gave a vote of confidence to the politicians who had been arrested. A day later, Svoboda traveled on a "visit of friendship" to Moscow, to discuss "questions of mutual interest to both sides." At his insistence, Dubček and other reformers who had been arrested participated in the negotiations, which seemed equivalent to capitulation.

Above: Memorial for Jan Palach on Wenceslas Square. Above right: Gustav Husák. Right: Michail Gorbachev.

Against resistance from the party and the people, the reforms were gradually abolished over the next few months, and the reform politicians removed from power. A few "realists," including Husák, Černík and Štrougal, let themselves be steered onto an opportunistic course. Nearly half a million members were either turned out of the Communist Party or turned in their Party books of their own accord; 30,000 Czechs and Slovaks left their native land. The student Jan Palach expressed the helplessness of resistance against the invasion, burning himself to death as a gesture of protest on January 16, 1969.

All that remained of the "Prague Spring" was a law about the national organization of the Republic that took effect on January 1, 1969: the Slovaks, at least on paper, were given full equality with the Czechs. On April 17, Dubček had to resign his office in favor of Gustav Husák, who had been in the resistance during World War Two, and been arrested and sentenced in 1951 in the course to Stalinist purges. Now, he became an aid to carrying out Brezhnev's policies.

There ensued a period of "normalization," lasting more than twenty years, during which the country seemed veritably crippled. The regime tried to keep the population happy and quiet with a modest, but apparently stable program of "prosperity." Attempts at open criticism were suppressed, but private life was given little, if any, attention. The Party "dogmatists," who called for reformers to be more severely persecuted, were held in check by the "pragmatists" around Party Head and Head of State Husák and his ministers.

The new Federalist order did little to change the actual centralist practices of the Czech planning authorities. The Slovakian state's authority was limited anew in 1970 – ironically enough, by Husák, the first Slovak to hold the office of President of the Czechoslovakian republic.

Nonetheless, the imbalances between the two parts of the country were gradually being leveled. Not only in industry and agriculture, but also in education, the Slovaks were beginning to catch up.

Overall, however, Czechoslovakia's economic development was stagnating as a consequence of poor planning decisions and a low morale among workers that bordered on sabotage. Two years after the European Security Conference in Helsinki, the opposition in Czechoslovakia took a public stance for the first time. "Charta 77," signed by 257 citizens, including intellectuals and writers such as the playwright Václav Havel, demanded that the human rights promised in Helsinki be extended to Czechs and Slovaks as well. The regime reacted with house-searches, arrests, and other outrages promptly made public by the Western media. As a result, the Communist party's authority gradually dwindled away to nothing.

This process was accelerated by Gorbachev's ascension to power in the Soviet Union. The anti-reformers who had taken power in Prague in 1969 could not support, much less implement, Gorbachèv's programs of *glasnost* and *perestroika*. Even changes in personnel, such as Husák's being replaced as Party Head in 1987 by the colorless Miloš Jakeš, did nothing to alter this. Attempts to restructure the economy, furthermore, showed no significant results, and led to Minister President Štrougal's leaving office and being replaced by Adamec. In spite of the peaceful process of democratization taking place in neighboring countries like Hungary, Poland, and even East Germany, things stayed remarkably quiet in Czechoslovakia for a long time.

It was the violent put-down of a student demonstration in Prague on November 17, 1989 that unleashed the "Velvet Revolution," which within three weeks had swept away the Communist regime. Czechs and Slovaks reacted to the events in Prague with a wave of protest demon-

strations, both spontaneous and organized, openly demanding an end to
Communist rule. The activities in Bohemia and Moravia were coordinated by the
"Citizens' Forum," founded in 1988 and
led by Václav Havel; in Slovakia, they
were headed by a group called "Public
Against Violence," which saw itself as a
collective movement of all opponents of
the regime.

The Soviet Union made it clear that, in
spite of their military presence, they
wouldn't interfere in the domestic affairs
of the Czechoslovakian Republic. The
ruling Communists, therefore, gave way
more and more, and the opposition demanded more and more, so that efforts to
negotiate a compromise at a hastily-or-
ganized "round table" remained fruitless.
In the end, the Communist-dominated
National Assembly not only rendered in-
active the Constitutional clause which

had previously been in effect, about the
leading role of the Communist party, but
even elected Václav Havel the new President on December 29. The path to a new
democracy for Czechoslovakia was clear
at last.

Problems of the Present

Now that they'd come to power, President Havel and other members of the
citizens' reform movement saw their first
and most important task to be that of se-
curing their hard-won democracy both
inside and out. In February, 1990, Czechoslovakia applied to enter the International Monetary Fund and the World
Bank in order to control its problem of
foreign debt. The republic distanced itself from the crumbling East Bloc as
quickly as possible, nullifying its mutual-
aid pact with the Soviet Union and requesting the Red Army to leave the
country. The Warsaw pack dissolved itself on July 1, 1991; in fact, it had by then
already ceased to exist.

Above: During the Velvet Revolution, Novem-
ber, 1989. Right: Václav Havel.

President Havel's motto became "Back to Europe," back into the community of democratic nations. Czechoslovakia, consequently, applied to enter the European Union and NATO; and neighbor and friendship treaties were signed with France and Germany. In the course of these, Václav Havel formally apologized to the Sudeten Germans for their expulsion in 1946/47, a move which was regarded with horror by many of his compatriots. The Sudeten Germans' continued demands for restoration of their property or payment of damages, however, were denied. In light of the difficulties of reorganizing the national economy, the Czechs weren't in a position to make redress, even had they wished to do so.

In the Parliamentary elections of June 1990, which saw a voter turnout of nearly 97%, the citizens' movements which had led the "Velvet Revolution" won in both sections of the country: the "Citizens' Forum" in the Czech areas, "Public against Violence" in the Slovakian ones. Yet soon enough, huge differences of opinion became evident, and problems began to arise.

In Slovakia, a movement began to grow up around the leading politician of "Public against Violence," Minister President Vladimír Mečiar, which, steadily gaining in support, demanded independence for the Eastern part of the country. Dissatisfaction with the Slovakians' political disadvantage was compounded by fears that the region would be marginalized, economically speaking: because of the heavy concentration there of armaments and heavy industries, unemployment in Slovakia was considerably higher than in Bohemia or Moravia. The Czechs tried to pacify the Slovaks by turning various Federal powers over to the states, but to no avail.

In 1992, former Finance Minister Václav Klaus was elected in the Czech part of the country. This meant the rise to

power of a politician who was no longer prepared to compromise with the Slovaks, particularly with regard to economic policies. What began as negotiations between the Czech Václav Klaus and the Slovakian Vladimír Mečiar about a workable program of government rapidly degenerated into negotiations as to how to dissolve the "marriage" between the two regions in "a civilized manner."

After several attempts, the Federal Parliament succeeded in coming up with a constitutional law about the division of the joint nation. Therefore, the separation of the Czech and Slovak Republics on January 1, 1993, was not only peaceful and democratic, but completely legal. There was, however, no popular referendum held to determine the will of the people, even though the constitution of July, 1991, demanded this for all "fundamental decisions about the state." According to opinion polls, even a majority of the Slovak people were against the division.

EXPLORING PRAGUE

CASTLE / HRADČANY
MALÁ STRANA (LESSER CITY)
STARÉ MĚSTO (OLD TOWN)
JEWISH QUARTER (JOSEFOV)
NOVÉ MĚSTO (NEW CITY)

THE CASTLE AND HRADČANY

Standing watch high over the city of Prague, the castle, Hrad, has always been a synonym for whatever secular power happens to be ruling the country at a given time. Counts and margraves, princes and kings, emperors and presidents have governed Bohemia from this fortress, the focal point of the district of Hradčany, though not to be confused with it. Hrad has seen popular heads of state, such as Tomáš G. Masaryk, the founder of the republic in 1918, who was affectionately referred to as *tatíček* (Papa); and it has seen very unpopular ones, such as the imperial governors Martinitz and Slavata, who, three hundred years earlier, were summarily tossed from its windows. Then as now, Prague's castle has served not only as the seat of the secular government, but also as a religious center, as evidenced by St. Vitus's Cathedral and its chapels, or the museum-like St. George's Basilica. Over the last few decades, many of the palaces on the castle grounds have become worthy homes to museums of culture,

Preceding pages: Bridge over the Moldau. Marionettes in front of St. Nicholas Church. Left: Window by Alfons Mucha in St. Vitus's Cathedral.

while the little shops on Golden Lane (*Zlatá ulička*) bustle with thriving, and sometimes dubious, commercial activity.

Constructed in the 9th century, the castle began as a wooden fortress surrounded by earthen bulwarks, and gradually transformed itself to assume the imposing form it has today, an appearance it took on during the reign of Maria Theresa in the 18th century. "I see a ship; its mast is Hradčany...," wrote the poet Vítězslav Nezval (1900-1958).

About three dozen secular and sacred historical sites located within the Prague castle make this the country's most important cultural monument. If you'd like to examine it in depth, allow at least half a day (which doesn't include time for museum visits), and start in the **first castle courtyard**, reached by way of *Hradčanské náměstí* (Castle Square).

The entrance with its magnificent iron grille gate, flanked by two sentries from the castle guard, is adorned with two oversized statues of fighting giants (copies). The original statues were designed in 1769 by Ignaz Platzer the Elder, who also designed the vases and figures around the top of the palace and on the so-called **Matthias Gate** (*Matyášova brana*). The allegorical figures above the gate represent war and peace. The sandstone gate itself was carved in honor of

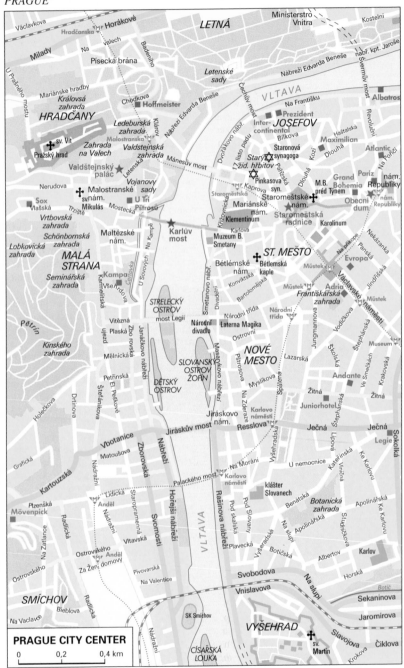

PRAGUE CITY CENTER

0   0,2   0,4 km

King Matthias around 1614. The coats-of-arms symbolize the countries which were at the time part of the Habsburg empire. The Viennese court architect Niccolò Pacassi designed the court of honor, also called the first courtyard. If the flag is flying over the presidential wing, you'll know that the Czech president is there. The changing of the guard takes place every hour on the hour, from 5 a.m. to 11 p.m.; at noon, there's a ceremonial parade as the new guards march in to take up their duties and the old ones retreat.

A small gate leads to the **bastion gardens** (*Zahrada Na baště*). Commissioned by Maria Theresa, Pacassi also created the **second castle courtyard** by filling in the castle moat. Some of the rooms in the surrounding buildings have been converted for state purposes, and are therefore no longer open to the public; among these are the legendary Rudolph's Gallery with its elaborate stucco work and the huge Spanish Hall, 157 feet (48 m) long, 78 feet (24 m) wide and 39 feet (12 m) high. Two fountains and a well are found in the second courtyard: the lion fountain from 1967, the bubbling fountain from 1686, and the draw-well with its handcrafted wrought-iron grille (1702). The **Picture Gallery** (*Obrazárna Pražského hradu*) forms the north side; this building was once used to house the magnificent imperial carriages. Czech art historians lament the fact that all that's left today are fragments of what was once a phenomenal collection of paintings assembled during the reign of Emperor Rudolph II (1575-1611) in the middle of the 17th century, which was later scattered far and wide. Nevertheless, the gallery attempts to present an exhibit of Renaissance art, supplemented by Baroque and Rococo elements. Among the prominent Italian artists represented here are Jacopo and Francesco Bassano, Titian, Jacopo and Domenico Tintoretto as well as Paolo Veronese. A monumental painting by Peter Paul Rubens, *Meeting of the Olympian Gods*, is found in room IV. Paintings by Peter Brandl and portraits by Jan Kupetzky demonstrate the local variant of High Baroque. And statues created in Bohemia by Matthias Braun are representative of Prague's golden age.

The **Chapel of the Holy Rood** (*kaple svatého Kříže*) was designed in the second half of the 18th century by Anselmo Lurago; the decorative figures on the high and the side altars are the work of Ignaz Platzer. The prolific Franz Xaver Palko painted the pictures in this chapel, which houses the cathedral treasury. Remodeled in the mid-19th century, the chapel contains cult objects spanning an entire millennium: relics, shrines, busts, crucifixes, vestments, monstrances, bibles, paintings, plaques, jewels and even gold- and silver-plated weapons.

After the founding of the Czechoslovakian Republic in 1918, archaeologists began excavating within the castle walls. In the **third castle courtyard**, they uncovered early medieval earthen bulwarks as well as fragments of Romanesque and Gothic buildings; these finds are now protected by a cement wall. Dominating not only the third courtyard but the entire city is **St. Vitus's Cathedral** (*chrám svatého Víta*), the pride of the Czech people. The main steeple with its four Renaissance bells is Prague's highest tower, measuring exactly 325.7 feet (99.6 m). The church is also an impressive size: 405 feet (124 m) in length, with a transept 196 feet (60 m) wide, and 108 feet (33 m) high. 28 pillars support the vaulting. The rose window above the west portal is 34 feet (10.4 m) in diameter. The cathedral saw the coronations of the Bohemian kings, as well as their interments; and it was also the repository for the crown jewels. Charles of Luxemburg, later elected King Charles IV, had this Gothic church built on the site of a former Romanesque basilica between 1344 and 1352. After the death of the first

architect, Mathieu de Arras, the cathedral was finally completed by the German architect Peter Parler and his sons around 1420. Bonifatius Wohlmuth added a Renaissance dome to the main steeple in 1554. The busts in the triforium, including those of Charles IV and his four wives as well as the architects Mathieu de Arras and Peter Parler, date from the 14th century. The high altar and several of the 21 chapels are neo-Gothic (built 1868-1875). One of the cathedral's gems is the **Wenceslas Chapel** (*kaple svatého Václava*), built by Peter Parler from 1362 to 1364, in honor of Václav, the patron saint of the Czechs. Even more magnificent than the Passion cycle by an anonymous 14th-century master are the inlays of more than 1,300 semiprecious stones: amethyst, agate and jasper stones were pressed into the wet plaster. Just as in a fairy tale, the crown jewels – the Wen-

ceslas crown, studded with sapphires, emeralds and crystal, from 1346; the Imperial orb and scepter; and the golden sword – are sealed in a treasury with seven locks and seven keys. Each key is safeguarded by one of seven different state institutions, so that access to this priceless treasure is a joint venture in the most literal sense. This, the country's second most important cultural treasure, is only displayed on important state holidays during leap years.

The cathedral houses art from every age. There are some Gothic tombs in the chapels. Johann Fischer von Erlach designed the Baroque silver tomb of St. John of Nepomuk. The organ loft by B. Wohlmuth is in Renaissance style. There are also several works by important Czech artists from between the two World Wars, including Alfons Mucha, Max Švabinský, and Karel Svolinský. Above the Golden Portal on the south side of the cathedral is a restored mosaic of *The Last Judgment* from around 1370, during the reign of Charles IV. The oft-

Above: Prague Castle with St. Vitus's Cathedral, as seen from the Lesser City.

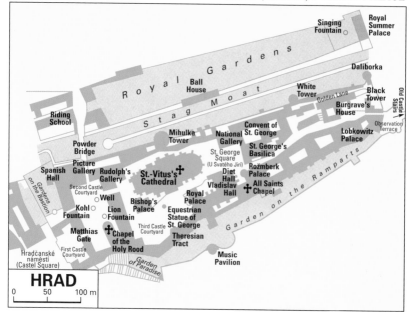

restored equestrian statue of St. George, created by the brothers Georg and Martin Klausenburg (Cluj, Romania), also dates from this epoch. The royal crypt contains the coffin of Charles IV as well as those of many other rulers (though some are merely symbolic). Nestled up against the cathedral is the *Staré proboštství*, the old bishop's residence, which received a Baroque face in the 17th century.

Also located in the third courtyard is the entrance to the President's office. In the former **Royal Palace** (*Královský palác*), which served as the residence until well into the 16th century, the so-called Bohemian Chancellery was the seat of the Habsburg governors. One of the castle's most impressive rooms is found here, the magnificent Vladislav Hall (*Vladislavský sál*), built by Benedikt Ried between 1486 and 1502. It is 203 feet (62 m) long, 52 feet (16 m) wide and 43 feet (13 m) high and bears the name of the Bohemian King Vladislav of the Polish Jagiello dynasty. It is here that the head of state takes the oath of office. The

Czech Parliament meets in the *Stará Sněmovna*, the Old Diet Hall, built 1559-61 by B. Wohlmuth. Leading up to Vladislav Hall, the huge stairway with its late Gothic rib vaulting is truly impressive. Here, too, is All Saints Chapel, rebuilt after a fire in 1541. Chr. Dittmann painted the dozen scenes from the life of the Bohemian medieval national patron Prokop (1669). From here, you can see the Mihulka Tower, a part of the fortress dating from the 15th century and now used for exhibitions.

Just a few steps on you we reach St. George Square (*U svatého Jiří*), flanked by the former Institute of Gentlewomen (*Ústav šlechtičen*) in Rožmberk Palace and the Convent of St. George. The square is dominated by **St. George's Basilica**, one of the oldest structures on the castle grounds – or, for that matter, in the whole city. Although this church was built in the middle of the 12th century, a much smaller one already stood on this site 200 years earlier. Today's basilica, which appears Romanesque, is the result

of restoration done in 1897-1907. The structure exhibits traces of every stylistic period. The early Renaissance portal stems from the workshop of Benedikt Ried; the Baroque facade was added in 1678. František Maximilian Kaňka added the Nepomuk chapel onto the basilica between 1718 and 1722: this chapel's frescoes and altarpiece are by Wenzel Lorenz Reiner; while its statue of Nepomuk was created by Ferdinand Maximilian Brokoff, one of the sculptors responsible for Charles Bridge. The Chapel of St. Ludmila dates from the 13th/14th centuries; the frescoes in the Renaissance vaulting are 16th century.

The Benedictine Convent of St. George is considered to be the oldest in Bohemia; it's said to have been founded in the 10th century. In 1782, it was secularized by Joseph II; thereafter, it occasionally saw use as a barracks. In 1974,

Above: St. George's Basilica. Right: Along Golden Lane and in the "New World."

after extended renovations, it became home to a part of the collection of the **National Gallery** (*Národní galerie*), exhibiting Czech art works from the Gothic period to the Baroque. The early Gothic panel paintings and the medieval Madonnas are of particular interest.

During the 16th century, one of the most important Bohemian aristocratic families, the Lobkowitz family, built a magnificent palace. Today this palace (on Jiřská) serves as a branch of the National Museum, displaying important objects from throughout Czech history which are interesting even to foreign visitors.

Since the 16th century, the former **Burgrave's House** has served a variety of functions. This Renaissance structure has been used as a law court, a residence, and, under the Communist regime, the "House of Czechoslovakian Children." Not far away is the **Black Tower** (*Černá věž*), whose small platform provides a lovely panorama. The other two towers, also the remains of the former fortifications, are the **White Tower** (*Bílá věž*)

and the **Daliborka** (featured in Smetana's opera *Dalibor*). You can descend from the castle by the Black Tower via the **Old Castle Stairs** (*Staré zámecké schody*), but if you do, you'll miss a major attraction: **Golden Lane**, *Zlatá ulička*. The tiny houses directly against the castle wall were built as of the end of the 16th century; today, they harbor flourishing souvenir shops. House 22 was once the home of Franz Kafka.

The castle is surrounded on several sides by well-tended gardens that have only recently been opened to the public. These are lovely oases in the often smog-filled Bohemian capital. The **Paradise Gardens** (*Rajská zahrada*) were documented as early as the 16th century, while the **Garden on the Ramparts** (*Zahrada Na valech*) was laid out during the last century. The most expansive public park, the 16th-century **Royal Gardens** (*Královská zahrada*), contains three buildings with landmark status. The sgraffito-covered **Ball House** (*Míčovna*), built by Bonifatius Wohlmuth 1567-69,

houses Flemish Gobelin tapestries from the 17th century. The **Singing Fountains** (*Zpívající fontána*) were also created during this period, based on a design by Francesco Terzio. The Italian architect Paolo della Stella designed the **Royal Summer Palace** (*Letohrádek*), also known as **Belvedere**, for Anna Jagiellonska, wife of the Habsburg Emperor Ferdinand I. This Renaissance structure, today used for art exhibits, was completed in 1563 by Wohlmuth. The former **Riding School** (*Jízdárna*) has served as a gallery for 20th-century Czech art since the end of the 1940s. It was built at the end of the 17th century by Jean B. Mathey, an architect who was active throughout Bohemia. The Powder Bridge (*Prašný most*) leads over the former Stag Moat (*Jelení příkop*) which served as a barrier between the gardens and the royal game preserve.

A **New World** – this is how the street name *Nový Svět* translates – opens up just a few hundred meters further on. Around 1600, the famous royal astronomer

Tycho Brahe lived in house No. 76 – *U zaetého noha*, to the Golden Griffon – ; The Baroque building next door is the restaurant House of the Golden Pear (*U zlaté hrušky*). Also Baroque is the House of the Golden Plow (*U zlatého pluhu*) from the second half of the 17th century. Finally, there's the house called At the Golden Grape. A monument to Kepler and Tycho Brahe stands on *Parléřova ulice* at Pohořelec.

At *Kanovnická ulice*, you have a choice of two routes through Hradčany. If you go left, you'll pass the Austrian Embassy and the Nepomuk Church (*kostel svatého Jana Nepomuckého*) on the way up to the castle; the right-hand route passes *Loretánské náměstí*.

In 1598, Hradčany became Prague's fourth independent city. In addition to numerous churches, it is dominated by the splendid palaces of wealthy aristocrats from the 16th and 17th centuries.

Above: An up-to-date reflection of a Prague city palace (Tuscany Palace).

The square *Hradčanské náměstí* is surrounded by more than half a dozen magnificent structures. The Schwarzenbergs, one of the wealthiest dynasties in Europe, had two palaces; one of them now houses a **Museum of Military History**. The 16th-century Renaissance structure (it once belonged to the Lobkowitz family) is one of the city's most impressive palaces, not least because of its sgraffito decorations. The interior is also worth a look, as are the displays of weapons and tools of war from over eight centuries and every corner of Europe. The Tuscany Palace (*Toskánský palác*), an early Baroque edifice built in 1690 by Jean B. Mathey, now belongs to the Foreign Ministry. Before 1694, this Burgundian architect had also remodeled the **Archbishop's Palace** (*Arcibiskupský palác*) across the square; the Rococo façade was added (Johann Joseph Wirch) in 1764-65. Every year, on the Thursday before Lent, the Cardinal opens a few of the splendidly decorated rooms, resplendent with paintings, tapestries, Gobelins and

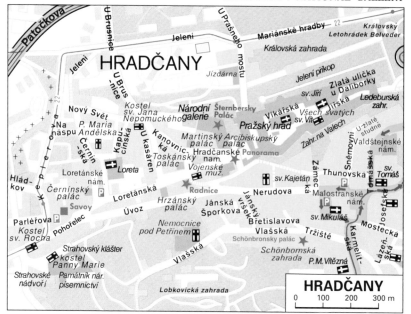

HRADČANY
0   100   200   300 m

porcelain dating from several centuries, as well as frescoes and plaster-work, to the public. The *Martinický palác* is closely linked with the name of Governor Martinitz, who was unceremoniously thrown out of the castle window onto a pile of manure in 1618. This seemingly minor incident led to the disastrous Thirty Years' War. Today, concerts are held in the palace's grand hall. Slightly hidden behind the Archbishop's Palace is the **Sternberg Palace**, once home to the wealthiest family in Bohemia. This splendid palace (built by Alliprandi and Martinelli, 1698-1720) is presently the seat of the administration of the equally splendid fine arts collection of the **National Gallery.** At the beginning of the 1990s, the collections included 400,000 graphic works and drawings, about 14,000 paintings and over 6,000 sculptures; among these are 8,000 works of Oriental art. The National Gallery's collections are world-renowned, even though after the advent of democracy in 1990 some works had to be given back to

their original owners, who had lost them when private property was confiscated after 1945. One strength is Italian art of the 14th to 18th centuries; also notable are the German and Dutch paintings of the 15th and 16th centuries, 16th- and 17th-century Flemish paintings, and French art from the last two centuries.

After taking in all this, the eyes deserve a rest. From the terrace of the castle square you have a lovely view across the spires and rooftops of the Lesser City, the old town and the new town, all the way to the industrialized suburbs. This is surely one of the loveliest panoramas in Prague.

Passing by Hradčany's **Town Hall** (*Radnice*), a Renaissance structure with sgraffito, and the *Hrzánský palác*, which is closed to the public, we continue on toward the quarter of Pohořelec (Place of Fire). The uneven street of Loretánské náměstí is dominated by the ***Černínský palác***, built by Count Czernin around 1669, and repeatedly renovated and expanded until the 1930s. Today this build-

53

ing, 491 feet (150 m) long, houses the Foreign Ministry. The palace has a tragic history as the site of Prague's last defenestration. In 1948, Foreign Minister Jan Masaryk, popular son of the even more popular founder of the Republic, met his death here under mysterious circumstances which remain unexplained to this day. Appropriately enough, there's a ceiling fresco over the stairway, executed in 1718 by Wenzel Lorenz Reiner, called *The Fall of the Titans*.

After a detour to the Capuchin **St. Mary's Church**, housing a lovely nativity scene with life-sized figures, we arrive at the historical pilgrimage church **Loreta**. Christoph and Kilian Ignaz Dientzenhofer designed the Baroque facade in 1720, the statues are by Josef B. Kohl and Andreas Ph. Quittainer. Every half hour since the 17th century, religious melodies have chimed from the steeple. Notable is

Above: Tower of the Loreta church. Right: Golden Prague: the castle at night.

the Casa Santa (G.B. Orsi and A. Allio, 1626-31), in the inner courtyard. In addition to the Baroque Nativity Chapel, the focal point of this church, which was built in 1626 with funds donated by Countess Lobkowitz, is the **Loreto treasure**, housed on the upper floor of the cloister. Most of the sacramental gems and jewels date from the 17th and 18th century; the monstrance, set with over 6,000 diamonds and weighing over 26 pounds (12 kg) is of inestimable value. This gilded silver masterpiece was made in Vienna in 1699.

Once a suburb of Hradčany, **Pohořelec** burned down several times, whence its name (*hořeti* means burn). Nevertheless, several Baroque buildings still remain (*Kučerův palác, Široký dvůr, U zlatého stromu*). The route leads past two churches. **St. Rochus Church** (*kostel svatého Rocha*) was built by Emperor Rudolph II after a plague epidemic in 1612; **Mary's Church** (*kostel Panny Marie*) was constructed on ancient Romanesque foundations.

Strahov Monastery, founded in the 12th century by Premonstratensians, has undergone numerous changes in the years since. Among the most significant were those made by Giovanni Domenico Orsi (1671-79), who, with his **Theological Hall**, created one of the most magnificent rooms in Prague, a city certainly not lacking in architectural splendors. Aside from valuable folios and prints, the library contains huge globes presenting a marvelous image of science in the 17th century. The room was expanded at the end of the 18th century through the addition of the Philosophical Hall, with ceiling frescoes executed by Franz Anton Maulbertsch. The National Museum of Texts contains incunabula and scripts from eight centuries, ranging from early medieval manuscripts to 130,000 works of non-fiction as well as pamphlets and Samisdat (underground) literature of Communist Czechoslovakia.

LESSER CITY / MALÁ STRANA

Even if you only have one day to spend in Prague, don't miss the opportunity to spend a few hours on the other side of the Moldau in the Lesser City. This romantic quarter boasts half a dozen official national cultural monuments; a historic center of Prague, it's said to be the largest urban district bearing landmark status in the world, measuring as it does a total of 1,875 acres (750 hectares) in area. It would be difficult to imagine the unique silhouette of the castle or Hradčany's churches and palaces without all the towers and steeples of the Lesser City.

In brief, the history of this part of the city is as follows: the Lesser City first came to prominence as *Civitas nova Pragensis* after 1257, when the area below the castle was inhabited by German settlers. The first stone bridge connecting the old town with the Lesser City, the now-vanished Judith Bridge, had already been built a century earlier, around 1170. This bridge was washed away in a flood in 1342, to be replaced by a second stone bridge begun in 1357. The newer edifice, also linking the Lesser City with the Old City and New City on the other side of the river, was built by order of Charles IV, but has only borne his name since 1870. In the year 1541, a disastrous fire destroyed a large number of the buildings in the Lesser City; after the quarter was rebuilt, it became, in the 17th century, the district of choice for diplomats and trade missions from around the world. When Joseph II decreed the Lesser City's incorporation into the city of Prague in 1784, the quarter was finally, completely integrated into the capital, administratively as well as emotionally. And since this 18th-century bureaucratic step, in fact, there's been hardly any major new building in the Malá

Left: Picture within a picture on Charles Bridge.

Strana. It looks much as it did during the Baroque era – except, of course, for the traffic!

The Lesser City offers a wealth of treasures to anyone interested in architecture. Wander through its narrow streets one by one, taking time to examine the facades, peer into courtyards, survey quaint, quiet squares, or unwind in one of its terrace-like parks. A hike up to **Petřín** is also worthwhile; this hilly area above the Lesser City, reachable via a cable car, was known for centuries as Mount St. Lawrence. The observation deck shaped like a miniature Eiffel Tower (*rozhledna*), 196 feet (60 m) high, offers a lovely panorama of the surrounding region. Churches and chapels, the Hunger Wall (part of the medieval city fortifications), the pleasure palace Vila Kinských. and the extensive park lands make Petřín a favorite with Prague residents.

Because of the fan-like layout of the Lesser City, it is difficult to recommend one particular route. **Charles Bridge** (*Karlův most*) is a good orientation point. Despite numerous repairs over the past six centuries, this is still one of Prague's most impressive structures.

The first house at the end of the bridge is a Renaissance building dating from the end of the 16th century, which incorporates a 13th-century Romanesque relief. The shorter of the two bridge towers is a remnant of the original Judith Bridge; it dates from the 12th century and is thus one of the city's oldest extant structures – despite the Renaissance dome that was plopped atop it at the end of the 16th century. The taller of the two towers was built under King George of Poděbrady in the year 1464 as a counterpart to the Old City Bridge Tower on the opposite bank. It was re-Gothicized by Josef Mocker from 1872-84. From its gallery, you have a lovely view of the hustle and bustle on the Charles Bridge, and can also survey the city districts on the other side of the Moldau. The **Lesser City Gate** (*Malos-*

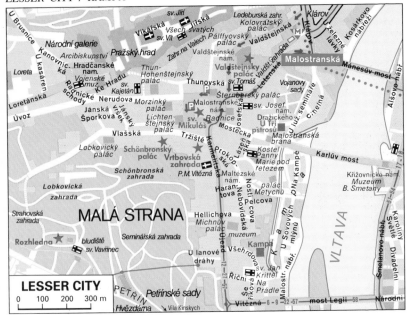

y

transká brána) is Gothic. Some of the coats-of-arms are testimony to the regency of Wenceslas IV at the beginning of the 15th century.

From the bridge, you can see **Kampa Island**. A number of mills used to operate on the banks of this tongue of land, which is divided from the mainland by the narrow Devil's Brook (*Čertovka*). This latter is, in effect, Prague's Grand Canal, lined with two rows of houses to create an idyll that's caused locals to dub this area *Benátky* (Czech for Venice). The island has always been a tranquil oasis for Prague residents. The Kampa ceramics market, was extremely popular at the end of the Middle Ages; but attempts to revive this old tradition in modern times have been rather unsuccessful.

One of the oldest structures in the Lesser City, first mentioned in the 12th century, is **St. John's Church** in *Říční ulice* (River Lane). Its nave dates from the 13th century; the presbytery was not added until 1641-44. A small infirmary and cemetery were also part of the parish. After the secularization, the church became, of all things, a public wash house, and was promptly nicknamed "House of Bleach" (*Na prádle*). In 1935, the church was completely renovated and turned over to the Czechoslovakian Hussite congregation. The courtyard of house No. 437 on *Všehrdova ulice* looks like it could be a set for a film about old Prague.

The **palace** of the **Michna** family (*Michnův palác*) in Újeyd Street, built by Francesco Caratti between 1640 and 1650, is characterized by the clear divisions of its facade. This Late Renaissance structure was used in the 19th century as, among other things, an arsenal. After the Czechoslovakian Republic was founded in 1918, the building came under the direction of the national "Body Fitness Association" Sokol. It now bears the name of the political leader of the "Falcon Federation," Dr. Miroslav Tyrš (*Tyršův dům*).

Right: View of Prague's Lesser City.

Wending your way along Karmelitská, you'll arrive at **Maltese Square**. When the knights of Malta arrived in Bohemia in 1169, they immediately established their headquarters here on *Maltézské náměstí*. The knights of the order of Malta had their own mill on Devil's Brook (*Čertovka*), at house number 489. The palace of the Grand Prior of this order was built by Thomas Haffenecker between 1728 and 1731. Bartolomeo Scotti later made several changes. Adjacent to the monastery is one of the public gardens where open-air concerts of classical music have been held for the past several decades. The **Church of St. Mary under the Chain** (*kostel Panny Marie pod řetezem*) in neighboring Bath Lane (*Lázeňská ulice*) evolved from a Romanesque basilica. The Gothic sections were also integrated into the Baroque remodeling carried out by Carlo Lurago in the middle of the 17th century. In 1660, Count Nostitz had his *Nostický palác* built on Maltese Square based on plans drawn up by Francesco Caratti. The effect of the High Baroque façade is enhanced by the Rococo portal created by Anton Haffenecker (1757). Today, the Netherlands Embassy is housed in the palace, as well as a library. Haffenecker, the father-in-law of Christoph Dientzenhofer, was one of the owners of a house in Nostitz Lane which he himself built in 1682; in 1689, it saw the birth of Christoph's son Kilian Ignaz, who was later to achieve equal fame. The focal point of Maltese Square is a statue of John the Baptist by Ferdinand Maximilian Brokoff.

The **House of Painters** is popular with Prague residents. Built atop a Gothic foundation, this well-preserved Renaissance structure today provides an ideal setting for a wine tavern named after the 16th-century painter Johannes Schütz. The entrance to the birth house of the composer Josef Bohuslav Foerster (1859-1951) is located behind the Baroque portal of the **Palace of Mettych** on *Velkopřevorské náměstí*. The prolific Foerster composed several operas, numerous oratorios, songs, works for

chorus and orchestra, pieces for piano and chamber music.

Before returning to Karmelitská, detour to Josefská. **St. Joseph's Church** (consecrated in 1692) was the Carmelite monastery's first house of worship. Matthäus Wenzel Jäckel, a local sculptor and painter, was responsible for the interior.

In 1720, the architect Franciscus Maximilian Kaňka designed one of the city's loveliest gardens (*Vrtbovská zahrada*), within view of the **Church of the Virgin Victorious** (*Maria Victoria*), for the burgrave Josef Vrtba. Matthias Bernhard Braun and Wenzel Lorenz Reiner added sculptures, vases and frescoes to this masterpiece of landscape gardening. The statues, representing heroes from ancient mythology, confer a kind of Mediterranean atmosphere upon this terraced park. The above-mentioned Baroque church (*kostel Panny Marie Vítězné*) was built by Prague's Lutheran congregation

Above: The Infant Jesus of Prague. Right: Night in the Lesser City.

between 1611 and 1613. Just a decade later, in the course of re-Catholicization, it had to be returned to the Carmelites. In honor of the victory on White Mountain, the church was named Maria Victoria. Peter Brandl created the opulent interior decorations around 1700, after the small wax statue of the **Infant Jesus of Prague** (*Pražské jezulátko*), donated to the Carmelites in 1628, had attained a kind of legendary status among Latin American Catholics as the "*Bambino di Praga.*"

The marketplace (*Tržiště*) was established here as early as the 14th century. It is flanked by several historically important houses, including the **House of the Golden Scale** (*U zlaté váhy*) as well as the **House of the Infant Jesus** (*U Ježíška*). This building with the pious name dates from the second half of the 17th century; its Baroque façade was added in 1704-05. It has particular significance for locals because the historian František Palacký lived here from 1823 to 1825. Amidst the wealth of Renaissance and Baroque buildings around the marketplace, a Classical house dating from around 1812 takes on a special, almost festive appearance. Its core dates back to the Renaissance, but it was later remodeled in Baroque style, as were so many houses on both sides of the Moldau. Clearly the most significant building here, however, is **Schönborn Palace**, completed in 1656, and renovated by Giovanni Santini in 1715. The palace, today home to the US Embassy, has one of the most lovely and well-tended gardens (*Vratislavská zahrada*) of the city. "For reasons of security," only a portion of the gardens are open to the public.

The **Lobkowicz Palace** in Vlach Lane (*Vlašská ulice*) was built by Giovanni B. Alliprandi from 1703 to 1707. Today this magnificent structure is home to the German Embassy. On the sala terrena of the lovely gardens there's stucco work by Tomasso Soldati. The public section of the park commands a lovely view of

Hradčany; the park itself, landscaped in the first half of the 18th century, contains Prague's first alpine garden.

After the beginning of the 16th century, the area around Vlach Lane was inhabited by Italians, whence the street's name: in Czech, *Vlach* means Italian. This densely-populated neighborhood, inhabited mainly by architects, artists and craftsmen, even had its own hospital (designed by Domenico Bossi, 1620), one of the first Baroque buildings in Prague, which became an orphanage after 1804. Around 1664, Santino Bossi built a palace in *Šporkova ulice* for Count Piccolomini; later dubbed **Sporck Palace**, this was expanded in 1730, and also became an orphanage around 1850.

Fronted by a statue of Nepomuk, the **Stonemason House** (*Kameníkův dům*) in John Lane (*Jánská ulice*) presents a picturesque aspect. In 1726, the architect and stonemason Andreas Kranner provided this lovely Renaissance building with its marvelous Rococo facade. On a small rise of land known as John Hill (*Jánský vršek*) stand two beautiful Baroque houses from the early 17th century, facing Nerudova.

Typical of Prague: The **New Castle Stairs** (in Nerudova) leading up to the castle (the sign is confusing) are actually older than the Old Castle Stairs beside the Black Tower (*Černá věž*). The first documentation of **Nerudova** dates from 1278; four centuries later, the stairs were renovated and renamed the New Castle Steps. The first houses along this romantic path were built in the 16th century, if not earlier. Only a few steps away is Nerudova ulice, site of one of Prague's most renowned houses. Originally an early Baroque structure, the legendary **House of Two Suns** was remodeled in 1693 to receive its present appearance. Locals connect the house with the author Jan Neruda (1834-91) whose *Tales of the Lesser City* is a standard work in the literature about fin-de-siècle Prague. The stories have been translated into every major language. In honor of this author, the street was renamed Nerudova ulice. The

1971 winner of the Nobel Prize for literature, the Chilean Pablo Neruda, took his name from the Prague author.

Giovanni Santini, architect of numerous Bohemian structures, created one of his most beautiful works in 1720-25 when he built the **Thun Palace** for Count Kolowrat. Although this building, which today houses the Italian Embassy, is not open to the public, the statues by Matthias B. Braun above the portal give some impression of the grandeur of 18th-century Prague. Across the street, the **Morzin Palace**, constructed for Countess Morzin in the short time of just two years (1713-14), is another proof of Santini's talents. Today housing the Romanian Embassy, the building is ornamented with larger-than-life figures of Moors, featured on the Morzin coat-of-arms and created in the workshop of Ferdinand Maximilian Brokoff. This famous sculptor also crafted the Baroque busts *Day and Night* as well as the depiction of the four regions of the earth that were recognized at that time. Santini lived for two decades in the Valkoun Renaissance house which was remodeled by Christoph Dientzenhofer in 1704 in Baroque style. **The House of the Three Violins** (*U tří housliček*) next door is a favorite subject for photographers; for over a century it belonged to a family of violinmakers. On the other side of the Dientzenhofer house is the **House of the Golden Goblet** (*U zlaté číše*), named in memory of a family of goldsmiths.

Before continuing down to Malostranské náměstí, go over to *Thunovská*. Near the House of the Golden Carp, with its lovely 16th-century Renaissance gable, you can see the quarters of the British Embassy: the **Thun-Hohenstein Palace**. The Salzburg archbishop Guidobald Thun-Hohenstein had this palace expanded in the years after 1659. This is one of two Thun palaces in Prague. One of the Lesser City's most beautiful pa-

Above: House emblem on Nerudova. Right: In the garden of Wallenstein Palace.

laces was built by Ignazio Palliardi in the 1780s for Count Czernin. The palace was later owned by the Kolowrat family. The atmosphere is simply infatuating: across the way is a wing of the Waldstein Palace, and nearby is the palace of the Pálffy family, who once had extensive land holdings in upper Hungary. The Kolowrat gardens in Waldstein Lane (*Valdštejnská ulice*) are considered to be one of the last Baroque parks in Prague (land-scaped around 1780); this fanciful facility even includes a small observation tower. The square *Valdštejnské náměstí* is the site of one of the city's main attractions, the **Wallenstein** (or Waldstein) **Palace**, built 1623-30. In the middle of the tumult of the Thirty Years' War, in which Duke Albrecht von Wallenstein served as an imperial general, the duke commissioned the architects Andrea Spezza, Giovanni Pierroni and Nicola Sebregondi to build him a mighty palace within sight of the castle. The construction of the Wallenstein Palace represented a turning point in the development

of the Lesser City. The middle portal on the front is a part of the former Trčka Palace, the original Renaissance residence which served as the core of this monumental palace. In his delusions of grandeur, Wallenstein had scenes from the Trojan War painted in the sala terrena. As the palace was being built, the splendid gardens (*Valdštejnská zahrada*) were also laid out. Records show that a total of two dozen houses, three large gardens and a brick works had to be razed to make way for the palace and its grounds. The original sculptures, created by Adrian de Vries of Holland, were carried off by the Swedes as part of the spoils of the Thirty Years' War. Today they decorate the park of the Drottningholm Royal Castle near Stockholm, and what you see here in Prague are merely well-made copies.

Passing through *Letenská ulice*, you approach the **Lesser City Ring** (*Malostranské náměstí*). **St. Thomas Church** was a part of the convent of the Augustinians who settled in Bohemia at the end

63

of the 13th century. Their place of worship (*kostel svatého Tomáse*) was renovated in Renaissance style in the late 16th century; between 1723 and 1731, Kilian Ignaz Dientzenhofer bestowed on it the Baroque style seen today. In 1639, two paintings by Peter Paul Rubens – *The Torture of St. Thomas* and *Portrait of St. Augustine* – adorned the main altar; today, these are displayed in the National Gallery in the Sternberg Palace. The interior of the church is also opulent Baroque. The frescoes of Augustine by Wenzel Lorenz Reiner include *The Baptism* and *The Apotheosis of the Saints* Anyone who feels in need of a rest at this point might want to try the dark strong beer served in the monastery's tavern.

Only a streetcar track separates St. Thomas Church from one of the **Lobkowicz Palaces**. This Renaissance structure, later redone in Baroque style, had a

Above: St. Nicholas Church at the heart of the Lesser City. Right: One of the Lesser City's marvellous Renaissance houses.

number of aristocratic owners before it was turned into a school.

The original floor plan of the late Renaissance **Town Hall** (*Radnice*) of the Lesser City, built 1617-22 by Giovanni Bossi, is, despite later renovations, still evident. The stairwell has Rococo sculptures by Ignaz Platzer dating from the second half of the 18th century. At that time, **Lichtenstein Palace**, built by one of the leaders of the Counter-Reformation, was serving as a post office; a century later it was a military command post. Today's classical façade was added to this monumental palace in 1791. The **Sternberg Palace**, built at the end of the 17th century, dominates the north side of the Lesser City Ring. In 1541, the neighboring house, *On the Bastion*, was the starting-place of a catastrophic fire which not only destroyed large sections of the Lesser City within a matter of hours, but also took its toll on Hradčany and even the castle. The late Renaissance palace of the Smiřický family, known as the **Monday House**, served in the 17th century as headquarters for the Bohemian aristocracy's rebellion against the Habsburgs.

The Lesser City is dominated by one of Europe's loveliest buildings, on which a number of first-rate Baroque artists demonstrated their talents: **St. Nicholas Church** (*kostel svatého Mikoláše*), built for the powerful Jesuit order. This church, with its Italian influence, was completed in three phases. Christoph Dientzenhofer began construction in 1704-11. His son Kilian Ignaz added the presbytery and the dome (1737-52) and son-in-law Anselmo Lurago built the steeple in 1755-56. Particularly noteworthy, a true gem of Baroque art, is the 1,500 sq. meter (almost 1/3 of an acre) ceiling fresco, one of the largest on the Continent. Johann Lukas Kracker worked on this painting, depicting the life of St. Nicholas, for almost ten years. Franz Xaver Palko painted most of the altarpieces, while the *Pietá*, the fresco in the cupola and the decoration of the lofts are by Karel Škréta. Ignaz Platzer the Elder as well as Richard and Peter Prachner crafted the statues and pulpit. The Jesuit College next to St. Nicholas Church was built between 1676 and 1690 by the Italian Domenico Orsi. It was disbanded in 1773. The **Column of the Holy Trinity** in front of the church is the work of yet another Italian, Giovanni Alliprandi (1714).

One of the well-preserved Renaissance houses along the Lesser City Ring is the **House of the Golden Lion** (*U zlatého lva*). Today the popular wine restaurant *U mecenáše* (House of the Patron) is housed under the vaulted ceiling of the ground floor, while there are private living quarters upstairs. Dating from 1608, this house is also known as "Trost House" for its one-time owner Wenzel Trost of Tiefenthal. The classical house next door was originally Baroque, built by Christoph Dientzenhofer.

Experts consider the Renaissance **House of the Golden Swan**, dating from

1689 and located on Five Church Square (*Pětikostelní náměstí*), to be the most beautiful patrician house in the Lesser City. Built by the architect Ulrich Avostalis, it was beautifully renovated in the 1950s. The Renaissance **House of the Three Roses** (*U tří růží*) was remodeled in Baroque style. Nearby are two other palaces: the Ledebour Palace, with a Baroque façade by Ignazio Palliardi, and the Auersperg Palace.

Anton Schmidt built a Rococo urban palace for Count **Kaunitz** in Bridge Lane (*Mostecká ulice*) between 1773 and 1775. The statues are the work of Ignaz Platzer. On *Dražického náměstí*, at the Charles University School of Medicine, there's a statue of Saints Cosmas and Damian (1709). Johann Fux, royal supplier of plumes, had the unusual **House of the Three Ostriches** (*Dům u tří pštrosů*) built just below Charles Bridge in 1585. It was here that the Armenian merchant Damayan served the first coffee in Prague. Now renovated, it houses a first-class hotel and well-known restaurant.

OLD CITY / STARÉ MĚSTO

One landmark that marks a way into the oldest enclosed quarter of the city of Prague is the **Powder Tower** (*Prašná brána*), which stands at the beginning of the so-called King's Way leading through the old town and up to the castle. But another classic way to enter this part of the city is to cross **Charles Bridge**, one of Prague's major attractions. *Karlův most*, as the bridge has been known since 1870 when it was renamed in honor of Emperor Charles IV, is one of the country's national landmarks. Charles IV, well aware of the strategic significance of Prague with its location at the crossroads of important trade routes, had this stone bridge built in 1357 after an earlier bridge on the site had been washed away (see the chapter on the "Lesser City," p. 56). "His" architect, the German Peter Parler, who was also working on St. Vitus's Cathedral, drew up a plan for a bridge with 16 arches stretching some 3/10 of a mile (516 m) across the river, and almost 33 feet (10 m) wide. This site, where today crowds of tourists jostle and photograph, once served as a marketplace and jousting field. Prague Bridge, as it used to be more simply known, was even said to be used for executions.

Some decades ago, Charles Bridge was open to automobile traffic, and served as a major transportation artery between the Old City and the Lesser City; today, it's restricted to pedestrians. Crossing on foot is certainly the best way to see, not only the marvelous views of the city from the bridge, but also the statues which line it. Oldest of these is the statue of Nepomuk, cast in Nuremberg (based on a design by M. Rauchmüller and Johann Brokoff's subsequent model) in 1683. During the Baroque period, Bohemia's leading sculptors were asked to create statues for

Left: The Old City Ring with Týn Church.

the sandstone brid... sponded to this ap... are Johann Brokof... dinand Maximilian... chael, as well as N... hann Friedrich Kc... Jaeckel. Most of their original statues, badly damaged by smog and acid rain, have since been replaced by copies. More statues, many of them by J. and E. Max, were added around 1850, including that of the national patron saint Václav (St. Wenceslas). The most recent sculpture group, depicting the saints Cyril and Methodius, was created by K. Dvořák between 1928 and 1938. Some of the bridge's most impressive sculptures overall are the depiction of the Ottomans guarding the captured Christians (F.M. Brokoff, 1714), the vision of St. Luitgard (Braun, 1710), and the crucifix by Hans Hillger (1629).

An integral part of the bridge is the restored **Old City Bridge Tower** (*Staroměstská mostecká věž*). This, too, was designed by Peter Parler: the east façade and the webbed vaulting in the tower's archway are the work of this German architect. On the right side of the portal is a portrait of the eponymous Charles IV, king and emperor; the figure on the left is his son Wenceslas IV (Václav).

Focal point of the piazetta *Křížovnícké náměstí* (**Crusaders Square**) is yet another statue of Charles IV, unveiled in 1848 in honor of the 500th anniversary of the founding of Prague's Carolinum University. Two religious structures enhance the architectural beauty of the square. The first of these, **St. Francis Church** with its adjacent Monastery of the Crusaders (design: Carlo Lurago), the only order founded in Bohemia during the crusades, has stood here since the middle of the 13th century. In the crypt of this church, designed by Jean B. Mathey and built by Domenico Canevale in the 1680s, you can still see the remains of an early Gothic Church of the Holy Ghost.

Above: In the Great Hall of the Clementinum.

In addition to the building's sculptures, both inside and out, and the paintings around the altar, a noteworthy art work here is the fresco of *The Last Judgment* by W.L. Reiner (1722). The second, **St. Salvator Church**, originally built in Renaissance style and later renovated in Baroque, is part of the Clementinum. The figures on the front façade are by Johann Georg Bendl. Just a few steps further is the **Old City Water Tower** dating from the end of the 15th century. The former city waterworks, with its impressive sgraffito decorations, was converted in 1936 into one of Prague's most popular museums, devoted to the composer Bedřich Smetana. Between the two buildings is a little oasis, a café where you can sip your coffee on the banks of the Moldau.

From here, you can plunge into the bustling heart of the Old City. Once a center for the Jesuit order, the **Clementi-num**, Prague's largest complex of related buildings apart from the castle, today contains the church of the Greek Orthodox congregation. *Kostel svatého Klimenta*, **St. Clemens Church**, was built by Kilian Ignaz Dientzenhofer between 1711 and 1713, and elaborately appointed by a number of artists: the sculptures are by Matthias B. Braun, the altarpiece by Peter Brandl, and the ceiling frescoes by Johann Hiebl.

After 1653, the Jesuit College expanded steadily on its 5-acre (2 ha) site, creating a veritable fortress of spirituality. Some parts, such as the hall of mirrors or the astronomers' tower, are the work of Franciscus M. Kaňka. Today the Clementinum is considered a gem of the Baroque and Rococo. Especially notable are the reading room (formerly the refectory) and library, with their decorative stucco work and frescoes. The Great Hall (1722) houses old clocks and outsized globes from the 17th and 18th century.

Although tens of thousands of Italians visit Prague each year, the 1590 **Vlach**

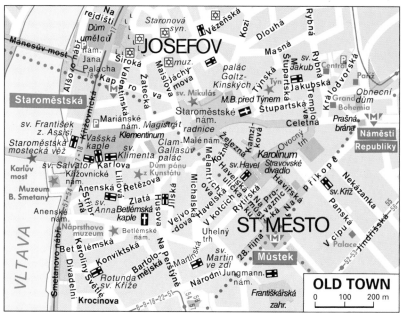

Chapel (*Vlašská kaple*) dating to 1595 remains a well-kept secret, largely owing to the fact that this former church of Prague's Italian congregation on Karlova ulice is usually closed. The corner house, **House of the Golden Snake** (*U Zlatého hada*) on Liliová ulice is popular with photographers. Nearby is Chain Lane (*Řetězová*). The **U Čapků** or **Dům pánů z Kunštátu** mansion is one of the most significant Romanesque secular buildings that's yet been excavated in Prague. A number of rooms provide a good impression of life in the Middle Ages. In fact, several dozen Romanesque buildings, or their foundations, have been unearthed over the last couple of decades, showing how modern-day Prague was built one "floor" above these Romanesque houses.

Back to Karlova: Passing several former palaces (Colloredo-Mansfeld, Pötting) and venerable houses such as the House of the Blue Pike (*U modré štiky*) or the House of the Golden Spring (*Uzlaté studně*), we arrive at Husova třída,

site of one of the Old City's most magnificent palaces. The **Clam-Gallas Palace** was built 1713-19 by Johann B. Fischer of Erlach for Count Gallas, who served as viceroy of Naples. He commissioned only first-class Baroque artists. Matthias B. Braun sculpted the giants beside the portal as well as the Triton fountain statue in the first courtyard and the figures in the stairway (stucco work by G. Fiumberti, R. Boll); Carlo Carlone produced the frescoes in the stairway and in the reception rooms. Shortly after its completion, the palace passed into the hands of Count Clam. Today it houses the Prague city archives, with hundreds of thousands of documents and valuable Prague ephemera. On the palace's outer garden wall on Mariánské náměstí (St. Mary's Square) is an allegorical fountain (cast in 1812 by W. Prachner) of the Vltava (Moldau).

Back on Husova, you'll find, besides a couple of old residential houses, one of the loveliest churches in Prague: *kostel svatého Jiljí* (**St. Giles's Church**). This

69

ary between the Old City and the New. Originally dating from the late 12th century, this Romanesque church was renovated in Gothic style after 1350 and again around 1490. Both the Gothic and the Romanesque elements are still visible, particularly the lovely Gothic web vaulting. Administered by the Congregation of Bohemian Brothers, the church has great historical significance for Protestants. It was here, in 1414, that communion was offered for the first time to everyone, not only to priests. The chalice has been a revolutionary symbol for the Hussites ever since.

From here, it's only a matter of steps to the historic **Coal Market** (*Uhelný trh*), at the center of which is the splendid Wimmer fountain (which Jakob Wimmer commissioned from F.X. Lederer), representing an allegory in praise of viticulture and agriculture. Charcoal was sold here from the Middle Ages until the beginning of the 19th century. A memorial plaque on **Platýz House** notes that Franz Liszt once stayed there. Of the many lovely houses here, the **House of the Three Golden Lions** (*U tří zlatých lvů*), which houses a wine tavern, is particularly notable. The building belonged to the Dušeks, who once hosted W.A. Mozart. A relief and a memorial plaque commemorate the composer's visit in 1787.

Romanesque edifice was renovated between 1339 and 1371 in Gothic style and used by the Hussites. In 1625 it was taken over by the Dominicans who turned it into a Baroque jewel. The carved confessional from 1720 is particularly impressive. Wenzel Lorenz Reiner (he is buried here) created the altarpiece and the ceiling frescoes. Reiner (1689-1743) lived nearby, in the House of the Dukes (*U Herzogů*), the so-called **Pernstein House** at 5 Na Perštýně. Because of the classical façade, added in the 17th century, you can hardly tell that the original house was Gothic. Next door is the popular restaurant **House of the Small Bears** (*U medvídků*).

From here we make a brief detour to Martinská, where you can see one of the oldest churches in Prague: *kostel svatého Martina ve zdi* (**Church of St. Martin in the Wall**). This used to mark the bound-

In the history books, the name Bartholomew is linked to the St. Bartholomew Massacre in Paris in 1572. In Prague, however, the name, associated with the street *Bartolomějská*, calls up associations, not of blood, but of the sleepless nights spent in the prison here by opponents of the Communist regime. Still, the street boasts two noteworthy sights: the Jesuit commune (consecrated in 1660) with its concert hall and the High Baroque **St. Bartholomew's Church**. The latter was built between 1726 and 1731 according to plans drawn up by Kilian Ignaz Dientzenhofer, and decorated with frescoes by W.L. Reiner.

Above: Arched passageway through the house Betlémské náměstí. Right: Jan Hus teaching; a fresco in the Bethlehem Chapel.

One of the oldest examples of Romanesque art in the Old City is on Světlá Street, where the popular storyteller and novelist Karolina Světlá (1830-99) was born. The early-12th-century **Holy Cross Rotunda** (*Rotunda svatého Kříže*) was saved from the wrecker's ball in the 1860s, and has since been restored. The frescoes which remain, however, are Gothic. Two tiny streets, Konviktská and Betlémská, lead to Betlémské náměstí. The magnificent **Náprstkovo Museum** is located in the house *U Halánků*. It contains a respectable collection of ethnography, started in the last century by the Náprstek family, and including works from Oceania, Africa and Asia as well as pre-Columbian America.

The reformer Jan Hus, who was the rector of Charles University before his exile, is even more revered in the Bohemian states than, for example, Martin Luther is in Germany. When he refused to follow the Pope, his summons to appear before the Council was inevitable. Despite his promise of safe conduct, Emperor Sigismund ordered Hus burned at the stake in Constance in July of 1415. This date is now an official holiday in the Czech Republic.

The **Bethlehem Chapel** (*Betlémská kaple*), a national landmark, is an authentic replica of the original late 14th-century church in which Jan Hus preached between 1402 and 1413. During the Counter-Reformation, Jesuits took over the church, and in 1786 the chapel was torn down, leaving only the surrounding walls standing. A residential house was later built on the site. In the early 1950s, archaeologists discovered, during reconstruction work, fragments of earlier inscriptions. Although the Communist regime preached the doctrine of atheism, a pilgrimage to the Bethlehem Chapel was practically a compulsory excursion for grade-school children.

Strolling on through the characteristic narrow alleys of the Old City, you'll come to *Anenské náměstí* and the Dominican **Convent of St. Anne**. This 14th-century building with its original Gothic roof timbering, renovated in Baroque style in the 17th century, houses the remains of the Romanesque Laurentinus Rotunda discovered in the 1950s. Christoph Willibald Gluck played here. Both Mozart and Beethoven resided in the palace next door (*Pachtovský palác*) during their stays in Prague. Across the street is the **Theater on the Balustrade** (*Divadlo na zábradlí*), formerly one of Europe's leading theaters by virtue of its trailblazing productions. The intimate house *U zelenho kloboučku* (House of the Green Hat) was also made famous by the pantomime ensemble of Ladislav Fialka.

Coincidentally, Fialka was also the name of the architect who, in 1893, designed the Old City **market halls** (*Staroměstská tržnice*) in Rytířská (Knights Lane). A conglomerate of several styles (Gothic, Renaissance, Baroque) can be seen in the House of the Old City Magistrate (*Staroměstská rychta*). The same is true of **Hrobčický Palace** and *U modrého sloupu* (**House of the Blue Column**) and *U zlatého kola* (**House of the Golden Wheel**). The Communists used two splendid palaces here for propaganda purposes. The neo-Renaissance building of the Prague Savings Bank served as a Klement Gottwald Museum, while the former Baroque Monastery of the Mendicant Carmelites for decades housed the "House of Soviet Science and Culture."

Wandering through Melantrichova, past a couple of historic, originally Gothic residences and businesses with names such as **House of the Golden Chalice** (a popular wine restaurant), or the Romanesque-Gothic St. Michael's Church with its monastery, you'll come to the Gallus neighborhood, originally settled by German immigrants in the 13th century. This neighborhood encompassed the coal market and fruit market squares as well as the streets Rytířská and

Havelská. The latter, the quarter's main axis, is the location of **St. Gallus Church** (*kostel svatého Havla*). Originally a Romanesque structure, the church was Gothicized in the first half of the 14th century, and later adorned with Baroque elements. The lancet arch portal and the cross-rib vaulting are particularly noteworthy. The talents of prominent artists and the architect Giovanni Santini, who redesigned the main façade just before 1738, can be seen here. Also in the church is the tomb of the prolific Baroque painter Karel Škréta. The arcades of Havelská, which have often served as a backdrop for historical films, still convey a sense of the city's past appearance, an impression supported by buildings such as the House of the Golden Scale, *U Bruncvíka*, or the House of the Bohemian Crown.

The **Fruit Market** (*Ovocná trh*) is again part of the Old City's urban zone. The former early Baroque **Kolowrat Palace** (Domenico Orsi, 1697), which has preserved its original appointments, now houses the Estates Theater. Focal point of this district is the national landmark of the **Carolinum**, the oldest extant university in central Europe, founded in 1348 by Charles IV. The lovely Gothic oriel, all that's left of the university chapel dedicated to Sts. Cosmas and Damian, is the only architectural feature of note. The Carolinum was able to withstand the pressure from the Jesuit college in the Clementinum, which was founded to serve as a counterweight to this secular educational institution during the Counter-Reformation. Throughout the Bohemian states, receiving a diploma in the auditorium of the Charles University has always been considered one of the greatest honors to which one can aspire, and a truly unique personal experience.

Linger a while in Iron Lane (*Železná ulice*). Between 1781 and 1783, a century before the National Theater was built, Anton Haffenecker built a theater here

Right: Fruit market in Havelská with St. Gallus Church in the background.

for Count Nostitz. At first named for the count, the building was later renamed the German Theater, and then became the **Estates Theater** (*Stravovské divadlo*; a name it's resumed today). In 1834, the theater presented the Singspiel *Fidlovačka* by František Škroup, with a libretto by Josef Kajetán Tyl. Tyl's poem *Kde domov můj* (Where is my home, my native land?) became the Czech part of the Czechoslovakian national anthem in 1918, and in 1949 the theater, now a part of the National Theater, was renamed the Tyl Theater (*Tylovo divadlo*) in his honor. An even more important world premiere here was that of Mozart's *Don Giovanni* in 1787.

Continuing through the lively pedestrian zone of Celetná, with its lovely historic residences and former palaces, you'll pass the *House of the Three Queens,* where Franz Kafka lived from 1896 to 1907, and the Cubist house *U Černé Matky boží*, built in 1912 by Josef Gočár, and decorated with a Baroque statue of the Black Madonna. At the end

of the street, you'll come to the **Powder Tower** (*Prašná brána*). Once a city gate, the tower was built around 1478 according to plans by Matěj Rejsek, a Moravian architect from Prostějov. It took on its present appearance, however, in 1875-6, when Josef Mocker re-Gothicized the tower.

Now as ever, the only term for the **Repre** or Municipal Building, Prague's representative Art Nouveau house (*Obecní dům hlavního města Prahy*) is "culture center." The Repre houses a concert hall and café, ballroom and billiard hall, meeting hall and exhibition space. It was built between 1906 and 1911 and leading local artists, including Aleš, Mucha, Myslbek, Šaloun, Švabinský and many others, considered it an honor to help in its construction.

Passing the architecturally playful *Hotel Paříž*, you come to Malá Štupartská and the Gothic **St. Jacob's Church** with its Minorite monastery. In the late 17th and early 18th centuries, this 14th-century church, a popular venue for con-

73

certs, was given a new Baroque face by J.S. Pánke. Peter Brandl and W.L. Reiner painted most of the pictures for its 21 altars. The frescoes in this church, Prague's second-largest, are by F.Q. Voget, who also decorated the rooms of the cloister.

The narrow alleys around **Týn Court** (also called Ungelt) set the perfect tone for exploring one of the oldest documented sites in Prague. Until well into the 16th century, newly-arrived merchants lodged here – for a fee – under the patronage of the reigning king. The royal court had a vested interest in trade (and the resulting customs duties, of course, until 1774). The Renaissance loggia in the Granovský Palace is from 1560.

Týn Church (*kostel Panny Marie před Týnem*), its steeple measuring over 260 feet (80 m) and its Madonna visible far and wide, is one of Prague's most impressive churches. Parts of this structure, where Danish astronomer Tycho Brahe

was laid to rest in 1601, were built by craftsmen from the Parler workshop. The interior is partially Gothic; Baroque elements were added later. Karel Škréta, who was born not far from this site, painted the altarpieces (before 1660). For the Czechs, this church with its three presbyteries played a significant role: up until the Thirty Years' War, it served as headquarters for the Protestants.

In recent years, the **Old City Ring** (*Staroměstské náměstí*) has become a lively pedestrian center at the heart of the city. This urbane square is completely surrounded by historic buildings. In the **House of the White Unicorn** (*U bílého jednorožce*), for example, a Romanesque room was excavated; atop this is a Gothic arcade with well-preserved cross-rib vaulting. Bedřich Smetana established a music school in the **House of the Golden Unicorn** (*U zlatého jednorožce*) in 1848. Restored frescoes by Mikoláš Aleš adorn the publishing house Štorchův dům, while the **House of the Golden Angel** (*U zlatého anděla*) sports a Baroque statue

Above: The Old City Town Hall. Right: Astronomical clock on the building's façade.

of St. Florian by Ignaz Platzer. Until the mid-19th century, the Týn School occupied the Renaissance building beside the Goltz-Kinsky Palace. Romanesque and Gothic elements testify to its age. The Gothic **House of the Stone Bells** (*U kamenného zvonu*), extensively renovated, now houses the Prague City Gallery. The National Gallery exhibits its collection of graphic works in the city's most beautiful Rococo palace (*palác Goltz-Kinských*), built in 1755-65 by Anselmo Lurago based on plans by Kilian Ignaz Dientzenhofer and decorated with sculptures by Ignaz Platzer. In this house was born Countess Kinsky (1843-1914), who under her married name, Bertha von Suttner, became famous for her work *Lay Down Your Arms!*, which protested the insanity of the arms build-up. This pacifist and author was awarded the Nobel Peace Prize in 1905.

Dominating the center of the Old City Ring is a statue of the reformer Jan Hus (by Ladislav Šaloun, 1915), a national landmark. Every schoolchild in Bohemia knows Václav Brožík's painting entitled *Jan Hus in Front of the Council of Constance*, which hangs in the **Old City Town Hall**. In the assembly room here hangs the same artists's monumental *The Election of Jiří von Poděbrady as King of Bohemia*. Another well-known painter, Josef Mánes, painted the calendar on the **astronomical clock** (*Orloj*) in 1866. The twelve apostles and the figures to the left and right of the carillon were badly damaged during the war and were replaced by new carvings, crafted in careful detail based on historical documentation so that the town hall clock looks much the same as it has for the past 500 years. Dating originally from 1410, it was reconstructed in 1490 and mechanized in 1560. The town hall itself consists of several buildings built over the years since the 14th century. A wedding ceremony held in the town hall is considered an important social event. One building in the complex stands out: the Renaissance *U minutky* (**House of the Minute**), covered with sgraffiti. Literature fans will want to visit the house where the reporter Egon Erwin Kisch was born, just a few steps away. The **House of the Two Golden Bears** (*U dvou zlatých medvědů*) in *Kožná* (Leather Lane) boasts a marvelous, if shabby, Renaissance portal.

Kostel svatého Mikuláše (**St. Nicholas Church**), not to be confused with the church of the same name in the Lesser City, was built in the amazingly short span of four years (1732-35) and is considered another masterpiece by Kilian Ignaz Dientzenhofer. The octagonal cupola of the opulent church – today belonging to the Hussite congregation – was frescoed by Cosmas Damian Asam.

Not far from the overrun Old City Ring, the **Lesser Square** (*Malé náměstí*) seems a quiet oasis, underlined by several old houses with lovely façades, which invoke the atmosphere of earlier centuries. Gone forever, however, is the historic world of the Prague ghetto.

JOSEFOV / THE JEWISH QUARTER

There are two figures which are practically synonymous with Prague's Jewish quarter. One is a real-life figure whose life's work was long treated as a phantom, and the other is a phantom whom most people claim to have seen spooking around at night in the gas-lit alleys and passageways of the old town. The characters in question are Franz Kafka and the Golem. Kafka (1883-1924, buried in the family plot in the Jewish Cemetery in Olšany) was a literary *persona non grata* in Communist Czechoslovakia up until 1963, when that the Prague German scholar Professor Eduard Goldstuecker finally restored Kafka to grace at a literary conference in Liblice with the air of a magician pulling a rabbit out of a hat. Much more popular at the time was the relatively harmless mystical figure of the homunculus Golem, created in the waning years of the Middle Ages and first introduced into literature in the 18th century. English-language readers may be familiar with him through the stories of Isaac Bashevis Singer; the figure's alleged original creator was Jehuda ben Bezalel, also known as Rabbi Loew. The rabbi's memorial, in the form of a statue by prominent sculptor Ladislav Šaloun, stands on the square Mariánské náměstí, in front of the Old City's new town hall.

Between these two poles – the myth of the ghetto and the reality of Jewish life and suffering in the 20th century, including the Holocaust of tens of thousands at the hands of the Nazis – lies the history of the Old City district known as Josefov, or the Jewish quarter. The district was dubbed "Joseph's town" in 1850 in honor of Emperor Joseph II, who also became king of Bohemia in 1780. This son of Maria Theresa instituted reforms which

Left: An Art-Nouveau relief, one of Prague's many turn-of-the-century documents.

helped to ease living conditions for the city's Jewish population. Jews, for example, were no longer forced to wear the yellow mark; they could now work without restrictions as craftsmen; they could attend public schools and the university. In 1788, Prague University awarded degrees in medicine to the first two Jewish doctors. Nevertheless, Jews in Bohemia and Moravia were repeatedly reminded of the fact that they were only a tolerated minority, albeit relatively strong in number. What this meant in practice was the publication of lampoons and anti-Semitic pamphlets, which were then circulated between Prague and Vienna, denouncing the "uselessness and perniciousness of the Jews in the kingdom." In 1783, there were 8,532 Jews (and nine Christians) registered in the Prague ghetto. A hundred years later, only one-third of the inhabitants were Jewish. You can get a good image of the Old City and the ghetto in the year 1834 from Anton Langweil's 20-square-meter (215 sq. feet) model, which took him eight years to build. Made of cardboard, wood and paper, this model reproduces in detail no fewer than 2,200 buildings. It is on display in the *Muzeum hlavního města Prahy* (**Museum of the Capital City of Prague**).

An important turn of events in the history of the ghetto occurred in 1787 with a prohibition on further burials in the **Old Jewish Cemetery**. With its forest of more than 12,000 gravestones, darkened with age, overgrown with moss, leaning at crazy angles, the cemetery seems shrouded with the hush of respect for those long dead. This aura prevails in the face of thousands of tourists who regularly tramp through – for the cemetery is now considered a museum – to view the stones, often without the kind of respect or piety the site merits. The grave inscriptions are all written in Hebrew; taken together, they make up a kind of stone picture-book of history. If you can read

Hebrew, you'll be able to decipher not only personal data, but also lyrical texts in praise of the dead; but you don't need to know the language to see the symbols (animals such as bears or deer, hands raised in blessing, grapes, crowns, branches and many more) which also allude to the deceased person's name and profession. There's nothing lyrical about the **Pinkas Synagogue** at the edge of the cemetery, a memorial to the Jewish victims of the Nazis. Carved into the wall, in alphabetical order, are 77,297 names – surnames first, followed by first names – 77,297 birth dates, and 77,297 deportation dates or dates of death: in short, 77,297 scant bits of data which are all that remain of Moravians and Bohemians who lost their lives under the brutal extermination policies of the Nazis, in the concentration camps of Auschwitz, Bergen-Belsen, Majdanek, Mauthausen, Oranienburg, Sachsenhausen, Theresien-

stadt/Terezín or Treblinka. This commemorative site and synagogue in *Široká ulice* (Broad Lane) also holds a melancholy record: it has the longest grave inscription in the world. Rabbi Pinkas founded the synagogue in 1479, and his grandsons had it enlarged in 1535. Subterranean rooms, including a ritual bath (*mikwe*) and a spring were discovered during renovation work. Archaeologists date these back to the late 11th and early 12th centuries. The Renaissance prayer room with its cross-rib vaulting and the women's gallery (both from the 17th century) are well preserved. This synagogue, the ghetto's second-oldest, was the focal point of a district that was home to several hundred members of the congregation as evidenced by the distribution of seats.

Back in the labyrinth of gravestones, weathered and askew, search out the four most famous among them. The oldest tomb is that of the poet Avigdor Kara, dating from 1439. Rabbi Mordechai Maisel (died 1601), the astronomer and histo-

Above: The old Jewish cemetery, a great memorial to Jewish life in Prague.

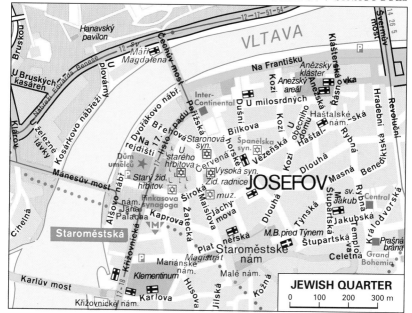

rian David Gans (1613) and the scholar Rabbi Loew (1609) all have striking gravestones which have become places of pilgrimage for Jews and Gentiles. Non-Jews often follow the Jewish ritual of laying a small stone on the grave, simply because it seems the thing to do.

The burial hall at the entrance of the old cemetery brings us back to the reality of the 20th century. Primitive drawings by children interred in the concentration camp Theresienstadt (Terezín) provide a chilling insight into the situation of these young victims of Nazi racism.

The **Cell Synagogue** (*U starého hřbitova*) derives its name from the tiny cell-like rooms of the Talmud school and the prayer room. After several restorations and much remodeling over the last 300 years, this synagogue now houses an exhibit of old manuscripts and prints as well as artifacts of Jewish rites and culture.

There was already a synagogue here as early as the 11th century, when the first Jews settled on the Moldau, in the street today known as Široká. Later it was referred to as the Old Synagogue. Today only fragments of this building remain. On this site, the oldest of the ghetto, new synagogues were repeatedly built over the centuries, replacing those which had fallen victim to fire or pogroms. In 1868, a design by the architect Vojtěch Ignác Ullmann was accepted for a magnificent synagogue built in the then-fashionable Moorish-Oriental style. The **Spanish Synagogue** is a reminder that the Sephardic Jews originally came from the western regions of Europe. The opulently-decorated interior enhances the exterior design. For the Czechs, the Spanish Synagogue is significant because of the fact that the organist here for 12 years was – remarkably for a synagogue – the non-Jewish composer František Škroup, who wrote what would later become the Czech national anthem. Today this synagogue, with its wealth of ornamentation and stucco work, houses an exhibit of religious textiles (Torah wraps, curtains, embroidery, woven material) from over five centuries. These stem – as do all of

79

the many articles in the Jewish Museum – from a collection established in 1906 by Prague Jews. Ironically, the collection was expanded during the Holocaust as Adolf Eichmann "added" to it items from destroyed communities with a view toward establishing a "World Museum of Anti-Semitism."

The **Old-New Synagogue** (*Staronová synagoga*) in Červená, built around 1270 in early Gothic style, is the last remaining original synagogue in the ghetto. Despite later additions, it provides a good picture of the Middle Ages. The impressive brick gable at the front was added at the end of the 15th century, the women's gallery in the 17th and 18th centuries. The Torah shrine for the five books of the Old Testament, the chancel (Hebrew = *almemor*) as well as the beautifully-crafted 15th-century grating are particularly noteworthy. The Old-New Synagogue in Red

Above: The Old-New Synagogue. Right: In front of the Rudolfinum.

Lane and six other synagogues are, aside from the town hall, the only remaining structures of the historic ghetto. The rest were destroyed at the turn of this century, the victims of "*Assanierung*," the Austrian term for "improving buildings for reasons of hygiene, society, or other considerations." Where today there are ten streets, there were 31 alleyways in the 1890s; where 80 buildings now stand, there were once 290. The population density in the Jewish district was the highest in Prague, with more than 1,820 people per hectare (2.5 acres). The death rate was 50% higher than in the other city districts. The "improvements" created the main thoroughfare of **Parisian Boulevard** (*Pařížská třída*), 78 feet (24 m) wide. Some of the architects and artists who designed this street tried to break new ground in a figurative and literal sense, and succeeded in creating a functional city plan which works to this day. This short but magnificent boulevard has become one of the top addresses for Prague's international business world.

In this setting, the **Jewish Town Hall** in Maislova is somewhat of an anachronism. Its clock (created in 1764 by Sebastian Landesberger) runs "backwards": not only is it counter-clockwise, but the big hand shows the hours and the little hand the minutes. The street on which the town hall is located was once the main street of the ghetto. It was first documented in the 16th century with the notation that it had been expanded after a fire. Another fire in 1689 destroyed the new structure. In the middle of the 18th century, the Jews were driven out of Prague and the town hall no longer served any function. Today it houses Prague's rabbinical offices. In the main hall, which has lovely stucco ornamentation, there's a kosher restaurant.

Next door is the **High Synagogue** (*Vysoká synagoga*), also known as the Town Hall synagogue. Originally built around 1570, it burned in 1689 and was later rebuilt. Late Gothic elements are mingled with Renaissance ones. The main hall's finely-crafted stucco work and ornamental decorations, which were integrated into the renovations of 1883, are particularly noteworthy. The neo-Gothic appearance of the synagogue today dates from the turn of the century. Today it houses part of the collections of the Jewish Museum, which for the past thirty years has displayed a collection unique throughout the world: silver from Bohemian and Moravian synagogues, precious metal confiscated by the Germans and brought to Prague from a total of 153 houses of prayer as well as many households. Rituals, customs and daily life come to life through the filigree work, candelabras and torah crowns, some dating back more than 500 years.

AGNES MONASTERY

Not far from the ghetto is the **Convent of St. Agnes** (*Anežský klášter*), a national landmark with lovely cloisters. In the

1230s, two orders, the female Poor Clares and the male Minorites, founded a double monastery here, a virtually unique historical phenomenon. Next door, in one of the oldest remaining religious complexes of the city, there were once two churches (Sts. Barbara and Franciscus); these were secularized in the year 1782. After long years of neglect, the buildings now house exhibits of the National Gallery, including local 19th-century art and temporary exhibits from the collection of the Museum of Decorative Arts.

Before the turn of the century, the architects Josef Zítek and Josef Schulz, who built the National Theater, designed the **Rudolfinum**, also known as House of Artists (*Dům umělců*), on the banks of the Moldau. This building on Náměstí Jana Palacha, with its many statues, was constructed in honor of the crown prince Rudolph. Housing an assembly hall and a gallery in neo-Renaissance style, this structure has been one of the city's most popular concert venues since the day it was built.

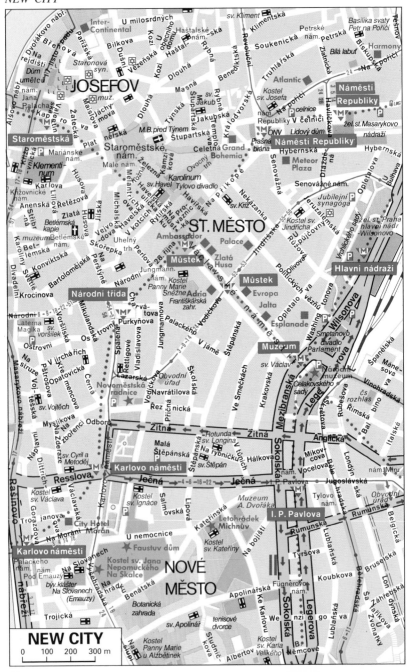

NEW CITY

0   100   200   300 m

NEW CITY / NOVÉ MĚSTO

Paradoxical as it may sound, Prague's new city is actually old. In 1998, it will celebrate its 650th birthday. What was the purpose of founding this town? Because the Bohemian King, Charles IV of the House of Luxemburg, was also the Holy Roman Emperor, it was imperative that he make a great display of his might and of his glory. He decided to make Prague the capital of his realm. Not only did he have the cathedral built in the castle, Hrad, but he also built the bridge between the Lesser City and the Old City. In 1348, furthermore, he established central Europe's first university, the Carolinum, which bears his name. And, carrying through on his strategy of attracting settlers to the new capital, he issued an order in that same year that a new town of Prague was to be established outside the gates of the Old City. The imperial-royal command was unequivocal: "Anyone who receives permission to build must begin construction within one month and must be finished within 18 months." Of course the king did not want to alienate the town councilors of the Old City, and he therefore granted the Old City's residents several important privileges. They were to have the right of free passage at all times, and they were even to be responsible for closing and opening two of the new town's city gates themselves. Charles' offer to resettle Old City artisans and craftsmen who were "loud" or forced to work in cramped quarters into the New City went over well. Many street names clearly refer to this Imperial policy: Blacksmith Lane (*Kovářská*), Potter Lane (*Hrnčířská*), In the Tannery (*V jirchářích*), Furrier Lane (*Kožišnická*), Clothmaker Lane (*Soukenická*), Foundry Lane (*Pasířská*), Carpenter Lane (*Truhlářská*), Ropemaker Lane (*Provaznická*), Butcher Lane (*Řeznícká*) or Between the Bakers (*Mezi pekaři*). Three large markets (livestock market, horse market and hay market) also contributed to the New City's economic importance.

Before the cornerstone of the New City (*Nové Město*) had been laid, or even that of its Town Hall, two churches had already been built: the Church of the Virgin Mary in Snow (*kostel Panny Marie Sněžné*) and the Slavic monastery with its own church, *Klášter na Slovanech-Emauzy*, commonly known as Emmaus because the scripture "Jesus' encounter with the disciples in Emmaus" was read at its consecration. Services in this church were popular because they were held not in Latin but in Old Church Slavic. The church changed hands numerous times; its owners ranged from the congregation of the Hussite brothers to Spanish Benedictines. The entire complex was given its Baroque face-lift in the mid-17th century; around 1880, German Benedictines from Beuron renovated it in neo-Gothic style. The church's rather extravagant appearance today, however, is a result of renovations undertaken in 1930. Today, the cloister of this national landmark houses the Institutes of the Czech Academy of Science.

Not far away is one of the most beautiful of Kilian Ignaz Dientzenhofer's churches: the rarely-visited *kostel svatého Jana Nepomuckého Na Skalce* (**Church of St. John of Nepomuk on the Rock**), which took the Prague Baroque architect nearly ten years to complete (1730-39). The wooden statue of its patron saint was carved by Johann Brokoff (1682).

From here, a short detour brings you to the botanical gardens (*Botanická zahrada*) and two old churches of the Virgin in the street *Na slupi*, as well as to the *kostel svatého Apolináře* in the street of the same name and the church of Charlemagne in Karlov. To elaborate, a bit more slowly: the Servite church *kostel Panny Marie Na slupi* (*slup* means fishtrap) dates from the 14th century, while its neo-Gothic monastery is from 1858. The neighboring Elisabethine monastery,

with its Order hospital, was originally Baroque but was modernized in the 1930s. Its church (*kostel Panny Marie u Alžbětinek*), on the other hand, is another work by Kilian Ignaz Dientzenhofer (1724-25). The frescos in the St. Tekla Chapel are by Johann Lukas Kracker (around 1762). The Church of St. Apollinarius houses the Psychiatry Department of Charles University; this single-nave Gothic church was built in 1390, during the reign of Charles IV, and its frescoes date from the same period. The **Church of Our Lady and Charlemagne** (*kostel Panny Marie a Karla Velikého*) was consecrated in 1377 in honor of the patron saint of the emperor and king. This oft-remodeled church has been a popular place of pilgrimage since the 18th century. On *Kateřinská,* you can see a Baroque church of the same name which,

built by Franciscus Maximilian Kaňka, is one of the loveliest churches not only in the New City, but in all of Prague.

Now we approach a simple but prominent site. The *Tavern U Kalicha* (**House of the Jug**), located on *Na Bojišti* (**On the Battlefield**), is the site of many key scenes in the immortal anti-war novel *The Adventures of the Good Soldier Švejk*. In this book by the Prague humorist Jaroslav Hašek (1883-1923), the rheumatic dog dealer Josef Švejk carries out his battle of wits against the imperial army with naiveté and cleverness, with innocence and flair. A true literary monument; and so permeated with a unique Prague atmosphere that it would have been impossible for this book to have been written anywhere else.

Another gem by Kilian Ignaz Dientzenhofer, this time a secular structure, is the **Pleasure Palace of Count Michna** (*Letohrádek Michnů*), built 1712-20, also called "Villa America." Today it houses the Antonín Dvořák Museum. The frescoes are by J.F. Schor, while the statues

Above: Church of Our Lady and Charlemagne. Right: Prague tradition: Švejk in the inn "At the Goblet."

are from the workshop of Matthias B. Braun. Dvořák (1841-1904), who lived at Žitná ulice 14 from 1877 until his death, is, along with Smetana, the most important and most popular Czech composer. The museum in the Michna Palace exhibits a cross-section of his life and work.

The best approach to the *Faustův dům* (**Faust House**) at the south end of Charles Square is through the clinic district. Tradition has it that mysterious creatures dwell in this 16th-century Renaissance building with its Baroque elements. When Goethe updated the Faust legend, the educated citizens of Prague took this as an opportunity to create an aura of mystery around this old apothecary's house. **Karlovo náměstí**, formerly the site of a livestock market, is the largest enclosed square in Prague, larger even than Wenceslas Square, and one of the largest in Europe. One attraction here is a church dedicated to St. Ignatius of Loyola (*kostel svatého Ignáce*), which served as the seat of the New City Jesuits until their order was disbanded. Carlo

Lurago selected a lavish mixture of Baroque and Rococo elements for this church (1665-77). Visible from afar is the statue of the saint with a halo, which dates from 1671. The neighboring Jesuit College was built a few years earlier.

The national landmark *Novoměstská radnice*, the **Town Hall of the New City**, has been renovated repeatedly since the 14th century; but its tower has managed to preserve its mid-15th century appearance. Extensively renovated in 1905, the town hall today is used for administrative purposes; it also contains some elaborate reception rooms. Standing in the park on Charles Square in front of the Town Hall, with its many statues of Czech writers, scientists and artists, you could easily forget that just a century and a half ago wood, coal, livestock and salt herring were being bought and sold here. At the time, The New City had a monopoly on the sale of herring. The former character of this district is also apparent in the street names *Ječná* (Barley Lane) and *Žitná* (Grain Lane). Still, it's astounding

85

to learn that there were, during that period, some 150 pubs on this square and in the surrounding area. This is a vivid illustration of the fact that, then as now, the Czechs are among the leading consumers of beer in the world. Another reminder of the area's merchant and commercial past is the measuring stick (*loket* in Czech) affixed to the façade of the Town Hall, establishing the official standard of measurement for Bohemia. And speaking of measures, there's also a piece of a chain attached here, testifying to the security measures practiced in medieval times.

If you don't want to detour to see the 12th-century Romanesque St. Longinus Rotunda, head down Resslova, named after the Bohemian inventor of the marine propeller, Joseph Ressel (1793-1857). Large Romanesque fragments can be seen in the Gothic **Wenceslas Church** (*kostel svatého Václava*). The Gothic-era frescoes in the presbytery date from around 1400. Today, the church known as *kostel svatého Cyrila a Metoděje* is the seat of the local Orthodox congregation; but when it was built in 1730-36 by Kilian Ignaz Dientzenhofer it was dedicated to St. Charles Borromeo. As a memorial plaque here shows, the church is also remembered as the site of the last stand of the group of parachutists who, in 1942, assassinated the hated Nazi official, "Imperial Protector" Heydrich, took refuge in the church basement, and fought until every one of them had been killed.

The New City is divided from the Old City, both historically and administratively, by **Národní třída**, or National Street. The name of this boulevard set the tone for a truly "new" wind blowing through Prague after it became the capital of a new nation in 1918: a new sense of self-respect was evident in a city which the Habsburgs had "demoted" to the status of a mere royal residence, which

Right: The opera house, a great stage for great music.

Prague residents took as a real put-down. Similarly new, for example, was the **National Theater** (*Národní divadlo*), which documented the Czech population's desire, long before the turn of the century, to have their own voice within the German-language center of Prague. The tones emanating from the theater (designed by Josef Zítek and Josef Schulz) were also new: Bedřich Smetana's national opera *Libuše* was staged in 1883 at the theater's reopening (the first building having burned down). Today, the National Theater is still the pride of the city, a gilded wonder created by the most important artists of that era. Patriots see it as a cradle of national culture.

Just a few steps away is the **Ursuline Convent** (*klášter voršilek*) with its church of the same name, designed by the architect Marc Antonio Canevale, 1702-04. The interior of the church is magnificent. The statues are by F. Preiss, Peter Brandl painted the main altarpiece, and the ceiling frescoes are by Johann Jakob Steinfels.

The sculpture group of John of Nepomuk in front of the monastery buildings is by Ignaz Platzer the Elder (1747). Not that this church is only for art lovers; wine connoisseurs are happy to stop in at the monastery's wine tavern (*klášterní vinárna*), steeped in tradition.

Buildings dating from the 18th, 19th and 20th centuries line both sides of Národní třída, including the magnificently restored Topič Publishing House (1908), the Baroque palace of the architect Franciscus Maximilian Kaňka (1740) and the Adria Palace dating from 1925, once home to the Laterna Magika, which is now housed in the National Theater. The route passes through the lovely piazzetta of *Jungmannovo náměstí*, an oasis in the city's tumult. A bit further on is Prague's tallest church – "tallest" here applying to the church itself, not to its steeple. It is the *chrám Panny Marie Sněžné* (**Church of the Virgin Mary in Snow**), commis-

sioned by Charles IV. The church's high altar is also a superlative: the tallest altar in Prague. The arches of this Franciscan church are Renaissance, while the frescoes and the altarpieces – one of which is W. L. Reiner's painting of the *Annunciation* – are Baroque.

Můstek (small bridge) is what the residents of Prague call the busy spot where people used to cross the trench (*Na příkopě*) separating the Old City from the horse market (today's *Václavské náměstí*). From here, you can either follow the pedestrian zone of Na příkopě or wend your way up Wenceslas Square.

The Classical **Holy Cross Church** (*kostel svatého Kříže*) is a popular place of worship in downtown Prague. The **Sylva-Taroucca Palace**, one of Prague's loveliest palaces, was built by the ubiquitous Kilian Ignaz Dientzenhofer (1743-51), and later expanded by Anselmo Lurago. Just a few steps away is the late 18th-century **Slavic House** (*Slovanský dům*), a multi-cultural center with restaurants. The elegant boulevard of Na

příkopě is similar to Národní: both are lined with galleries and department stores, souvenir and gourmet shops, cafés and foreign-language bookshops, banks and restaurants, combining to create a distinctive atmosphere. One of the more noteworthy buildings is the neo-Renaissance *Zivnostenská banka* (**Merchants Bank**), built at the end of the 19th century by Oswald Polívka.

Republic Square (*Náměstí Republiky*) is dominated by the Capuchin church of St. Joseph (with two altar paintings by Karel Škréta) and its former monastery, which later served as a barracks. The playwright Josef Kajetán Tyl wrote the poem *Kde domov můj?* here in 1834 (Where is my home, my native land?), which later became the Czech national anthem.

Those interested in art history should take note of three buildings here. The graphic artist Wenzel Hollar (1607-77) was born in the house at Soukenická ulice 13, while **St. Clemens Church,** belonging to the Protestant Church of the

Bohemian Brothers, is in Klimentská. This re-Gothicized building was originally Romanesque but has several 14th-century Gothic elements. In Petrská, you find the **Church of St. Peter na Poříčí,** a Romanesque structure with two towers. It was renovated in Gothic style in the 14th and 15th century; turned into a Baroque structure in the 18th century; and in the second half of the 19th century restored to its Gothic roots.

The **Sweerts-Sporck Palace** in Hybernská was remodeled as a bank by Josef Gočár in the 1920s. It was originally built by Anton Haffenecker and Ignazio Palliardi, while Ignaz Platzer the Younger crafted the statues on the façade. In the Middle Ages, this street was an important route into and out of the city. The early Baroque **Kinsky Palace**

Above: Pure Art Nouveau on the central train station commemorates the founding of the Republic on October 28, 1918. Right: National Museum on Wenceslas Square.

in the new town (not to be confused with the Goltz-Kinsky Palace on the Old Town Ring) was built by Carlo Lurago in Empire style. The palace was remodeled in the first decade of this century and re-named *Lidová dům* (**House of the People**) when Bohemia's Social Democratic party established its headquarters here in 1907.

When the first train arrived in Prague in 1845, the city's first train station was ready and waiting. Built in classical style, it now once again bears the name *Masarykovo nádraží* in honor of the founder of the Republic, Masaryk.

The Moorish-Oriental **Jubilee Synagogue**, built by the architects W. Stiassny and A. Richter in 1905-06, is located on Jeruzalémská. Just a short distance away, on Jindřišská, is one of the New City's oldest churches, **St. Henry's Church** (*kostel svatého Jindřicha*). Like St. Peter's church mentioned above, this originally Gothic church was remodeled in Baroque style and then re-Gothicized in the middle of the 19th century.

On Třída Politických vězňů, parallel to Václavské náměstí, you'll find the former Gestapo headquarters. It was here that many members of the Czech resistance were tortured. Today the building (built 1923-29) is a **Monument to National Resistance**.

Even downtown Prague has a number of parks. One of the more popular is *Vrchlického sady* near the restored **Central Railway Station** (*Hlavní nádraží*), named after President Woodrow Wilson. This monumental building (architect J. Fanta) with its oversized decorative statues was built in 1901-09 in the Prague Secession style. Heading from here toward the National Museum, you'll pass the popular **State Opera**, built in 1886-88 as the German Theater. The architects were Ferdinand Fellner and Hermann Helmer of Vienna, in their day the busiest architects you could find between Odessa and Hamburg.

The Parliament of the former Federal Assembly of the Czechoslovakian Republic on Wilsonova třída was completed in 1972 after 15 years of construction. The **National Museum** (*Národní muzeum*), its façade measuring more than 325 feet (over 100 m) in length, took only five years (1885-90) to build under the architect Josef Schulz. Because of its artistic ornamentation, this neo-Renaissance building is another of the Czech Republic's national landmarks.

The terrace of the museum provides a lovely view of **Wenceslas Square**, which is almost 2,500 feet (750 m) long and 195 feet (60 m) wide. Until the middle of the last century the Horse Gate was located here, the boundary of the traditional Horse Market. Today, the square is the pulsing center of the metropolis. And what would a square named after the national patron saint Václav, Wenceslas, be without a huge statue of this man? Created by Josef Myslbek in 1912-13, this statue has stood at the focal point of Czech history ever since. Even more so than at the castle, Prague's sense of democracy and nationalism have been at home here throughout this century.

Transportation

Within Prague's inner city, it's best not to use a car. The streets here are narrow and crowded; garages are expensive, and the police aren't shy about ticketing or towing illegally parked cars.

In addition, most of the sights are so close together that you can easily reach them on foot. There are, furthermore, three subway lines that run through the city until midnight, and there are also plenty of streetcars and buses. Taxis are easy to hail and relatively inexpensive, by Western standards, as long as you agree on the regular local fare before you set out on your journey. After the subway closes at night, buses run out to the suburbs every half-hour or hour.

Accommodations

Although we've tried to be as accurate as possible, many Prague telephone and fax numbers have been or are about to be changed. When in doubt, you can always call International Information. We haven't been too strict about organzing hotels according to city district, since this would mean in some cases separating hotels that are across the street from each other, but happen to lie in two different administrative districts of the city.

Botels are a holdover from the bygone Socialist administration, introduced to try to make up for a huge deficit in tourist accommodations that was present even before that fateful November of 1989. What they are, simply, are hotel buildings floating on the Moldau, which have a moderately boat-like character without ever having actually travelled the river.

You can't simply camp whereever you please, and there aren't any campgrounds in the immediate vicinity of the city center. We've listed a **campgrounds** from the outlying districts around the city. Since November, 1989, countless agencies have sprung up specializing in finding **private rooms** for visitors. The official Prague Information Service (PIS) also locates private rooms; see below for addresses.

There are, furthermore, a number of agencies for **Bed & Breakfasts**. Best-known is the **Prague B&B Association**, P-5, Kroftova 3 (formerly Rosy Luxemburgové), Tel: 54 93 44, Fax: 54 78 06.

HRADČANY AND LESSER CITY

LUXURY: **Savoy**, P-6, Keplerova 6, Tel: 2430 2430, rooms with private butlers on request, next to the castle. **Diplomat**, P-6, Evropská 15, Tel: 2439 4172/3, Fax: 2439-4215, meets Western standards with pool, sauna, fitness room, close to the subway. **Hoffmeister**, P-1, Pod Bruskou 9, Tel: 5731 0942,

Fax: 5732 0906. **U tří pštrosů** (At the Three Ostriches), P-1, Dražického náměstí 12, Tel: 5732 0565, Fax: 5732 0565, in a historic old building right be Charles Bridge, with marvelous ambience and the accompanying crowds.

MODERATE: **U páva** (At the Peacock), P-1, U lužického semináře 32, Tel: 5732 0743, Fax: 53 33 79, comparable with the "Three Ostriches," but quieter. **Kampa - Stará zbrojnice**, P-1, Všehrdova 16, Tel: 2451 0409, Fax: 2451 0377, located in a former weapons depot in a side alley, now renovated to no-nonsense, functional comfort.

BUDGET: **U raka**, P-1, Černinská 1093, Tel: 2051 4792, Fax: 2051 0511, beautifully renovated with a romantic garden near the castle.

OLD CITY AND JOSEFOV

LUXURY: **Intercontinental**, P-1, náměstí Curieových 43/5, Tel: 2488 1111, Fax: 2481 1216, large, wiht lovely views, pool, fitness room, sauna, near the Jewish Museum. **Grand Hotel Bohemia**, P-1, Králodvorská 4, Tel: 2480 4111, Fax: 2329 545, very comfortable; the neo-Rococo banquet room "Boccaccio" has served as a film set; near the Powder Tower. **Paříž**, P-1, U Obecního domu 1, Tel: 2422 2151, 2422 5280, Fax: 2422 5475, held to be Prague's loveliest Art Nouveau hotel, with a stylish café. **Renaissance** (formerly Penta), P-1, V celnici 1, Tel: 2180 1100, Fax: 2182 2200, modern, with pool, sauna, fitness room.

MODERATE: **Meteor Plaza**, P-1, Hybernská 6, Tel: 2419 2111, Fax: 2421 3005, formerly the Hotel "City of Vienna," Imperial lodging with 14th-century wine-tavern. **Central**, P-1, Rybná 8, Tel: 2481 2041, Fax: 232 84 04, near the Jewish Museum. **U zlatého koníčka** (At the Golden Horse), P-1 Husova 18, Tel: 2400 9459, Fax: 2400 9299, renovated, reservations essential as it's very popular due to its central location.

BOTEL: **Albatros**, P-1, nábřeží L. Svobody, Tel: 2481 0547, Fax: 2481 1214, a bit cramped, and not for those bothered by noise.

BUDGET: **Unitas**, P-1, Bartolomějská 9, Tel: 232 7651, simple and clean, no alcohol allowed on the premises.

LOWER (eastern) NEW CITY

LUXURY: **Esplanade**, P-1, Washingtonova 19, Tel: 2421 1715, 2421 3696, Fax: 2422 9306, traditional, comfortable; Thomas Mann once stayed here; near Wenceslas Square. **Jalta**, P-1, Václavské náměstí 45, Tel: 2422 9133, Fax: 2421 3866, for anyone nostalgic for the days of Socialism: this was once the luxury hotel for prominent artists, since newly renovated. **Palace**, P-1, Panská 12, Tel: 2409 3111, Fax: 2422 1240, Art Nouveau façade, modern and unpretentious interior, sauna, near Wenceslas Square. **Adria**, P-1, Václavské náměstí 26, Tel: 2421 9274, 2422 7685, Fax: 26 34 15, functional. **Ambassador - Zlatá usa** (Golden Goose), Václavské náměstí 5-7, Tel: 2419 3111, 2421 8104, Fax: 2422 6167, traditional, but modernized.

MODERATE: **Atlantic**, P-1, Na poršíčí 9, Tel: 2481 1084, Fax:2481 2378, pleasant atmosphere. **Harmony**, P-1, Na poříčí 31, Tel: 232 0016, Fax: 231 00 09, renovated, now conforms to Western expectations. **Evropa**, P-1, Václavské náměstí 25, Tel: 2422 8118/9, Fax: 2422/4544, lovely, slightly lived-in Art Nouveau hotel with an interior straight out of a film: for tolerant nostalgia buffs. **Juliš**, P-1, Václavské náměstí 22, Tel: 2421 7092, Fax: 2421 8545, quite all right, and near the night life.

BUDGET: **Yaha**, P-1, Vác-lavské náměstí 64, Tel/Fax: 2421 6399.

UPPER (southern) NEW CITY

LUXURY: **City Hotel Moráň**, P-2, Na Moráni 15, Tel: 2491 5208, Fax: 29 75 33, historic building under Austrian management.

BUDGET: **Páv**, Křemencova 13, P-1, Tel: 2491 3286, Fax: 20 17 13, small and cozy.

Youth Hostels

CKM, P-2, Žitná 10-12, Tel: 2912 40-221, open 7 am-7 pm, near Charles Square; this office books the cheapest accommodations in Prague, particularly for young people. During university holidays, you can also book rooms here in the student dormitories behind Petrín.

Campgrounds

Because of the good transportation connections (bus and boat) to the city center, a whole series of campgrounds have sprung up in Troja. Best-known is **Sokol Troja**, P-7, Trojská 171a, Tel: 688 11 77, open April – Oktober (trees and bushes surround the level field).

Autocamp, **Hájek** and **Herzog** are also located on Trojská. Herzog also offers regular (indoor) accommodations.

In the south, between the Moldau and a sport club, is the pleasant campground **Intercamp Kotva**, P-4, U ledáren 55, Tel: 46 17 12, Fax: 46 61 10, open mid-April - Oktober (tennis courts, bike rental, near the expressway).

Additional campgrounds or camper facilities:

PRAGUE 5: **Eva**, Strojírenská 78, Tel: 301 92 13, a level meadow with fruit trees. **Motol**, Plzeňská,

Tel: 52 47 14, terraced meadow on a hill, with trees, near the streetcar. **Sportcamp**, Nad hliníkem 15, Tel: 52 18 02, Fax: 52 16 32, tennis courts, 700 m from the streetcar stop. **Karavan Park Císařská louka**, Císařská louka 599, Tel: 54 50 64, Fax: 54 33 05, on an island in the Moldau.

PRAGUE 6: **Džbán** (sk Aritma), Nad lávkou 3, Tel: 36 85 51, Fax: 36 13 65, also indoor accommodations, tennis courts, sauna, fitness room, small artificial lake, near the lovely Šárka gorge as well as the streetcar.

PRAGUE 8: **Na Vlachovce**, Zenklova 217, Tel: 688 02 14, near the streetcar, also regular accommodations. **Triocamp**, Obslužná 43, Tel: 688 1180, meadow with trees, bus and streetcar links. **Busek**, U parku 6, Tel/Fax: 859 18 52, meadow with bushes, sauna, tennis courts, near bus and streetcar stops.

PRAGUE 9: **Tj Sokol Dolní Počernice**, Nad rybníkem 290, Tel: 72 75 01, on a pond, with tennis courts, access to bus and subway. **Siesta**, Pod šancemi 51, Tel: 82 14 23, bus and streetcar access.

Tourist information

The newly-established city information agency PIS has gotten off to a good start and is doing a fine job, in several branches through the city, of helping out visitors. In addition, there are a host of private agencies, which you can't miss if you're walking along the "tourist mile" (Wenceslas Square – Na příkope – Celetná – Staroměstské náměstí – Karlova – Charles Bridge – Mostecká).

PIS, all in Prag 1, Na Příkopě, Tel: 26 40 22-3; Staromestské náměstí 22, Tel: 2448 2018; Malostranská Mostecká věž, Tel: 53 60 10; Hlavní nádraží (train station), in the main hall, Tel: 2423 9258.

Private Agencies: **AVE**, P-2, Wilsonova 8, Tel: 2422 3226, 2422 3521, Fax: 2422 3463.

ČEDOK, P-1, Panská 5, Tel: 2419 7615, 2421 0502.

Martin Tour, P-1, Štěpánská 61, Tel/Fax: 2421 2473.

Pragotur, P-1, U Obecního domu 2, Tel: 2481 6120, Fax: 2481 6172.

Top Tour, P-1 Rybná 3, Tel: 232 1077, Fax: 2481 1400.

Universitas Tour, P-1 Opletalova 38, Tel: 26 04 26, fax 2421 2290.

Ticket Offices

Ticketpro, branch offices: PIS - Staroměstská radnice, Staroměstská ámesti 1, Tel: 2448 2018; PIS P-1, Na Přikopě 20, Tel: 26 40 20, Lucerna, P-1, Štěpánská 61, Tel: 2421 2003.

Or-Fea, P-1, Dlouhá 10, Tel: 232 1919.

Bohemia ticket international, P-1, IFB, Václavské námesti 27, Tel: 2422 7253, 2161 2122/4.

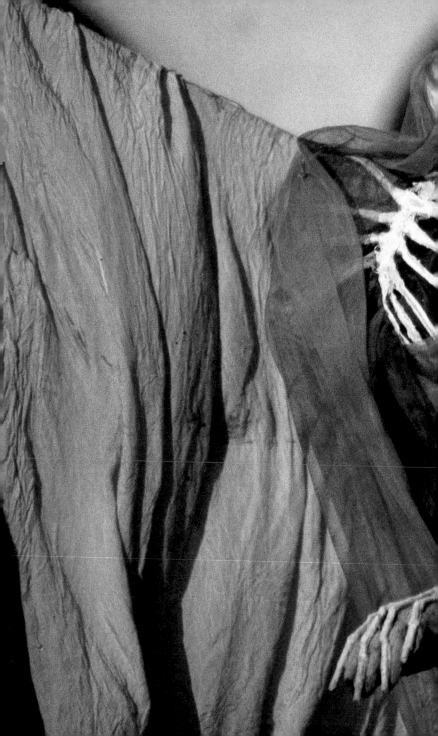

EXPERIENCING PRAGUE

FROM "KING'S WAY" TO
TOURIST ROUTE
PARKS / GARDENS / ISLANDS
GALLERIES / MUSEUMS
SHOPPING / DINING OUT
THEATER

FROM THE POWDER TOWER ACROSS CHARLES BRIDGE TO THE CASTLE

You won't find the **King's Way**, or **Coronation Way** (*Královská cesta* or *Korunovační*), on any Prague city map. These two names designate a lengthy route used by many Bohemian rulers since the Middle Ages. Is it mere coincidence that this historic route is almost identical to the "path of conquest" followed by today's camera- and video-laden conquistadors who descend on Prague from countries around the world? Of course not: the stations along the route are exactly those most popular with the tourists. Starting at the Powder Tower in the Old City (*Staré Město*), the route proceeds through U Prašné brány - Celetná ulice - Staroměstské náměstí - Karlova ulice - Karlův most (Charles Bridge). In the Lesser City (*Malá Strana*), it follows along Mostecká ulice - Malostranské náměstí - Nerudova Ulice - Ke Hradu. And, above the city, in Hradčany, the route runs across Castle Square (*Hradčanské náměstí*).

Preceding pages: Wintry mood on the island Kampa. Dance of death in a street theater performance. Left: A little night music.

Every month, hundreds of thousands of visitors from around the world trek along this trail. Entire school classes in full cry swarm through the narrow streets of the Old City; and high spirits are furthered by the Prague beer, relatively high in alcohol content and relatively low (for Westerners) in price.

There are, furthermore, certain historical parallels between the days of the "King's Way," when the splendid processions of foreign dignitaries visiting the sovereign traveled this route, and the years since 1989, since the "Velvet Revolution": now as then, the citizens of Prague are often thrust into the role of mere bystanders, observers of the pomp and foreign wealth. In fact, today's "foreign invasion" is resulting in an economic situation which threatens to estrange Prague's residents completely from the city of which they are so justly proud and which they so love. Everything which, less than a decade ago, made Prague so lovable and unique – the pubs and small restaurants, the typical pastry shops and the bookshops with their large selection of books in most major languages, the galleries and theaters playing mainly to the locals – is falling by the wayside, pushed aside by the advance of Western commerce and its sometimes dubious stratification of society.

97

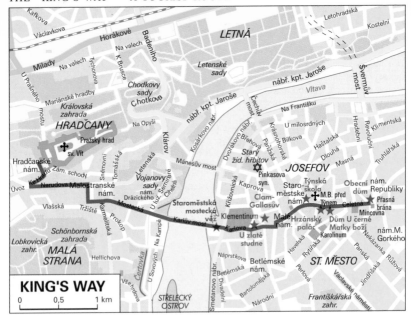

Soon, many fear, the center of Prague will look much like that of any western city, with the same chain restaurants or fashionable boutiques. Already – although the entire downtown area of Prague is a landmarked, thus a protected, area – many of the façades are being altered and disfigured by wooden mountings or neon lights, simply because these are supposed to act as more effective advertising. Marvelous Art Nouveau reliefs are concealed behind plastic awnings which allow customers to enjoy their food and drink outdoors even during rain showers. These urban sins have been given a new name: *servís* (service). Today, the insider notices things which would have been inconceivable in Prague a few years ago: orthographic or factual errors in the advertisements, exaggerated announcements with superlatives, none of which conform either to the city's image or to the fine, elegant structure of

the Czech language. Unconventional spellings have been adopted from Western languages, especially from German. Many of these cutesy slogans have been imported by entrepreneurs who are themselves former emigrés, and who find themselves today as much at odds with the Czech language as they once were with the ruling Communists.

Speaking of Communists: you see things going on today which no Party official would have dared to mix in during the Soviet Army's 20-year occupation in Czechoslovakia. Prague is doing a booming business in icons and matrjoschkas of all shapes and sizes; in jewelry from the Baltic states or Russia; and even in Russian objets d'art and paintings from Russian museums (rarely with a certificate of provenance). Western customers are delighted at the incredible range of items available here, which saves them the trouble of having to travel to Russia to make their purchases. Service is in English, German or Italian, as you prefer, and the currency is equally international.

Right: A steady stream of tourists flows across Charles Bridge.

Where there used to be bookstores or record shops, you now find antiques dealers – a questionable swap. Of course, you can also find a huge selection of high-quality products, but the prices are already, in places, comparable to those in Munich or Madrid: far too expensive, in any case, for Czech pocketbooks.

Although there still isn't, as yet, much animosity toward tourists, you do sometimes hear the occasional heated exchange of words, something unheard-of before 1990. It is important to realize that Prague's six-century-old revolutionary tradition is still very much alive in this city. The Hussite movement of the 15th century, the Prague defenestration of 1618 and the passive resistance in the era after 1968 are not just chapters in the history books, but are kept alive on an everyday basis. With a sense of responsibility to their tradition of liberty, Prague's citizens can't help but feel a certain amount of resentment toward the unabashed advance of the aggressive commercialism of a consumer society – even though the flip side of this are the renovations which have steadily been restoring Prague to its former elegance. All of which means that a stroll along the King's Way will lead you through a city in the throes of radical transition.

From the end of the 14th century until 1483, the royal court (*Králův dvůr*), established by Wenceslas IV (*Václav*), was located on the site of today's Art Nouveau structure *Reprezentační dům hlavního města Prahy* (**Community Center of the Capital of Prague**), 1905-11, with its magnificent Smetana Hall. It was here that the Old City bounded on the New City; and the former court is commemorated in the street name *Králodvorská ulice*. Constructed a fitting distance away from the Moldau, the court was not particularly well located from a strategic point of view. It was here, at the **Powder Tower** (*Prašná brána*), that royal processions always began. The late Gothic

gate, originally built by Matthias Reiseck and re-Gothicized at the turn of this century by Josef Mocker, was a part of the Old City fortifications. The tower, 213 feet (65 m) high, got its name in the 17th century when it was used to store gunpowder.

On the left side of the street Celetná, (this name is derived from the German word *Zeltner*, or pastry-maker), at čp. 587, you'll find the **New Mint** (*Mincovna*), a monumental city palace built in the mid-18th century by the architect J. J. Wirch, with sculptures by Ignaz Platzer. One of the most sensational examples of Cubist architecture is the **House of the Black Madonna** (*U černé Matky Boží*), designed by Josef Gočár in 1911-12. The name refers to the Madonna which decorated the façade of the Baroque palace which originally stood on this site; today, the building is a museum with changing exhibits and a permanent collection of Czech art. A religious motif also adorns the **House of the Golden Angel** (*U Zlatého anděla*) at čp. 588, which served

as a hotel in the 19th century. Three palaces on the right side of the street are noteworthy. **The House of the Black Eagle** (*U černého orla*) at čp. 593 was once Gothic but has been renovated several times. Beside this is the **Menhartovský dům Palace** at čp. 595, with Gothic and Renaissance elements. And just a few steps away is the **Caretto-Millesimo Palace**, a Baroque structure which integrates several Gothic windows from an earlier building on the site. Across from this is the Renaissance **Buquoy City Palace** (čp. 562), today part of Charles University, which received Baroque elements and, more recently, a classical façade. Further along on Celetná is the high Baroque **Hrzánský Palace** (at čp. 558) designed by Giovanni B. Alliprandi at the beginning of the 18th century. As are many of the Old City's palaces and patrician houses along King's

Way or Coronation Way, this splendid structure is also built atop the foundation of a Romanesque house. Also old is the Gothic **House of the Three Kings** (*U tří králů* čp. 602), with its cross-rib vaulting, which dates from the end of the 14th century. Its main claim to fame is the fact that Franz Kafka lived here with his parents as a teenager. The house next door, *U bílého jednorožce* (also called *Trčkovský dům*) at čp. 603, has Gothic and Baroque elements and a Romanesque foundation.

The next four buildings worthy of note are on the Old City Ring (*Staroměstské náměstí*). The Baroque **Sixta House** at čp. 553 was originally Romanesque. At the turn of the century, Mikoláš Aleš, one of the country's most popular painters, designed the façade of the **Stork House,** which was owned by a prominent publisher. The oversized fresco is an equestrian portrait of King Wenceslas I. **The House of the Stone Table** (*U Kamenného stolu*) at čp. 550 was originally Gothic, later Renaissance and today Ba-

Above: Old City Ring. Right: House of the Two Suns on Nerudova.

roque. The **Týn School** (*Týnská škola*) at čp. 604, also originally Gothic, today echoes the style of the Venetian Renaissance.

Passing the **Old City Town Hall** (see the chapter "The Old City," above), we arrive in Malé náměstí, also known as *Ryneček* (Small Ring), with a Renaissance fountain dating from 1560. The **House of Paradise** (*V ráji*) at čp. 144, one of Prague's oldest apothecaries, was originally Romanesque; on the ground floor, you can see a Gothic vaulted ceiling in the form of an eight-pointed star.

On Karlova, pass the Clam-Gallas Palace and take a look at the **House of the Golden Spring** (*U zlaté studně*), decorated with several statues of saints. Once Romanesque, the house is now in Renaissance style and houses a wine restaurant. The former Pötting Palace now houses a small theater. Passing the Clementinum, you'll come to the Old City Bridge Tower (see p. 67).

Charles Bridge is the number-one tourist attraction along the King's Way. It provides the loveliest panorama of the city, with its Baroque statues in the foreground, the Lesser City as the backdrop and behind everything the monumental castle, the destination of the processions which originally followed this route. The chapter on the Lesser City (see above) describes the individual sights along this historic trail. In this part of the city, the increase in commercialism is less noticeable, although street vendors line the tiny streets just as much as in the other parts of the city.

Nerudova has been taken over by speedsters, with or without diplomatic license plates. This is a pity, for the ideal vantage point from which to appreciate the façades and ornamentation on both sides of the street would, in a world without traffic, be the middle of the road. Particularly noteworthy here is the **House of the Two Suns**, once home to the author Jan Neruda. If you aren't in a hurry, take a breather in one of the galleries or cafés which have opened in recent years below the castle.

101

PARKS, GARDENS AND ISLANDS

Prague is an ideal place in which to roam about at a leisurely pace, letting yourself be carried along by the current. This is as true for the locals as for the tourists. Franz Kafka once wrote to his fiancée Felice Bauer, "What I like best is to meander through the parks and small streets."

Many visitors to Prague, wandering about lost in amazement at the beauty of the city, led by curiosity to explore one tiny alley after another, don't notice until too late just how hard the rough cobblestone streets can be on your feet. It is to these people that the following chapter is dedicated. For Prague is much more than merely an animated history lesson. It's also a city of peaceful gardens and parks, of islands and oases of tranquillity, of

Above: In the gardens on Petřín. Right: The Church of St. Lawrence appears at its best from a bird's-eye perspective.

birds chirping contentedly – and of young, or not-so-young, lovers.

The Gardens of Petřín

Let's start with an high point to which every visitor should ascend before the first signs of exhaustion set in: the gardens on the hillsides of Petřín. To the west of the Moldau, Prague is bordered by a range of hills running from Hradčany to Smíchov. Near the highest point of this range is an observation tower modeled on the Eiffel Tower in Paris. The easiest way to reach this iron structure, our first destination at Petřín, is via cable car. To get to this cable car, head south on Karmelitská, which begins at the Lesser City Ring, following it until it turns into *Újezd*. Shortly thereafter, after passing through an arch on the right, you'll arrive at the cable car's lower stop, where you can also buy tickets (they're the same as those for the streetcar). The ascending and the descending cable cars meet at a passing place halfway up the mountain. The restaurant **Nebozízek**, at a stop part way up the hill, commands a spectacular view of the city. Debarking from the cable car at the top, turn left to reach an observatory. A bit further in this direction is a rose garden enclosed by lilac bushes. A path to the left leads down the hill to the gardens of the Kinský Palace while the path on the right leads to one of Europe's largest stadiums, with seating capacity for 200,000 fans. What once served as a parade ground for Olympic-style games under the Communists is today being eyed by the national(istic) "Sokol" gymnastics movement, which is interested in obtaining the grounds for its own purposes.

To get to the 196-foot (60 m) high observation tower from the cable car station, follow a path leading off to the right. Along the way, you pass through an arch of the Hunger Wall. This wall was built under Charles IV as a means of providing employment during a time of famine. The workers were paid enough wages to keep them alive and, in return, constructed this fortification wall. Its purpose was to serve as protection to the southeast, closing the wall at this point, just as the completion of the wall at Vyšehrad did on the other side of the Moldau. Although you have to climb a total of 299 steps in order to reach the tower's observation platform at 164 feet (50 m), the view is worth the effort. You won't find such a complete panorama of the city anywhere else in Prague. It's especially nice because, as you're standing even above the castle, you can survey every one of Prague's major sights.

Before heading back down Mt. Lawrence (Petřín's other name) to the city, visitors might want to take a peek in the cabinet of mirrors (*Bludiště*). Inside is a labyrinth of mirrors, which is easy enough to master; a panorama picture which flows into a three-dimensional foreground, depicting one of the last battles of the Thirty Years' War on

Charles Bridge; and, to the delight of children, a Hall of Mirrors where you can laugh at your grossly distorted reflection.

Across from this is the **Church of St. Lawrence** (*kostel svatého Vavřince*). This Romanesque church was given a Baroque facelift in the 18th century by the Italian architect Palliardi. A winding path, in some places sorely in need of maintenance, leads down the mountain. During the spring and summer months the meadows on the mountainside are awash with colorful wildflowers, providing an almost rural landscape as the foreground to the cityscape. On the evening before May 1, tradition dictates that lovers lay flowers on the Mácha Monument, part way down the hillside. The poet Karel Hynek Mácha died at a young age, and most of his literary estate was composed of fragments; but he is renowned for the romantic epic poem *Máj*, in which he brings out all of the poetic beauty of the Czech language. "It was the first of May, the time for love," the poem begins: hence the offerings of flowers

ever since. Franz Kafka experienced (wouldn't you know it) an entirely different mood here. "Once, many years ago, I sat sorrowfully on the slopes of Mt. Lawrence, and considered what I wanted, what I hoped for, from this life." This is, in short, a great site for emotion, whether you're hopelessly in love or in the throes of spiritual crisis.

The Gardens of the Lesser City

From here, too, you can get a wonderful overview of the city, and in the loveliest of surroundings. In recent years, the gardens of Prague Castle have been restored with utmost care and opened to the public, and it is truly a royal pleasure to stroll through them. Looking toward the Lesser City, you'll notice there are a number of gardens here; many of these, however, are not open to the public, such

Above: Autumn in one of the city's parks.
Right: Devil's Brook separates the island Kampa from the Lesser City.

as that of the British Embassy in Thun Palace. Located at the bottom of the valley are probably the most beautiful of the public gardens of the Lesser City, the **Gardens** of **Waldstein Palace** (*Valdštejnská zahrada*). The entrance to the gardens is not far from the Malostranská subway station, at a bend in the street *Letenská*. At first, the garden seems small and intimate because of the high walls and central paths hemmed in by thick high hedges. To the right, however, the space opens up, revealing an enclosed square goldfish and carp pond at the edge of the gardens. Behind this is the former riding hall, which now houses temporary exhibitions. A path to the right leads to the palace, where, on the side facing the park, the building's most attractive façade includes a *sala terrena* in late Renaissance style, its design based on a northern Italian loggia. In the summer, this provides an architectural framework for cultural events. The garden is open daily from May to September from 9 a.m. to 7 p.m.

Anyone wishing to escape the throngs of tourists who'd rather find a place frequented by Lesser City residents themselves should head for the Moldau and follow the street *U lužického semináře.* Here, you'll find the **Vojan Gardens,** also hidden behind a high wall. Landscaped in the 17th century, they are today a veritable hive of activity.

Moldau Islands

One of the islands in the Moldau is a true gem. At first glance, you can't even tell that this is an island, which is why it is tagged onto the Lesser City in this and most other discussions of Prague. It is, of course, **Kampa Island,** so narrowly separated from the Lesser City by the narrow Devil's Brook (*Čertovka*) that you can hardly tell it's not the mainland. "Here it was tranquil, peace and water, and the lilac filled the air," wrote the Czech poet Antonín Macek in 1912; his description holds true today, particularly during the evening hours. Most of the southern part

of the island is a park; on the square near the bridge, under the shady trees, the atmosphere is peaceful. From time to time, a flea market is held here, and things liven up a bit. A holdover from days gone by, a large mill wheel, churns in the water.

Heading south from Kampa, you come to the **Legion Bridge** (*Most Legií*), built mostly of granite and erected at the turn of the century. A stairway leads down from the bridge to **Marksmen's Island** (*Střelecký ostrov*). A bit overgrown, this island is mainly visited by young people. It is a good place to stroll or simply sit under the green canopy of the linden, willow, chestnut and maple trees. At the island's northern tip, the roar of the water at the Moldau weir drowns out all the other noises of the city. From here, you have an expansive view along the river toward Charles Bridge. Police warn, however, that the island is not a safe place to be after the sun goes down. You can follow the example of the author Max Brod, who was as fond of the island

as was his friend Franz Kafka, and who preferred in any case to come here during the morning hours.

Another island, very close by, is linked to the Moldau's eastern bank by two bridges, actually footbridges. This is **Slavic Island** (*Slovanský ostrov*). Some people still refer to it as Sophie Island, named after the restored white-and-yellow palace here called the *Žofín* (**Sophie Hall**). Hector Berlioz and Franz Liszt both gave concerts in this hall, and balls were also held there. When the weather is good, the benches on this small island are usually full; you can also rent rowboats and paddle-boats at several sites on its shores. Sitting on a landing on the Moldau side of the island, sheltered from the city traffic, you can enjoy a peaceful drink. A statue in the park commemorates the most famous Czech storyteller of the 19th century, Božena Němcová, whose novel *Grandmama* (Babička) is

Above: In the National Gallery's painting collection in Sternberg Palace.

one of the most beloved works of Czech literature. A Constructivist exhibition hall at the southern tip of the island is dedicated to another artist: the painter and sculptor Josef Mánes.

There are very few parks and gardens on the eastern side of the Moldau, in the downtown area. Here, you have to content yourself with the pedestrian zones or Charles Square and the Vrchlického sady across from the main train station, which really isn't much of a park. Because of the noise of surrounding traffic, it can hardly be recommended as an oasis of quiet.

Charles Square (*Karlovo náměstí*) is certainly preferable, particularly owing to the fact that it is surrounded by a number of lovely buildings. The light of the setting sun falls on St. Ignatius and his golden halo on the gable of his renovated church, approximately in the middle of the square, on the eastern side.

At the southern end of the square is a Renaissance building, remodeled in baroque, the so-called Faust House (*Faus-*

tův dům). The Emperor Rudolph II commissioned an English alchemist who worked in this house to change worthless material into gold. His attempts, as we know, proved futile. Ever since, legend has had it that it was here that Dr. Faustus sold his soul to the devil. But there's no substance to this story, either.

GALLERIES AND MUSEUMS

Prague is a museum city in two senses. First, in that merely strolling through the city's streets is like leafing through a stone history book. Everywhere you look, your eye alights on ornamental details or architectural tidbits which are present in a seemingly endless wealth. Who could hope to count the atlases and caryatids straining to bear the weight of the city's houses? Just look around! But in addition to all of this, Prague has a large number of important museums. In most cases, the larger collections are dispersed among many buildings, often lying in different districts of the city. Rather than spend hours in a huge building, therefore, you'll generally take in the collections in bits and pieces, and it's easy to combine a museum visit with an exploration of a particular city district. There's only room here to mention a few of the city's legion, often very small museums; the subjective selection we present is meant simply to whet your appetite and send you out to discover more of the city's treasures on your own.

The National Gallery

The National Gallery consists of four institutions with permanent and occasional special exhibitions, as well as three galleries which only have temporary exhibitions. The permanent collections are in the Sternberg Palace, St. George's Monastery, the St. Agnes Convent and in Zbraslav Castle in the south of Prague. Indubitably the most international of these is in the **Sternberg Palace**. This Baroque building is tucked away behind the Archbishop's Palace on Castle Square. Focal point of the extensive collection is German medieval and Renaissance painting; 15th- to 17th-century Dutch and Flemish masters; the Italian Renaissance; and French painting of the 19th and 20th centuries. One of the most valuable works in the collection is Albert Dürer's *Rosary Festival*, painted in Venice in 1506. More popular, however, at least in terms of drawing crowds, is the collection of French painting, notably works by the Impressionists and post-Impressionists. These range from Eugène Delacroix through Gustave Courbet to Manet, Monet, Renoir, van Gogh, Toulouse-Lautrec, Gauguin, Henri Rousseau, all the way up to Georges Braque, as well as Chagall and Utrillo. During the Communist regime, visitors were always amazed at the extent of the museum's remarkable collection of modern art, particularly works by Picasso which were seldom, if ever, shown in the West. Outsiders tended to forget that Picasso, when in exile, was by no means on good terms with the Franco regime; but rather, as a member of France's Communist Party, was not exactly opposed to the former socialist state. But 20th-century Austrian and German art is also represented with works by Gustav Klimt, Egon Schiele, Oskar Kokoschka and Franz Marc. There are even some sculptures by Rodin, who had many admirers in Prague, not a few of whom attempted to follow in his footsteps.

St. George's Monastery is not far from the Sternberg palace, on the grounds of Prague Castle. If you undertake a visit through the exhibit here, you should come armed with a healthy interest in Christian paintings, from the Gothic age to the Baroque. This former Benedictine monastery houses, among other things, the world's largest collection of 14th-century panel paintings,

mainly works from Bohemia, Germany and Italy. Other works in the gallery range from Rudolphian Mannerism up to Late Baroque. Another branch of the National Gallery in the castle is housed in the former Riding School, which presents rotating exhibits of contemporary art.

Down in the city, near the Moldau and just east of Josefov, is the **Convent of St. Agnes**. The permanent collection here features works by Czech painters and sculptors of the 19th century, including many sculptures by the ubiquitous Josef Václav Myslbek, whose works are scattered throughout the entire city. Fans of figurative painting will enjoy the works by Josef Mánes and Mikoláš Aleš. Dandies should make sure not to miss the portrait of Hermína Brožíkova-Sedelmeyerová, and rationalists will ask themselves how Adolf Karásek managed to

Above: Functionalistic hall in the Great Exhibition Palace. Right: The National Museum. Far right: Musical instrument collection of the National Museum.

bestow such a supernatural aura on his painting *Winter Night*. A model of the National Theater shows how the architects solved the problem presented by an asymmetrical construction site.

The fourth museum of the National Gallery, *Zbraslav Castle* (**King's Hall**), can be reached by bus 129, 241 or 243 from the main bus depot Smíchov. The building, with its Baroque elements, is a former Cistercian monastery which was originally a hunting palace and a chapel. Noteworthy is the depiction of the founding of the monastery by King Václav II, shown in a ceiling fresco by Wenzel Lorenz Reiner in the main hall of the central wing. Sculptures by Czech masters of the 19th and 20th century are exhibited inside as well as outside in the park. The prolific Myslbek is represented in Zbraslav, as is Ladislav Šaloun, who sculpted the Hus Monument on the Old City Ring, and Bohumil Kafka, the artist who created the monumental life-like statue of Jan Žižka on Vítkov. If you're interested in learning more about the development of sculpture in Bohemia (influenced by such greats as Rodin or Maillol), make sure to have a look at this museum, even if it's a bit out of the way and lies in the rather less than attractive suburbs.

The galleries which show temporary exhibits are also worth mentioning. One is the **Kinský Palace** on the Old City Ring; its storerooms seem to contain an inexhaustible supply of drawings and graphics by masters from around the world from over the last five centuries, which are displayed in rotating exhibitions. Highlights include works by such artist as Dürer, Rembrandt, Goya and Dalí, to name but a few. The other gallery is the **Riding School** in the Waldstein Palace. Exhibitions here tend to be held on short notice.

Looking toward the future, great things are afoot in Prague, at least as far as lovers of modern art are concerned. The Great Exhibition Palace, near the train

underpass in front of the Old Exhibition Grounds on Stromovka, has finally been completely restored after having been badly damaged by a fire in 1974. This functionalist structure was for a time the world's largest exhibition palace after it was completed in 1929. It is still impressive today with its two spacious, high-ceilinged halls, used predominantly to display large machines and industrial objects. One would imagine that this building will be an impressive forum for the presentation of modern art in Prague.

National Museum

Like the architecture of the National Theater, the National Museum's construction has about it a sense of the nationalistic pathos that prevailed in the late 19th century, turned to stone. Even before you enter the exhibits, you're greeted by the statues and busts of important historic figures which line the stairway under the dome. This theme continued in the Pantheon, a kind of Czech hall of fame spread over two floors. Among all of these heroes, only two women are to be found, the authors Božena Němcová and Eliška Krásnohorská. All the other pedestals, and there are more than 40 of them, support figures of men, including the composers Dvořák and Smetana, the great reformer Jan Hus, the pedagogue Jan Amos Komenský (Comenius) and the first President of the Czechoslovakian Republic, Tomáš G. Masaryk.

Also on the second floor, you'll find a well-curated exhibit of the pre- and early history of the territory of the Czech and Slovakian states. Although there is a very general description in English of the individual cultural epochs, the detailed explanations are all in Czech, so if you're not well-versed in the language, it's virtually impossible to become too deeply involved. Other exhibits in this wing present the history of the currency as well as the more modern history of the Czech people since their sense of national identity began to develop in the 19th century.

The opposite wing houses an extremely detailed, not to say pedantic, collection of mineralogy and petrography. If you've never realized the myriad forms and colors which inanimate nature can present, this exhibit will be truly an eye-opener. It makes one realize that precious stones which we usually identify solely by their color actually exist in a variety of different colors and unusual forms.

One wing on the third floor has a zoological department; the other, a paleontological one. The exhibit of stuffed exotic animals in glass cases is somewhat less than exciting. It seems as though the curators were simply trying to find space for these specimens rather than arranging them in any kind of sensible order. For lovers of smaller creepy-crawly things, the National Museum has one of the world's largest insect collections. In the basement, as well as a salad bar, there is

Above: Special exhibition in the Museum of Decorative Arts.

also space for cultural, historical, or other relevant temporary exhibits.

Like the National Gallery, the National Museum also has branches throughout the city displaying parts of its collection. Music lovers are in for a special treat, for there are four museums in this category. Three of these are dedicated to single composers: the **Villa America** to Dvořák, the **Villa Bertramka** to Mozart and the former **Waterworks** to Smetana. At the time of writing, the fate of the Museum for Musical Instruments is still not clear. Heretofore, it's been housed in the Palace of the Grand Prior of the Order of Malta in the Lesser City, but it may be moved to Karlov Monastery.

The **Lapidarium** on the Exhibition Grounds (*Výstaviště*) houses a noteworthy exhibit of building fragments from historic houses which have been razed. History buffs will want to visit the **Lobkovicz Palace** when they're touring Prague Castle. In addition to the permanent exhibit documenting the most important epochs of Bohemian history, the building is also a venue for special exhibitions and concerts.

Other Museums

If you'd like to learn something about the city itself, stop in at the **Museum of the Capital City of Prague**, located north of the Florenc bus depot. The incredibly detailed model of the city depicts, for example, the layout of Josefov at the turn of the century, before its so-called *Assanierung* (the Austrian term for building improvements for reasons of hygiene or society). Here, too, is the original face of the large clock of the Old Town Hall, designed by Josef Mánes.

The **Museum of Decorative Arts** (*Umělecko průmyslové muzeum*) is located between Rudolfinum and the old Jewish cemetery. Fans of antique furnishings will particularly enjoy this museum. In addition to lovely pieces of furniture sporting exquisite stone and wood inlays, the museum also houses delicate double-walled glass containers with gold and silver foil between the layers, Meissen porcelain and majolica. There are descriptions of the exhibits in several languages. Hall IV offers a good view of the old Jewish cemetery. The museum also has a small café.

Finally, at the end of this small selection, a museum of a very special nature should be mentioned. This is the **Prague Police Museum** in the southern part of the New City, near the Villa America. Even more realistically than its American counterpart, the Chicago Police Museum, it displays the real-life face of a policeman's work. Particularly spectacular cases of criminal energy are documented here in interesting detail. Gangsters with unique "talents" even have their own showcases. To calm the fears of the timid, the police have already roped off and inspected the museum's chaotic and very realistic scene of the crime, and outlined the position of the corpse in chalk.

National Gallery (Národní galérie), exhibitions Tue-Sun 10 a.m.-6 p.m.: **Sternberg Palace**, P-1, Hradčanské náměstí 15, Tel: 2031 4599. **St.-George Monastery**, P-1, Prague fortress, Jiřské náměstí 33, Tel: 8732 0536. **St.-Agnes-Convent**, P-1, U Milosrdných 17, Tel: 2481 0628. **Castle Zbraslav**, P-5, Zbraslav; Tel: 5792 1638-9. **Riding School of Prague fortress**, P-1, U Prašného mostu 55, Tel: 2437 3232. **Wallenstein Riding School**, P-1, Valdštejnská 2, Tel: 53 68 14. **Kinsky Palace**, P-1, Staroměstské náměstí 12, Tel: 2481 0758.

National Museum (Národní museum): **National Museum**, P-1, Václavské náměstí 68, Tel: 2449 7111, Mon-Sun 9 a.m.-5 p.m. **Lapidarium**, P-7, Výstaviště, Tue-Fri 12 p.m.-6 p.m. and Sat.-Sun 10 a.m.-12 p.m. and 1 p.m.-6 p.m. **Lobkowicz Palace**, P-1, Prague Fortress, Jiřská 3, Tel: 53 73 06, Tue-Sun 9 a.m.-5 p.m. **Dvořák Museum**, P-2, Ke Karlovu 20, Tel: 29 82 14, Tue-Sun 10 a.m.-5 p.m. **Smetana Museum**, P-1, Novotného lávka 1, Tel: 2422 9075, call for opening hours. **Vila Bertramka** (Mozart-Museum), P-5, Mozartova 169, Tel: 54 38 93, Mon-Sun 9:30 a.m.-6 p.m. **Museum of Musical Instruments**, P-1, Lázeňská 2 or Velkopřevorské náměstí 4, Tel: 5732 0059, Tue-Sun 10 a.m.-5 p.m. (call ahead).

More Museums

Museum of the City of Prague, P-1, Na Poříčí 52, Tel: 2481 6772, Tue-Sun 10 a.m.-6 p.m. **Artwork Museum**, P-1, 17. listopadu 2, Tel: 24 81 12 41, Tue-Sun 10 a.m.-6 p.m. **Police Museum**, P-2, Ke Karlovu 1, Tel: 29 89 40, Tue-Sun 10 a.m.-5 p.m. **National Technical Museum**, P-7, Kostelní 42, Tel: 37 36 51-9, Tue-Sun 9 a.m.-5 p.m. **National Culture Monument Vyšehrad**, P-2, Soběslavova 1, Tel: 3966 5132, 9:30 a.m.-4:30 p.m. (cemetery 9 a.m.-4 p.m.). **Premonstratensian Monastery Strahov**, P-1, Strahovské nádvoří 1, Tel: 2451 0355, Treasures of convents from the Gothic to the romantic, Tue-Sun 9 a.m.-12 p.m. and 12:30 p.m.-5 p.m. **Museum of Czechoslovakian Manuscripts** is also here, Tel: 5732 0828, Tue-Sun 9 a.m.-5 p.m. **Star Castle** (Hvězda), P-6, Liboc 25c, Tel: 36 26 00, exhibition of A. Jirásek and M. Aleš, call for opening times (renovation). **Dům U Černé Matky boží**, P-1, Celetná 34, Tel: 2421 1732, Czechoslovakian cubism and exhibitions.

Art galleries of the city of Prague, every Tue-Sun 10 a.m.-6 p.m.: **Old town city hall**, P-1, Staroměstské náměstí 1, exhibitions, Mon-Sun 11 a.m.-5 p.m. **Stone bell tower** (Dům U kamenného zvonu), P-1, Staroměstské náměstí 13, exhibitions. **City library**, P-1, Mariánské náměstí 1, exhibitions. **Troja Castle**, P-7, Troja, Tel: 689 07 61, sightseeing, exhibitions. **Veletržní palác**, P-7, corner of Veletržní/Dukelských hrdinů modern art.

SHOPPING

Now that the Czech Republic has decided to embark on the road toward a market economy, with no ifs, ands or buts, you can buy everything in Prague that you can buy in any other commercial center throughout the globe. Many of these items, furthermore, particularly those manufactured in this country, are less expensive than they are in Western industrialized countries.

Market economy also means that not only can you buy more in the country's main centers of tourism, but things tend to be more expensive there. "More expensive" remains a relative term; even in Prague, prices are still lower than in the West. The most expensive area in Prague is in and around the so-called Golden Cross, the area which runs from Wenceslas Square and its northern extension

to the Old City Ring, with a horizontal axis formed by Národní třída and Na příkopě. Here, you can find everything from simple off-the-rack clothing to the choicest of Western luxury items. The farther you retreat from the center, the less expensive the shops become, and the better your chances of finding unassuming, unpretentious stores which, like fossils of a bygone era, exude the bleak flair of socialism. On their dusty, half-empty shelves are items that are often solid, practical, and useful, but have none of the design appeal or gloss to which western eyes are accustomed. But the days of these relics also appear to be numbered. Even in the remotest corners of the Czech capital, you see more and more often the occasional renovated facade standing out among the palette of gray tones: and this signals a modern boutique, an electronic game arcade, or a travel agency with plastic palms in the window, vying for the favors of old and new customers.

Some of the most popular souvenir items of the past can still be found today,

Above: A car from the Stone Age, a touch of France, and an empty store. Right: Onion-pattern china from Karlovy Vary.

and at relatively inexpensive prices. Among these are goods intended for immediate consumption such as Prague ham (*pražská šunka*); Znaimer and other sausages; Karlovy Vary wafers; Becherovka (a liqueur from the town of the same name); a variety of beers including, but not limited to, the famous Pilsner and Budweiser; and Moravian wine and fruit brandies such as *slivovice* or *borovička* (made of juniper berries). If you'd like to survey the full range of the hearty, tasty local edible delicacies, visit the gourmet shop across the street from the Art Nouveau Hotel Evropa on Wenceslas Square. Before making any actual purchases, however, do some comparison shopping and price the same items in the grocery sections of the large department stores or the supermarkets in the outlying districts of Prague. Nowadays, you can also get a full range of health food in Prague. One of the more "in" shops in this category, and accordingly expensive, is "Countrylife" on the street Melantrichova.

Just as popular now as under the Communists, and still relatively inexpensive, is the wide selection of Bohemian glass, porcelain and ceramics. In addition to traditional items such as hand-cut crystal or porcelain with the Karlovy Vary blue onion pattern, you can also encounter modern forms, particularly among the glassware and the ceramics. Anyone looking for a souvenir with a flavor of days gone by can find a range of chandeliers and mirrors that seem sprung full-blown from the last century. Once you've made the decision to purchase Bohemian glass, you'll quickly be overwhelmed at every turn with the sparkle of cut-glass and crystal twinkling from one shop window after another, until the entire city center seems a veritable palace of rock crystal. All the more reason, then, to take the time to do some comparison shopping, for the differences in price and quality are considerable. Sometimes it might even pay to take an excursion into the countryside around Prague and visit one of the manufacturers. If you're arriv-

ing in Prague by car, stop off at one of the many, clearly signposted glass factories on the way in to get an idea of the selection and the prices.

Bohemia is also known as a land of semi-precious gems; and you therefore find local jewelry in a wide variety of forms. In addition to the roving street vendors who have to display a license issued by the "Association of Artists on Charles Bridge and the Castle Hill" in order to sell their earrings and trinkets in this area, there are also jewelry salesmen plying local wares on and around Wenceslas Square. Perhaps they will be able to interest you in a garnet choker reminiscent of something your grandmother might have worn.

What is particularly cheap is casual clothing such as jeans, T-shirts and the like, sold in discount stores which seem to have sprouted up overnight. In general, clothing is inexpensive, but it also tends

Above: Marionette: a popular souvenir of Prague.

not to be very fashionable. The same holds true of leather clothing – relatively cheap, but without much style. On the other hand, if you're looking for a leather handbag, you may have more luck. Many of the new smaller dealers offer a wide variety of these. Anyone in need of new shoes should first stop in at Baťa on Wenceslas Square to check out their styles and prices. Then head for other shoe stores, or *Dům obuvi* (e.g. in Karmelitská/Újezd) to do some comparison shopping. Because Baťa also carries other famous brands, some shoppers may want to return there to make their purchases from the large selection offered.

Not only children are delighted by the dolls, marionettes and imaginative wooden toys found in Prague. This particular branch of commerce owes its seemingly unshakable position entirely to tourism. Anyone who can afford it should try to seek out unique, individually hand-crafted items, and avoid the usual gamut of stereotypical plastic kitsch.

Once, in the years before November 1989, Prague's bookstores contained a large selection of Czech as well as non-Czech books. Prominent among the latter were inexpensive German classics from the GDR. Nowadays, these are harder to find as the publishers as well as the bookshops have cut back on their supply. This loss has partially been made up for with English-language books or books from West German publishers, predominantly remaindered or surplus titles which are marketed cheaply. Some second-hand bookstores still contain buried treasure, although in the Golden Cross area this, too, has its price, since most of the clientele are Western tourists.

The same is true of antiques. One gets the impression that, because of the rising prices, the people of Prague now enjoy the possession of their family heirlooms solely through their ability to put them up for sale, knowing they'll be bought up eagerly by an entirely Western clientele. The prices certainly reflect this. If you're looking for a bargain, you'll have more luck if you venture into the suburbs. Bear in mind, however, that it is illegal to export valuable antiques out of the country.

Music and musical instruments remain popular with shoppers. From CDs, which are up to 50% cheaper than they are in the west, to scores to musical instruments, the selection in this area can fully compete with that at home in terms of quality, and generally wins out in terms of price. If you're looking to buy an instrument, you'll find that most of the products are local brands; which means that you have to be well enough informed to be able to ascertain the quality on your own.

For the rest, it's generally worthwhile simply to browse around. There are shops here specializing in articles for fishermen, equestrians, hunters, athletes and more. Stamp and coin collectors with a special interest in issues from the ČSR, ČSSR and ČSFR will be delighted with the selection here.

Stores and Shopping Centers
Kotva, P-1, náměstí Republiky 8, biggest department store, good groceries. **Tesco**, P-1, Národní třída 26, good clothes. **Nákupní galerie Myslbek**, P-1, Na Příkopě 19, shopping center, **Palace Koruna**, P-1, corner Václavské náměstí and, Na Příkopě, shopping center.

Shoes
Baťa, P-1, Václavské náměstí 6. **Italian Fashion**, P-2, Vinohradská 32.

Glass and Porcelain
Bohemia, P-1, Národní třída 43. **Bohemia Crystal**, P-1, Celetná 5. **Bohemia Moser**, P-1, Na Příkopě 12 u. Malé náměstí 11. **Český křišťál**, P-1, Celetná 26. **Jafa**, P-1, Maiselova 15. **Karlovy Vary Porcelain**, P-1, Pařížská 2. **Sklo Bohemia**, P-1, Na Příkopě 17, also mail-order. **Sklo exclusive**, P-1, Vodičkova 28, in the ABC arcade, also mail-order. **Caesar crystal**, P-1, Václavské náměstí 20.

Jewelry
Chiuri, P-1, Národní třída 31. **Exclusive**, P-1, Václavské náměstí 47. **Granát**, P-1, Václavské náměstí 8 and Dlouhá 28. **Luna**, P-1, Maiselova 17. **Shana**, P-1, Na Příkopě 31. **Vili**, P-1, Václavské náměstí 9 and 13. **Český granát**, P-1, Celetná 4 and Karlova 44. **Detail**, P-1, Haštalská 8 and Melantrichova 11. **Rapa**, P-1, Na Poříčí 13. **Tom-Bohemia**, P-1, Můstek 10 (glass and jewelry).

Sheet Music
Amistar, P-2, Francouzská 26. **House of Musical Instruments** (Dům hudebních nástrojů), P-1, Jungmannova náměstí 17. **Antikvariát Hudebniny** (used books), P-1, V Kolkovně 6. **Music Goca**, P-1, V Kolkovně 6. **Popron multimedia megastore**, Jungmannova 30, newest CDs, partially self produced. **234**, P-2, Bělehradská 234, rock-CDs. **Hudební nástroje**, P-1, Náprstkova 10. **Megastore Koruna**, P-1, Václavské náměstí 1. **Supraphon**, P-1, Palackého 1 (classical CDs).

Foreign-language Books
Cizojazyčná literatura, P-1, Na Příkopě 27. **Kniha**, P-1, Štěpánská 12. **Knihkupectví Franze Kafky**, P-1, Staroměstské náměstí 12, Kafka books. **Knihkupectví Kanzelsberger**, P-1, Václavské náměstí 42. **Kafkův dům**, P-1, U Radnice 5. **U Černé Matky boží**, P-1, Celetná 34.

Antiques
Antikvariát Keřnek, P-1, Celetná 31. **Athena**, P-1, U starého hřbitova 4. **Filip Jaeger antikva**, P-1, U Prašné brány 2. **Hodinářství**, P-1, Mikulandská 10. **Profoto**, P-1, Pařížská 12, old cameras and photographs. **Antique shop**, P-1, Národni třída 21 and Masarykovo nábřeži 36.

Toys, Dolls, etc.
Dřevěné hračky, P-1, Jilská 7. **Ivre Löfelmannová**, P-1, Jakubská 3 u. Veselavínova 3.

EATING OUT

As a rule, any judgments you hear on questions of gastronomy should be taken with the proverbial grain of salt – perhaps in a literal as well as a figurative sense. How much more true this is if you're trying to make generalizations about the cuisine of an entire city. Ask twenty people who've just eaten in the same restaurant and you're likely to get twenty different opinions as to its quality, each colored by the mood, expectations, and tastes of the individual in question. Everything you're about to read, therefore, is just one attempt to define the phenomenon of "Prague Cuisine," based on individual experience, boiled down to an unsteady idea of averages, providing rules or recipes for city dining which are spiced throughout with exceptions, changes, approximations.

Above: Eating in a square. Right: Perhaps the service compensates for a scanty selection.

Seen through the eyes of a fictive Lucullus, Prague's gastronomy ranges through every pinnacle and nadir of the business, although the pinnacles are rare, while the nadirs of the "actual socialist cuisine" of the past have all too often been replaced with mere profit-seeking carelessness. Finesse often costs more, but high costs by no means guarantee finesse. Cheap can often mean "not bad," but nearly everything offered cheap at the center of Prague is prepared with an eye to mass consumption, so that wet, limp salad and soft French fries seem to have become standard side dishes. The custom of using canned vegetables or terribly overcooking fresh ones is widespread. If you want to eat cheaply, look for local cuisine: that's a better bet than venturing into regions that are experimental for cook and diner alike. Some establishments offer lunchtime buffets, where food is kept warm under heat lamps; if you arrive a bit late, you won't generally even need to think about trying the meat or vegetables.

The country's opening westward has meant an influx, not only of fast-food chains, but of a whole spectrum of international cuisine; but these haven't pushed out the restaurants, so prized in the past, offering Eastern European specialties. It's virtually impossible to attempt any evaluation of the newer arrivals, particularly as the rate of fluctuation is high.

"Knedlíky" – local stuffing

If you're looking for something cheap and local, expect to find yourself in a narrow, smoky pub with simple furnishings. In many such places, the greasy mists of Socialist recipes still weigh heavily on the cast-iron cooking pots, which means that nourishing oneself is often equated with the mere purposeful intake of calories. Ideally suited to this purpose are the "knedlíky," or dumplings, prominently featured on every menu; they prove all too often to be tasteless sponges to soak up sauce, but are certainly more than filling. If you're lucky, the meat will be more or less free of gristle, and even be tasty – albeit slightly sour – thanks to the tradition of marinating it before cooking. White and red cabbage, the standard "two veg," as it were, of the pre-capitalist era, are still popular with many cooks. Some newer arrivals on the gastronomic scene seem to have noted the general absence of vitamins from the local diet, which has led to the institution of a few (overpriced) salad bars.

A sense of ideological continuity is provided by the fact that menus still often advertise the weight (in grams) of each portion of meat and fish. As Prague's relatively low prices seem to make most tourists more, rather than less, stingy, the whole city is waiting for the first Western tourist to show up with an electronic kitchen scale in his pocket, to make sure that his serving has lived up to its promise. However, having the waitress calculate

the final price from the actual weight of your portion, down to the last krone and heller, which was the custom during the Socialist period, is today practiced only outside the city center.

Apart from the fast-food establishments, where guests are handled with a businesslike professional élan, service is generally fair to good. This doesn't prevent appetizers and entrees, often as not, from being served together, without eliciting any great show of regret from the responsible waitperson. The waitperson in question will, however, tend to be stoic, helpful or even friendly, and try to compensate for any shortages with the appropriate speed, as far as it's within the power of the establishment to do so. In many eateries, the tableware is reminiscent of the selection one finds in the apartments of college students, a motley assortment lifted from various student dining halls; and you shouldn't expect to find toothpicks everywhere you go. And if you like to eat with your eyes as well as your mouth, your digestion may fre-

quently be disturbed by the sticky bottles of Worcestershire sauce and ketchup which grace many tables.

One real strength of Prague's gastronomy is its atmosphere. There really is something for every taste: historical, traditional rooms; cool, modern, fashionably-styled halls. Adding to the appeal, often enough, are lovely views of the Moldau, the castle, the bridges, or some facet of Prague's old architecture.

In Praise of Fine Vines

People generally say that Bohemia is beer country, but while there's truth to this cliché, there are also exceptions. Unlike beer, which is seen as a necessary dietetic staple, *víno* in Bohemia is understood as a rather exalted pleasure. Because of this association, many a *vinárny* has undergone a transformation, target-

Above: Wine-tasting with music by Charles Bridge. Right: Four drinkers – or one very thirsty consumer?

ing a more discerning (i.e. more well-heeled) public by developing from a simple tavern into a gourmet establishment. Only a few places have kept up the original tradition of only offering the wines of a given region, or even of a given vintner. Still, what you'll generally be offered are local wines from Moravia and from a few small wine-producing regions in Bohemia. Imported wines are certainly for sale, but imbibing them can quickly become an expensive pastime, as there's still a steep customs duty to be paid on EU wines. And because of this high tax, you'll find that, with the exception of the French establishment **U Malířů** and a very few others, the international wines on sale are seldom better than average.

If you wanted to make a list of the best wine-producing areas in the Czech Republic, it would be headed by the vineyards of southern Moravia. The names on everyone's lips – literally as well as figuratively – are Hodonín, Mikulov, Valtice and Znojmo. In Bohemia itself, the

vintages of the Žernoseky region in the Elbe valley vie with those of Mělník for the oenophile's attention.

Recommending a particular wine is not so easy, as various connoisseurs differ widely in their evaluation of various vintages. If someone names a leading red wine, it's likely to be the deep red, dry, strong *Frankovka*. *Vavřinec* also comes into the final round. Of the white wines, it's the rather dry *Rulandské* that can most honestly be recommended; other kinds tend to be too sweet. To be on the safe side, it's best to begin with a "deci" (0.1 liter), rather than ordering half a liter of something you turn out not to like.

Shortly after the grape harvest, you can find a kind of early green wine served in Prague. It's called *burčák*, is fairly sweet, goes down like grape juice, and will get you very tipsy very quickly if you don't watch out. When it arrives, there's such a rush on the wine-cellars that people end up standing around in the street to drink, toasting each other no less cheerfully for all that.

Beer, the elixir of life

The Bohemians belong to the ranks of the world's leading beer producers, something indicated by the fact that, like the Bavarians, Belgians, and Brits, their name begins with "B." Unlike their fellows, however, the object of their veneration does not begin with the same letter; but it does have an even greater etymological significance. In Czech, the word for beer, *pivo*, derives from *píti*, to drink – which makes it clear what, for the Czechs, represents the ultimate thirst-quencher.

Anyone who complains about the food in Prague may be right from an objective standpoint, but is wrong from the perspective of the local cultural mores; for in Prague, as any insider knows, a restaurant is not interesting because of what it serves to eat, but by virtue of its beer. To put it differently (and succumb, for a moment, to one of those generalities one tries so scrupulously to avoid): in Prague, people don't drink beer with their meal;

119

they eat in order to drink beer – if they can still afford to eat in a restaurant at all. What develops from this relationship is a fidelity, strengthened by many experimental dalliances to test the waters (or the beers), to one's own, tried and true house brand.

This fidelity can go to extremes. When the restoration of private property and privatization began in earnest, there was a threat of pub closures on a wide scale. One story with a happy ending was that of **U koucora** (At the Cat). A citizens' group formed to save this beloved, unpretentious establishment, which has always been held to be the pub that serves the best Pilsener in the city.

And this brings us to Bohemia's most famous beer, whose name has come to describe a type of beer known all over the world: **Pils(ener)**. Originally developed by a Bavarian brewer who had been

Above: In summer, the beer garden U Fleků is a place of pilgrimage for many tourists. Right: From the source.

brought into the country, the slightly bitter Pilsener Source has always been one of the republic's top exports. Only one beer can vie with its renown: the Budweiser from České Budějovice. Americans who confuse this with the Budweiser they know from home have a surprise in store: Czech Budweiser is a whole different ball game, with a stronger, punchier flavor. To Europeans, the difference is that the Czech variety is a real beer (beer having, like coffee, American and European incarnations, of which the European is far the stronger).

In Prague, there are a whole series of small and medium-sized breweries, each with its own regular clientele. The favorite, after the two top runners, is **Smíchover Staropramen beer**, with a malt content of 10 or 12%. **Pražan beers**, brewed in Holešovice, have the same levels. In Braník, the light and dark variants of **Braník beer** have malt contents of 10, 12, or 14%. Recently, the city's old, established breweries have gotten more competition from smaller labels from the provinces. You can't miss the label of the Grosspopowitzer brewery, a newly-ubiquitous billygoat (*kozel*) which advertises beer with a malt content of 12%. And the popularity of the 13% dark beer served in **U Fleků**, an establishment with many rooms and a large, tree-shaded beer garden, continues to grow unchecked. This beer has the shortest distance to travel from brewery to table, thence into the mouths of locals and tourists: it's brewed in-house. It does get its share of shaking up, however, comparable to that other beers receive in shipment, since things have been getting increasingly lively in the beer garden of late, with plenty of dancing and swaying to and fro both during and after consumption.

The alcohol content of beer, if given at all, is stated in very small print on the label; but you can arrive at an approximate figure by dividing the malt content by 3. For those who can't tell the quality of a beer by its taste, Prague's citizens have developed two methods of testing it: either you place a light heller coin on the foamy head of the beer, or you stick a match upright into the foam. If the coin or match remain standing for 10 seconds, the beer is capable of satisfying even the most discerning connoisseurs.

The general rule on pricing holds true for beer as well: the farther you are from the city center, the cheaper the beer. While many audacious bartenders are already asking up to 80 krone for a bottle of Pilsner Source, you can get a standing half-liter, the normal measure in the Bohemian regions, for about 10 krone in the suburbs.

Where has all the café culture gone?

At one time there was a good deal of uncertainty as to the future of one Prague institution which has gone down in the city's cultural history as a meeting-place for political dissidents. This is the **Café**

Slavia on the corner of Národni třída, opposite the National Theater. After the "Velvet Revolution," it was sold to an interested party from the New World; but the hope that the new owner would proceed to renovate and reopen this cult site with capitalistic haste was dashed at first. Quite the contrary: the café, which was an informal literary meeting-place for Czech writers with nationalist leanings as early as the beginning of the century, remained closed for months, without anything at all seeming to happen, and it was even feared that the site, once known widely as an anti-authoritarian enclave in the midst of the Socialist state, would have to be re-apropriated. The whole thing was escalated to the status of a government affair when Václav Havel wrote a letter to the new owner, requesting him to make a positive decision. As yet, nothing concrete seems to have happened. Prague's residents can sometimes be heard asking with melodramatic melancholy, "How long will the Slavia's empty windows continue to stare blindly

121

out over the Moldau?" On the other hand, such nostalgia is a bit surprising in light of the fact that the Slavia didn't enjoy a fabulous reputation when it was open: the coffee was supposed to be bad, the service unfriendly, and the music at night played dutifully, routinely, but without any interest or fire. But perhaps it was precisely its cheerless atmosphere that gave the establishment, which opened again at the end of 1997, its special flair.

Similar things are said of other cafés which are today surrounded with nostalgia, even at the acme of "café culture" at the beginning of the century. It was doubtless the relative cheapness of such establishments, and the hint of anti-bourgeois disrespectability, that helped them develop into central institutions for la vie bohèmienne – rather than such amenities as good coffee or a pleasant ambiance.

In Národní třída there were other cafés which also served as watering-holes for

Above: In Gany's. Right: Prague's coffee-house culture, modern version.

the Czech avant-garde. Not far away, opposite the Ursuline, people met in the Café **National**. The Union on the corner of Na perštýne, favorite hangout of Josef and Karel Čapek, Jaroslav Hašek and the poet (and 1984 winner of the Nobel Prize) Jaroslav Seifert, is no more; but there is, at least, a bookstore located in its once-smoky premises. One café that has seen an appropriate and happy resurrection under a new name is the former **Louvre**. In the days of Art Nouveau it was frequented by a circle of philosophical, mainly German-speaking intellectuals, including, briefly, Max Brod and Franz Kafka. Today, the café is called **Gany's**, located, like its predecessor, on the building's second floor. Its new interior is perhaps a bit heavy on the plastic, but still manages to create a pleasant atmosphere. One of the rooms is dominated by large-scale reproductions of old advertising posters.

Like the Slavia, the Café **Radetsky**, better known as *Malostranská kavárna*, a relic of the days of the monarchy, also reopened in 1997. It was here that the Prague poet Johannes Urzidil accompanied his father when he was a little boy, and received his first reading lessons from the café's tattered newspapers. Kafka, too, used to sit here after his long walks through the parks and alleyways of the Lesser City.

Many of the traditional coffee-houses have disappeared altogether. Take two cafés in Vodičkova, west of Wenceslas Square. The former café City is today home to a German bank, while the café Myšák is now a fashion boutique (only a few faded letters around the entrance bear testimony to its past). On Wenceslas Square, the Café Alfa, keeping in step with the times, has transformed itself into a pitch-black techno disco.

If you want to follow in the footsteps of Prague's German-speaking intellectuals, you'll find that here, too, little is left of the past. The Café Continental on

the second floor of the Kolovrat Palace on Na příkopě (number 17) was the hangout of the writer Gustav Meyrink (*The Golem*) and a meeting-place for many German Jewish emigrants who fled the country after Hitler was named Reichskanzler in 1933, who gathered here to discuss their situation; but the café was closed at the end of the war.

In addition to the Café Central, also long gone, one of the favorite haunts of German-speaking men of letters was Café **Arco** on Hybernská, founded in 1907. Among the first generation of "Arconauts," as they were jokingly termed, were poet and novelist Franz Werfel (later husband of Alma Mahler), whose much-lauded tenor voice provided additional atmosphere after a few drinks as the evening wore on; the journalist Willy Haas; the dramatist Paul Kornfeld, and the actor Ernst Deutsch. The artists didn't keep exclusively among themselves; Ernst Polak, a bank official, was also a regular member of their circle (he later married Milena Jesenská, herself event-

ually to gain world fame after Kafka's letters to her were published). Before World War I, Kafka himself, as well as authors Max Brod and Oskar Baum, also came here. The latter had lost his sight at the age of twelve in a fight with Czech youths, when a lens of his glasses was punched into his one good eye. Other occasional members of the Arconaut circle were the journalist Egon Erwin Kisch and the poet Rainer Maria Rilke.

Almost forgotten today, but greatly responsible for the flair of this and other cafés at the time, were the two rebels and dandies Victor Hadwiger and Paul Leppin, who tended more in the direction of esotericism and kitsch. The erotic escapades of these two, known to the whole city, played no small part in the antibourgeois reputation of the literary scene of the day. Both of these characters made the rounds of the city's establishments in big broad-brimmed hats and bright neckties; when they were in good form, they treated anyone in range to a torrent of punning, disrespectful, antic poetry.

123

If you seek out the Café Arco in the hopes of encountering its romantic past, however, you're likely to be disappointed by its new design. Corresponding to its decor, its new name, "Taifun," is an indication that the proprietors weren't exactly aiming to rediscover and reanimate the historic coffeehouse atmosphere. But if you're waiting for a train and want to play a game of billiards, you've come to the right place.

Today, the places that reawaken associations with the good old days described above are probably the establishments which summon up the spirit of the early days of this century in their appearance and decor. Leader among these is the **Café Nouveau** in the Municipal Building (*Obecní dům*) on Náměstí Republiky. The Art Nouveau ambiance, colorful and varied clientele, and nightly performances of live music, all at moderate prices, tempt one to linger for hours in

Above: The Art Nouveau café of the Hotel Evropa.

the true Prague coffeehouse tradition. Also beautiful, but almost too elegant, is the cafe in the **Hotel Paříž**. If you try to imagine what kind of literary figures might frequent these renovated rooms, it would probably be advanced sophisticates weary of urban doings and anxious to keep their distance.

Another establishment in this category is the **Café** in the **Hotel Evropa** on Wenceslas Square – although this café is less elegant and restrained, since it's usually filled to bursting with visitors. In the Hall of Mirrors here, the shy, very young Franz Kafka is thought to have given his only public reading of his works, presenting *The Trial*. Although it's slightly faded today, reminiscent of an old film set, this attractive salon is certainly worth a look, even if you have to pay an admission charge of 20 krone to get in.

Somewhat away from the main visitors' track, and still relatively new, although housed in a venerable building, is the **Café Savoy** in the Lesser City, right near the bridge Most Legií. This shouldn't be confused with the coffeehouse of the same name which served, in Kafka's day, as a stage for Jewish actors' troupes from Eastern Europe, whose productions of plays in Yiddish had a great effect on the young writer. Today's Savoy was used as a storeroom, and it was only recently that the turn-of-the-century ceiling decorations were uncovered.

If you'd like to find a taste of modern coffeehouse culture in the original tradition of unconventionality, the best place to look is in an underground café, **Café Velyrba**, in a small alley (Opatovická 24) south of Národní třída. There, people sit in the heavy fog of cigarette smoke and discuss God and the world: the Bohemians of Montparnasse have found their Central European resurrection. If you'd like things a little less smoky and a little less earnest, try **Hogo Fogo** on Salvátorská, north of the Old City Ring, where a small scene is starting to develop.

EATING OUT

Restaurants and Wine Bars

It is recommended to make reservations in advance at the following restaurants, especially on weekends, holidays and during the main tourist season, when the crowds can become overwhelming.

LESSER TOWN AND HRADČANY

EXPENSIVE: **U Malířů**, Maltézské náměstí 11, Tel: 5732 0317, French cuisine of the finest quality and most expensive, for example lobster; excellent French wines. **Lobkovická vinárna**, Vlašská 17, Tel: 53 01 85, French cuisine and Melniker wine. **U Zlaté hrušky**, Nový Svět 3, Tel: 2051 4536, Bohemian and French cuisine.

MODERATE: **Nebozízek**, Petřínské sady, Tel: 53 79 05, good food with an incredible view of the city. **U Mecenáše**, Malostranské náměstí 10, Tel: 53 38 81, almost 400 years old, cozy restaurant. **U ševce Matouše**, Loretánské náměstí 4, Tel: 53 35 97, good local cuisine.

ECONOMY: **U Vladaře**, Maltézské náměstí 10, Tel: 53 81 28, good local cuisine. **Jo's Bar**, Malostranské náměstí 7, Tel: 53 12 51, Mexican food and US-American customers.

DOWNTOWN AND JOSEFOV

EXPENSIVE: **Parnas**, Smetanovo nábřeží 2, Tel: 2422 1387, French and Italian cuisine, beautiful view of the Moldau and Hradschin from window tables. **U Sixtů**, Celetná 2, Tel: 2422 3906, Bohemian and French cuisine in historic building. **Opera**, Karolíny Světlé 35, Tel: 26 55 08, excellent appetizers along with piano music.

MODERATE: **Reykjavík**, Karlova 20, Tel: 2422 9251, very good fish restaurant. **V Dlouhé**, Dlouhá 35, Tel: 231 6125, good Bohemian cuisine. **Košer restaurant Shalom**, Maislova 18, Tel: 2481 0929, kosher food and piano music.

NEW CITY

EXPENSIVE: **U Šuterů**, Palackého 4, Tel: 26 10 17, steak specialties.

MODERATE: **Klášterní vinárna**, Národní 8, Tel: 29 05 96, steaks in a convent-like ambiance. **Pezinok**, Purkyňova 4, Tel: 29 19 96, Slovakian specialties. **Pod Křídlem**, Národní 10, Tel: 2491 2377, Bohemian cuisine and piano music.

ECONOMY: **Grill restaurant Pepino**, Jugoslávská 11, Tel: 2422 5415, interior like in a truck stop, but good food with the exception of the watery salads.

Beer Pubs

U Fleků, P-1, Křemencova 11, Tel: 2491 5118, self-brewed beer, very touristy. **U Kocoura**, P-1, Nerudova 2, Tel: 53 89 62, Pilsner Urquell. **U Zlatého tygra**, P-1, Husova 17, Tel: 2422 9020, with a cellar from the 13th century, now and then writers are customers there as well, Pilsner Urquell. **U Kalicha**, P-2, Na Bojišti 12, Tel: 29 07 01, Schwejk memorial bar, very touristy, Radegast beer. **U Malvaze**, P-1, Karlova 10, Tel: 2422 9252, beer from Holešovice. **U Vejvodů**, P-1, Jilská 4, Tel: 2421 0591, Smíchover beer. **U Černého vola**, P-1, Loretánské náměstí 1, Tel: 2051 3481, beer from Velké Popovice. **U Svatého Tomáše**, P-1, Letenská 12, Tel: 53 67 76, Braník-beer. **U Dvou koček**, P-1, Uhelný trh 10, Tel: 2422 9982, Pilsner Urquell. **U Medvídků**, P-1, Na Perštýně 7, Tel: 2421 1916, summer garden, Budweiser beer. **Krušovická pivnice**, P-1, Široká 20, Tel: 231 6689, lager beer from Krušovice, for night crowds.

Cafés

COFFEE HOUSES IN TURN-OF-THE-CENTURY STYLE:

Kavárna Obecní dům, P-1, náměstí Republiky 5, Tel: 2202 2763. **Hotel Evropa Café**, P-1, Václavské náměstí 25, Tel: 2422 8117.

Café im Hotel Paříž, P-1, U Obecního domu 1, Tel: 2422 2151.

Savoy, P-5, Vítězná 5, Tel: 53 50 00.

Café Rudolfinum, P-1, Alšovo nábřeží 12, very chic, only open until 8 p.m.

COFFEE HOUSES WITH A PAST:

Café Slavia, P-1, Národní třída 2, Tel: 2481 6772. **Malostranská kavárna**, P-1, Malostranské náměstí, Tel: 53 30 92.

CONTEMPORARY COFFEE HOUSES:

Café Lávka, P-1, Novotného lávka, Tel: 24214797. **Gany's**, P-1, Národní třída 20, Tel: 29 76 65. **Kavárna Velryba**, P-1, Opatovická 24, Tel: 2491 2391. **Hogo Fogo**, P-1, Salvátorská 4, Tel: 23 170 23. **Café in the Artwork museum**, P-1, 17. listopadu 2, Tel: 2481 1241. **Dolce Vita**, P-1, Široká 15, Tel: 232 9192, good Italian coffee. **The Globe**, P-7, Jankovského 14, Café with bookstore, predominantly US-American customers.

MORE CAFÉS:

Café Poet, P-1, zahrada Na Baště, Tel: 2051 5462, quiet and somewhat hidden position in the northwest part of the fortress. **Café Puškin**, P-1, Husova 14, Tel: 232 0482. **Kavárna u Týna**, P-1, Staroměstské náměstí 15, Tel: 231 0525, touristy. **Internet Café**, P-1, Národní 25, Tel: 2108 5284.

Tea Rooms

Dobrá čajovna, P-1, Václavské náměstí 14, Tel: 2423 1480. **Růžová čajovna**, P-q, Růžová 8, Tel: 26 27 91.

125

THEATER IN PINK AND GRAY

A first-time visitor to Prague could well gain the impression that the city is one giant theater. The buildings form the best stage set one could hope for. Small wonder, then, that throughout the city you run into fashion photographers and models, film and television teams from around the world, and artists of every imaginable description.

Occasionally, the city is also the site of special events or happenings that are worthy of a theater. The most famous, a political-aesthetic escapade of a statement, surrounded the pink tank on the former "Square of the Soviet Tank Fighters" in Smíchov. Overnight, the Prague art student David Cerny and a couple of comrades-in-arms provided the tank, set up in the square as a monument to the liberation by the Red Army, with a

Above: In the German Embassy: a memorial to the East German emigrants of 1989 by David Černý. Right: street theater.

coat of pink paint. Cerny was arrested for inciting public unrest, and on the anniversary of the liberation, the tank was repainted in its original shades of green-brown. As Cerny remained in custody, two or three dozen officials, protected by their immunity from arrest as members of Parliament, decided to stage the event anew, and lo and behold, the tank was pink once again. And pink it remains today, although it's been deposed from its pedestal and banished to the storeroom of the Air and Space Museum. The Soviet Army has, in the meantime, left the country.

Any performer who tries to play on the streets for money soon realizes that the competition is tough. Although crowds collect virtually at the drop of a hat, you have to come up with something truly creative and original if you want that hat to fill up with marks, dollars, and the occasional krone.

In light of the flourishing activity on Prague's streets, it's notable that many of the city's established theaters can't hold a candle to some of the street performers. Wonderful as Prague is, and wide as the range of musical and theatrical offerings in the city's theaters and concert halls, one has to note that much of what comes before the public is truly old hat. Some shows which have been particularly successful with audiences have been around for years, and have dated (or outdated) accordingly. Many of the performances, furthermore, are characterized by kind of amateur silliness which can still the laughter of even the most naive viewer.

Although Prague's theaters may be slumbering in something of a cultural coma, they're by no means financial flops. Hitherto, amazingly, people have paid the high ticket prices without a murmur, presumably eager for whatever crumbs of entertainment they could glean from these lackluster spectacles. But the word "tourist trap" is starting to make the rounds.

From the success of some of the finer street performers, you can see that the public is certainly ready to applaud more daring presentations. One example: a slender, small woman in ragged clothing, before the magnificent set of the Old City Ring, with the aid of a few unimpressive but effectively-chosen props, presents an imaginative revue, in mime and dance, which tells the story of a fallen woman and her unwanted, ugly, but ultimately beloved child. Her movements range from ghostly dream sequences with an umbrella which has become, through her motions, three flapping black ravens, through harmless raillery of her spectators, brought coquettishly into the action, to a ghastly necrophilic dance of death. The whole thing is supported with ballads and songs, ditties and klezmer music. The audience is pulled between shock, emotion, and enthusiasm, and finally rewards the actress with money and waves of applause. Why is it that the small local theaters are generally unable to present anything comparable to this? There are certainly enough topics, particularly in Prague.

And the argument that foreign visitors can't understand the local language, which is often brought up in this connection, holds no weight. For in the past, artists made a virtue of the necessity posed by the fact that any performance which aspired to international success couldn't rely too much on words: productions developed which concentrated more on pantomime, puppet theater, animated films, or dance. Yet in this realm, too, stagnation has set in.

Conventional as they may be, the productions in the big theaters are certainly impressive. However, there's no guarantee as to what the future will hold, for the houses or for their audiences. On the one hand, there's talk of diminishing state funding for the theaters, or even cutting it altogether; on the other, the National Opera (in the National Theater building

on Národní třída) and the State Opera (formerly the New German Theater, now the Smetana Theater on Wilsonova třída) have been officially separated and placed in competition with each other. In light of this and of the desire to be more international, both houses have let it be known that they have great plans in the way of spectacular innovations.

Let's start with the **National Theater**, which has classical dramas in the repertory as well as grand opera (usually with introductions in German and English). If you prefer to see stagings that are true to the composer's wishes, rather than the kind of interpretative readings one often encounters in Europe, has – until now, at any rate – come to the right place. This is where you should see *Dalibor* (by Smetana), *Rusalka* (by Dvořák), or other Czech opera classics. The elegant, festive, yet serious mood is underlined by the opulent decor of the neo-Renaissance building and the finery of local members of the audience. The same is true of the **State Opera**. Here, too, the architecture

127

emphasizes the character of the classical productions. Recently, however, this theater has seen some daring productions with new, international performers.

A truly historic site is the **Estates Theater** between Na příkopě and the Old City Ring, called the Tyl Theater for a period after the Second World War. Here, in 1786, Mozart's *The Marriage of Figaro* made such waves that the composer was able to report to Vienna that Figaro was all you could hear in the city. He was subsequently commissioned to compose an opera for the Estates Theater and returned to the site of his greatest success with a work called *Don Giovanni*. In October, 1787, he conducted the world premiere, thereby bringing the Estates Theater into the annals of history. For the more than two hundred years since, this has been a place of pilgrimage for Mozart aficionados; one reason why

Miloš Forman filmed parts of his movie *Amadeus* in this city. Even today, Mozart performances are among the highlights in this neo-classical theater. If you aren't bothered by the interference of synchronization, you can listen to performances with headphones, in English.

Mozart operas are also the core of the repertoire of the marionette theater *Národni divadlo marionet* on Žatecká. In two years, more than 60,000 visitors have seen *Don Giovanni*, and paid a pretty price to do so. The music is recorded; the clever, attractive puppet staging is calculated to win smiles from its audience. The same could be said of Prague's most famous marionette theater, the *Divadlo Špejbla a Hurvínka*. For decades, the expressive puppets here have been presenting light pieces dealing with the ever-popular subject of father-son relations.

Light, amusing entertainment can also be found at the **Karlín Music Theater** (*Hudební divadlo*), an Art Nouveau building on the edge of the city between the New City and Karlín, which spe-

Above: a puppeteer amuses his audience.
Right: the National Theater, sold out.

cializes in operetta and musicals. In the past, Prague's residents loved it for its enchanting operetta productions; today, its program seems rather traditional, focusing on works by Johann Strauss, Franz Lehár, and Emmerich Kálmán.

Among the best theaters which present works almost exclusively in Czech are the **Divadlo Na Vinohradech**, the **Studio Ypsilon** and the **Divadlo Za branou II**. It may be worth the effort to try to go to a play here, provided you already know the piece in question and will be able to follow to some degree. For fans of pure, slapstick comedy who understand Czech, there's a number-one destination in the suburbs, in Zizkov: the **Divadlo Járy Cimrmana** with its original, dilettantish, but nonetheless marvelous nonsense works.

Pantomime is to be found in the **Divadlo Na zábradlí** and the suburban **Branické divadlo pantomímy**; the former of these also presents regular plays. Director here is Ladislav Fialka, whose brand of pantomime, now become a classic, has placed him beside Marcel Marceau and Samy Molcho in the ranks of the greatest performers of wordless drama. The pantomime in Braník is in no way inferior. In the late autumn, this theater presents a renowned international festival (Mimos).

Prague's cinemas present international films in the original language with Czech subtitles, relatively soon after their release in their home country. Late shows are still uncommon, perhaps because few tourists have, until now, ventured into local movie theaters. To be recommended for their ambiance are the older cinemas in the arcades around Wenceslas Square, especially the **Lucerna**, which is basically a small city within a city. The founder of this entertainment complex was the grandfather of the country's current President.

Prague is a veritable El Dorado for classical music enthusiasts. There are performances nearly every day in many of the city's old palaces, historic buildings, and churches. Occasionally, an

afternoon performance is shoved in before the evening one, to meet the public demand. A highlight of the annual calendar is the festival called **Prague Spring**, which takes over the whole city so that it's impossible to see more than a portion of its offerings.

The city's best musical institution is the Czech Philharmonic, which regularly enthuses audiences in **Dvořák Hall** in the Rudolfinum on Jan Palach Square. The building itself is an impressive neo-Renaissance edifice which is also a venue for art exhibitions. Along the balustrade in Dvořák Hall are a row of sculptures representing the long line of great Central European composers. Behind the orchestra, a huge organ with classical ornamentation dominates the scene. An equally impressive space is **Smetana Hall** in the Municipal Building on Republic Square. Fabulous for its architecture and majestic

acoustic, as well as for the level of musical offerings, is **St. Vitus's Cathedral** in the castle, especially when the tones of organ and full chorus boom out and resound through the nave.

In season, there are several concerts a week in the Clementinum, sometimes as many as twice a day. You can also hear performances in Týn Church, St. Nicholas Church, or the Nicholas Church in the Lesser City.

The "Scene"

Hardly anything is as intangible as that element which we know as a city's "scene." Is "scene" the city's artists, young people with outlandish behavior, peripheral groups, outsiders, or the "in" crowd? Is the Hare Krishna disciples and their vegetarian club **Govinda** in the suburb of Liben? Or the science fiction fans who hang out in the **Klub Najáda** in Karlín?

Let's start at the bottom of the social ladder. The first thing a visitor who ar-

Above: Converting or concerting? Right: Young wild things.

rives in Prague by train notices is the number of homeless people and social outcasts, unknown in the days of Socialism, who frequent the park before the train station. Certainly, the unemployment rate in the Czech Republic is lower than in most other countries, but it's not zero, and those who are affected by it tend to converge on the metropolis in the vain hopes of there catching some of the crumbs from the table of the promised economic upswing. Those who have kept their honesty hunt for bottles and cans which they can turn in for the deposit, or anything else of value. Less evident, but present in ever-increasing numbers, are elderly people whose pensions are not at all adequate to their needs, which is why you sometimes see them searching through the garbage cans, as well.

In the wake of this new poverty have arrived dubious or shady forms of business which used only to be present in embryonic form. On Wenceslas Square and Na příkopě, above all, there are all kinds of money-making endeavors cropping up; and the border between them and outright criminality is fluid. Moneychangers and card sharks, pickpockets, street vendors and fences of stolen goods, and, toward evening, prostitutes frequent the pavement – which is, it must be conceded, still more of a pink- than a red-light district. Drugs are also beginning to play a role. The police keep a rather low profile; they seem still to be trying to come to grips with the nature of their new role. In some places, private police ensure the maintenance of whatever state of affairs is deemed desirable by their respective employers; this, for example, is how a measure of order is imposed on the weed-like growth of vendors and musicians on Charles Bridge. The advantages for those who do manage to stake out a place there, however, are all the greater.

The Englishman David, for example, has lived from his street music for seven years. A couple of years ago, he ended up

in Prague, and he's been appearing regularly on Charles Bridge ever since. His first CD is in the works. Also popular is the small, friendly Brazilian with the dark curly hair, whose simple chords and enthusiastic encouragement for audience participation draws hordes of teenagers to bop on the bridge. Local musicians and performance artists have to present really fabulous offerings in order to compete with these old-timers for the international, mainly western, public. Amazingly, it's the romantic old saws of the 1960s which are the most popular. In Prague's hippie-like ambiance, the Beatles and the Stones are still unbeatable.

But this is actually a holdover trend from the days of socialism; and one of its relics, the John Lennon wall on the island Kampa, where people leave songs and letters to transmit messages and wishes to the ultimate Beatle – now virtually sainted – in the Hereafter, is gradually falling into decay. New sites of pilgrimage or ecstasy today are the various cellar clubs. There, together with more recent

fashions you'll see plenty of local members of the "scene" still sporting the old '68, hippie look, ratty and longhaired. Prague's scene, in fact, seems as able to withstand postmodern trends as well as some of the city's architecture.

The true trend of the times, however, can be seen in one scene that believes in cutting a good figure. New yuppies and the unmistakable old yuppies aren't only to be found in the new shopping arcades and the chic and expensive watering-holes; the best place to sight them is in the fitness centers of the larger hotel complexes, where they work dutifully on weight and exercise machines to meet the new demands of a market economy. The subjects discussed here, such as the smoking question or cholesterol levels, are wholly unknown in other parts of town. Who knows where all this will lead.

Above: At least amusing: a motorized concert hall. Right: No laughing matter.

Since the fateful November of '89, the gay and lesbian scene has also been reborn. An umbrella organization of homosexual citizens, SOHO, puts out a publication called *SOHO Magazine* which includes listings of special events, clubs, and other meeting-places; it's on sale at most of the larger kiosks in the city center. The weekly publication called *Program*, a calendar of city events, also has listings for the gay scene.

A novelty in Prague's multicultural life, now grown a bit old hat, are the more than 20,000 Americans who've settled here and built up their own scene. An article in *Newsweek* drew the comparison between Prague and the spirit of the 1920s, and it didn't go unheard. Who could pass up the chance to live out the experience of a generation in the Golden City, like Gertrude Stein, Hemingway, Fitzgerald or Henry Miller in Paris? Dynamic youth began to arrive in the city; people in their early 20s founded the English-language papers *The Prague Post* and *Prognosis*, and helped form a base of American-style hangouts, from the *New York Pizzeria* and *Jo's Bar* to the laundromat *Laundry King*. But it wasn't only the young who arrived. Take the retired, but far from retiring, car designer who sold his house and all his possessions in Seattle and took off to discover new horizons on the banks of the Moldau. Today, he works as a designer for a Czech boat firm, and sings in his free time, appearing, for all who'd like to hear him, with his "Old Man's Blues" as the final number on the programs of local jazz combos.

The Nights Get Longer

Under the Socialist regime, the streets closed up by 11 p.m. at the latest. Only people who had connections or no commitments to the world of commerce and production whiled away the nights in bars of expensive hotels, in order to see the nights out and usher in the mornings in a state of alcoholization or in more or less amusing company. For those with Western currency, the **Alhambra** on Wenceslas Square, which still exists today, smacked a bit of a provincial Moulin Rouge or some other (dis)reputable night spot with a reputation for slightly shady adventures.

In the field of nightclubs, not much has happened, quantitatively or qualitatively, of late; but the disco field has seen considerable activity. Around Wenceslas square, there have always been a whole row of expensive dance spots, usually inundated with the combined forces of high school classes visiting from the West. **Carioca**, with its open-air balcony, broadcasts its music the lower part of the square, and is known today as the hit of the Golden Cross. But the real action goes on in other, more "in" spots.

Similar to the Wenceslas Square discos in terms of its public is the open-air disco of the **Lávka Bar** on Charles Bridge. On warm summer nights, the very very

young and the no-longer-so-young from the West can be found rocking on a small terrace in the shadow of the bridge. The music is dominated by oldie titles, and the site, all in all, is an ideal hatchery for teenage dreams.

Things are less romantic in the **Rock Café** on Národni třída. Ear-splitting live music deafens the ears of a public comprised, again, predominately of tipsy high-schoolers. After midnight, disco music takes over. If your ears need a break, you can recover in the adjacent basement rooms, buying souvenirs, sitting at the bar, or in the video room.

A comparable establishment is the well-known **Bunkr**, set up in a former atomic shelter on Lodecká. Some of the best bands in Prague, or, indeed, in the entire world, uphold the reputation of this bar, which is known today as one of the best clubs in Europe. You can find plenty of high-schoolers here, as well, but since the prices are still very reasonable, the local youth hasn't been driven away entirely. A ground-floor café, frequented by

a rather freaky clientele, provides refreshment between dances.

The dance floor of the club **Borát**, on Újezd Street in the Lesser City, is notable for its extreme smallness. This joint still draws a local crowd, whose hearts are still in the 1960s and 70s – as well as their outfits and their hairdos. On weekends, it's pretty hopeless to try to squeeze into one of the rooms here, which are more the size of a living room than a dance floor. Generally, therefore, everyone stands outside and gets acquainted.

Further south toward Smíchov on Zborovská, **Futurum** has taken over the building of a former movie theater. Only a few tourists find their way here. When no band is playing, a kind of elegiac air seems to prevail in the emptyish rooms.

In the Lesser City, directly on the Lesser City Ring, a club which is extremely reasonable and meets people's actual expectations, both in its prices and

Above: Live music in the Rock Café; after midnight, a DJ takes over.

in what it offers, has established itself on the upper story of a building that used to be the Town Hall for the neighborhood: **Malostranská beseda**. In addition to jazz, a lot of rock (or rock-like) music is performed here by local bands. There are performances nearly every evening, and the roomy foyer serves as a bar.

A special kind of Western enclave appears in the form of **Radost F/X**. This is a gathering-place for chic locals who want to treat themselves to a taste of America, as well as for a portion of the Americans who find Prague so chic that they've decided to settle down for a while. The music tries to satisfy every taste; the decor is opulent; and a vegetarian restaurant on an upper floor keeps the predominantly foreign clientele happy and healthy into the wee hours of the morning.

One of the loveliest places to go is the **Repre Klub** underneath the Café Nouveau in the Municipal, or Representational, Building. Here, a style that is usually protected with a museum curator's diligence from any kind of practical usefulness comes in regular contact with a cheerful, vibrant scene of young people: the club's Art Nouveau rooms house various young rock bands of various levels of ability, who quite literally shake the foundations of this venerable old building nearly every evening. The low admission fee means that the local scene flourishes here, fleshed out with only a minority of Western young people. Anyone who wants to talk rather than listen heads for the upholstered bar.

In the same building, on the corner, the bar **Formanka** has come to house a scene reminiscent of the Berlin bar scene in the early 1970s. In the crowded space, its air foggy with cigarette smoke, people talk, philosophize, and drink in ample measure. A plaster bust of Lenin in the window stoically, and uncomprehendingly, endures the cigarette butt that someone has forced into his mouth.

Opera and Theater

Národní Divadlo (National Theater), P-1, Národní třída 2, Tel: 2491 3437, opera, ballet, plays.

Státní opera (state opera), P-1, Wilsonova 4, Tel: 2422 7693 or 26 53 53, opera, ballet.

Stavovské divadlo (Estates Theater), Ovocný trh 1, Tel: 2421 5001, opera, plays.

Hudební divadlo v Karlíně (Karlín Music Theater), P-8, Křižíkova 10, Tel: 2421 0710, operetta, musicals.

Laterna Magika, P-1, Národní třída 4, Tel: 2491 4129, media mix of film, theater, dance, pantomime and music.

Divadlo Na Zábradlí (theater on site), P-1, Anenské náměstí 5, Tel: 2422 1933, plays, pantomime.

Černé divadlo Jiřího Srnce (Black Theater J. Srnec), P-1, Lucerna, Štěpánská 61, black theater, plays.

Studio Ypsilon, P-1, Spálená 16, Tel: 29 22 55, plays.

Divadlo Járy Cimrmana (also under Žižkovské divadlo TGM), P-3, Štítného 5, avantgarde comedy.

Činoherní klub (acting club), P-1, Ve Smečkách 26, Tel: 9622 2123, plays.

Divadlo Na Vinohradech (theater in Vinohrady), P-2, Náměstí Míru, Tel: 2425 7604 (plays).

Divadlo Spejbla a Hurvínka, P-6, Dejvická 38, Tel: 2431 6784, puppet theater.

Národní divadlo marionet (national marionette theater), P-1, Žatecká 1, Tel: 232 3429.

Branické divadlo, P-4, Branická 63, Tel: 462 779.

Opera Mozart, P-1, Novotného lávka 1, Tel: 232 25 36, modern opera.

Pyramida, P-7, Výstaviště, Tel: 37 11 42, musicals.

Spirála, P-7, Výstaviště, Tel: 2010 3214, musicals.

Selected cinemas and film clubs

Lucerna, P-1, Vodičkova 36, Tel: 2421 6972.

Institut Français, P-1, Štěpánská 35, Tel: 2421 6630/61, at 6:00 p.m., entrance free.

Dlabačov, P-6, Bělohorská 24, Tel: 311 5328.

Praha, P-1, Václavské náměstí 17, Tel: 26 20 35.

Ponrepo, P-1, Bartolomějská 11, Tel: 2423 1846.

Kino Mat, P-2, Odborů 7, Tel: 2491 4604.

U Hradeb, P-1, Mostecká 64.

Concert Halls

Dvořák-Hall in Rudolfinum, P-1, náměstí Jana Palacha, Tel: 2489 3352.

Smetana-Hall in **Representation House** (Obecní dům), P-1, náměstí Republiky 5, Tel: 232 2501.

Stone bell tower (Dům U kamenného zvonu), P-1, Staroměstské náměstí 13, Tel: 2482 7526.

Hall of mirrors in **Klementinum** (Zrcadlová síň Klementina), Marianské náměstí, tickets at the box office.

Lobkowitz-Palais (Burg), P-1, Jiřská 3, Tel: 53 73 06.

Nostitz-Palais, P-1, Maltézské náměstí 1, Tel: 5731 1590.

Vila Amerika (Dvořák-Museum), P-2, Ke Karlovu 20, Tel: 29 82 14.

Vila Bertramka (Mozart-Museum), P-5, Mozartova 169, Tel: 54 38 93.

Atrium, P-3, Čajkovského 12, Tel: 627 04 53.

Kongresové centrum Praha (formerly the Palace of Culture), P-4, ul. 5. května 65, Tel: 6117 2711.

Clubs and Discos

NIGHTCLUBS:
Alhambra, P-1, Václavské náměstí 5, Tel: 2421 0463. **Black & White**, P-5, Štefánikova 7.
Lucerna Bar, P-1, Vodičkova 36, Tel: 2421 7108.

DISCOS:
U bílého koníčka, (the white horse), P-1, Staroměstské náměstí 20, Tel: 235 89 27.
Lávka, P-1, Novotného lávka 1, Tel: 2421 4797.
Modrá terasa, P-1, Na Můstku 9, Tel: 2422 6288.
Arkadia, P-1, Na Příkopě 22, Tel: 2421 3091.

ROCK- AND POPCLUBS:
Klub Újezd, P-1, Újezd 18, Tel: 53 83 62. **Bunkr**, P-1, Lodecká 2, temporarily closed. **Futurum**, P-5, Zborovská 7, Tel: 54 44 75. **Malostranská beseda**, P-1, Malostranské náměstí 21, Tel: 53 86 51 bzw. 53 90 24. **Radost F/X**, P-2, Bělehradská 120, Tel: 25 47 76. **Rock Café**, P-1, Národní 20, Tel: 2491 4416. **Roxy**, P-1, Dlouhá 33, Tel: 2481 0951.

JAZZCLUBS:
Agharta, P-1, Krakovská 5, Tel: 2221 1275. **Café de Paris**, P-1, U Obecního domu 1, Tel: 2422 5475. **Obecní dům-vinárna**, P-1, náměstí Republiky 1, Tel: 2200 2130. **Metropolitan**, P-1, Jungmannova 14, Tel: 2421 6025. **Reduta**, P-1, Národní 20, Tel: 2491 2246.

GAY SPOTS:
Drakes, P-5, Petřínská 5, Tel: 53 4909. **David**, P-8 Sokolovská 77, Tel: 231 78 82. **Maskot**, P-2, Kolínská 11. **Whiskey Club Old England**, P-2, Šafaříkova 6, men and women.

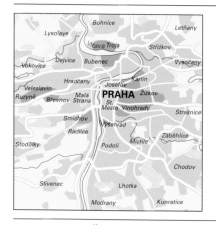

THE OUTLYING DISTRICTS

VYŠEHRAD
VINOHRADY / ŽIŽKOV
LETNÁ / TROY
WEST OF THE MOLDAU
SMÍCHOV

VYŠEHRAD

Hrad Castle was not the only castle in Prague. Up the river from Prague, on a promontory jutting over the Moldau's left bank, a neo-Gothic church of blackened stone towers over an entire city district. According to legend, Prague's first fortress stood on this cliff. It was known as Vyšehrad, the "upper castle" and is said to have been home to the legendary patron figure of the city, Libussa (Libuše). Archaeologists, however, still believe that Hrad is the older castle, dating the foundations of Vyšehrad back to about AD 930 Nevertheless, the upper castle did replace Hradčany as the sovereign's residence between 1070 and 1140. The reason for this was a dispute between the Duke of Bohemia, Vratislav II (who became King Vratislav I in 1085) and his brother Jaromír, Bishop of Prague, about who was head of the church of Prague. Vratislav, who had been installed as the representative of Rome by the emperor, claimed the Prague's bishop's seat for himself. As he was unable to win out over his brother, however, he therefore proceeded to establish his own cathedral

Preceding pages: Modern architecture in Golden Prague. Left: Bronze Art Nouveau beauty on the Svatopluk-Čech bridge.

branch on Vyšehrad, where he saw himself as holding power only by virtue of the authority vested in him by Rome. It is for this reason that the Vyšehrad coat-of-arms depicts St. Peter's crossed keys to the gates of heaven. It was under Vratislav that the first church was consecrated here, a Romanesque structure dedicated to the apostles Peter and Paul. Buildings for the royal court were constructed around the church, as was a modern rampart which were defensively far superior to the clay ramparts of Hrad Castle. After 1140, the castle began to decline in significance and fall into decay. Not until Charles IV came to power did it gain renewed strategic importance as a means of protection for the New City which he founded in 1348. The walls of Vyšehrad were joined with the new walls being constructed around the city. Nine churches were built within the fortress, manned with 100 priests. During the first Hussite war, the army of the Reformation attacked this bulwark of Catholicism in 1420, destroying all of the buildings except St. Martin's Rotunda and the Church of Sts. Peter and Paul. In the 17th century, the fortress was renovated for the last time, expanded into a huge bastion. You can still see traces of this remodeling in the layout of the castle grounds. The last fortification element, a large brick

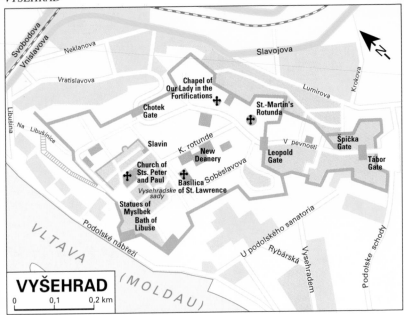

VYŠEHRAD (MOLDAU)

0   0,1   0,2 km

gate (*Cihelná brána*), was built here in 1841 in Empire style; an edifice which also marked the end of the city's construction of defensive fortifications. Vyšehrad was incorporated into Prague as the sixth city district in 1883, and a cemetery of honor was laid out atop the cliff.

Surrounded by tales and legends, the cliff of Vyšehrad has entered the annals of story. Some of its most famous cultural appearances are Bedřich Smetana's opera *Libuše* and Franz Grillparzer's play *Libussa*. Smetana's first work in his *My Fatherland* cycle, moreover, is entitled *Vyšehrad*. In Adalbert Stifter's historical novel *Witiko*, the princes of the empire assemble in the palace at Vyšehrad.

Today, Vyšehrad, with its park-like grounds, is a popular excursion site for Prague residents. It's easy to reach on the subway, which stops at Vyšehrad station. From there, head west past the modern

Right: St. Martin's Rotunda, Vyšehrad. Arcade in the cemetery of Vyšehrad.

culture palace (which affords a good view) and along the old fortifications to the early Baroque Tábor Gate (*Táborská brána*, built in 1655). This is an outpost of the fortifications which were disbanded in 1866. After passing through the gate, you can see the remains of the late Gothic main gate (Špička Gate) on your right, and the defensive wall erected under Charles IV. The fortress begins at the Leopold Gate (*Leopoldova brána*, built in 1678). Beyond that, on the right, is the oldest structure of Vyšehrad, **St. Martin's Rotunda** (*Rotunda svatýho Martina*). The chapel, a Romanesque rotunda, was built after King Vratislav I made Vyšehrad his residence. It is the only structure still remaining from this era; although it did, admittedly, undergo a course of restorations in 1878-89, when a new south portal was added in place of the original west portal. Very nearby, to the north, is the **Chapel of Our Lady in the Fortifications**. Until 1784, this chapel was a site of pilgrimage; worshippers flocked to see the statue of Our Lady

of Loreto. Closed for a hundred years, it was consecrated anew at the end of the 19th century.

Heading west from the rotunda, one arrives at the former **Canons' House** dating from the year 1770; today, it houses an exhibit about the history of Vyšehrad with explanations in Czech and English. West of this is the **Church of Sts. Peter and Paul** (*kostel svatýho Petra a Pavla*). Its tower, overlooking the Moldau Valley, was not completed until 1902. The Romanesque structure dating from the time of Vratislav I was remodeled as a five-aisle basilica under Charles IV. Thereafter, the church underwent three more radical remodeling: one in Renaissance style, one in Baroque and finally, between 1885 and 1887, the final transition into the neo-Gothic edifice you see today, which has become something of a Vyšehrad landmark. Above the main entrance is a relief of the Last Judgment. In the interior, the first chapel of the southern side aisle has a Romanesque sarcophagus which probably contains the mor-

tal remains of one of the Přemyslid rulers.

Slavín, the cemetery of honor, which is also a national cultural monument, is located north of the church. It is surrounded on three sides by arcades which are reminiscent of the Campo Santo in Pisa. More than 200 important artists are buried here, many in very artistically designed graves. Among these are the composers Antonín Dvořák and Bedřich Smetana, the authors Jan Neruda, Karel Čapek, and Božena Němcová, poet Karel Hynek Mácha, the violinist Jan Kubelik, the artist Alfons Mucha, the sculptors Josef Myslbek, Bohumil Kafka and Ladislav Šaloun and many more. Some of the artists mentioned here designed a number of the gravestones in this cemetery, including those marking their own last resting-places.

In the north, toward the Moldau, is a copy of the equestrian statue of St. Wenceslas. The original, which J.G. Bendl created in 1678, originally stood on Wenceslas Square. Further to the south is a

group of statues by Josef V. Myslbek depicting themes and figures from Bohemian legends, including Libuše and her husband Přemysl as a ploughman.

Before leaving Vyšehrad, take the opportunity to enjoy the lovely view. The panorama encompasses the Moldau Valley, Hrad Castle across the river and, to the east, the city districts of Nusle and Vinohrady. You can make your exit from the castle through the brick gate on the north side of the grounds. In one of the old casements here is another small museum with information about the fortress's history and development. You then complete your tour by returning to the banks of the Moldau and boarding streetcar number 17, which delivers you back at Charles Bridge. If you're interested in modern architecture, however, take a short detour to the street Neklanova before getting on the streetcar.

Above: Unusual doorhandles in the Cubist style. Right: Cubist house on Neklanova by Josef Chochol.

House number 30 here is an outstanding example of Cubist architecture by Josef Chochol. The same architect also designed the Villa Kovařovic in nearby Libušina and three houses on Rašín Quay on the Moldau. Continuing up the Moldau, one sees, shortly before the tunnel which cuts through the cliff on which the Vyšehrad fortress stands, a flat complex. House no. 42, on the other hand, is a mighty structure exhibiting a touch of Art Deco.

VINOHRADY, ŽIŽKOV AND THE EASTERN DISTRICTS

The city district (*Královské*) to the east of the National Museum is called Vinohrady, a name which hearkens back to the time when the royal vineyards were located here. Almost all of the houses in this district date from the turn of the century. In addition, the district boasts two parks. The first, **Riegrovy sady**, is nestled between patrician houses sorely in need of restoration. From here, one has a lovely view of the city center and the castle. To the south, in the other park, **Havlíčkovy sady**, you can even still find a few grape vines, testimony to Vinohrady's past. Visitors interested in Art Nouveau will want to stroll around the district southeast of *Náměští Míru* (**Freedom Square**): Korunní and the streets to the south, Moravská, Budečská, Lužická, Šumavská and Chodská, are lined with a number of houses sporting Art Nouveau ornamentation.

One sight you can't overlook is the tower that looks like a bunch of metal asparagus spears, thrusting into the Prague smog over the region east of Riegrovy sady, toward Žižkov. This is the 706-foot (216 m) television tower, constructed in 1990. The imposing modernistic structure seems somewhat out of place against the city's graceful silhouette. The grounds around the tower were originally purchased by the Jewish community to serve as a cemetery for plague victims; it was later used simply to supplement the cemetery in Josefov. In the 18th century, a Christian cemetery for Czech and French victims of two influenza epidemics was tacked on. A small part of the cemetery has been preserved at the edge of the grounds, which now serve as a park.

Prague's **Main Cemetery** and the **New Jewish Cemetery** are located further east, in Olšany, which is actually a part of Žižkov. Both cemeteries are noteworthy for their gravestones, some of which are very artistic and some of which are simply gaudy. One of the main attractions in the New Jewish Cemetery is the grave of Franz Kafka. The simple gravestone is on the right after you enter the cemetery, in a row near the wall. Many of the inscriptions on the gravestones are in German, testimony to the days when Prague was a city of three cultures.

Žižkov, a working-class district to the northeast, is named after the aristocratic general of the Hussites, Jan von Trocnov,

also known as Žižka. He managed to unite moderate Utraquists and radical Taborites into a formidable army, which he stationed atop St. Vitus's Hill (Vítkov) to the east of Prague to awaited the troops of King Sigismund, which had already conquered Hrad Castle and the fortress on Vyšehrad. The royal crusaders, who outnumbered the Hussites, approached steadily; but Žižka's troops waited to attack until the moment when the royal troops thought they had already conquered the hill. Caught thus by surprise, Sigismund's troops were slaughtered by the thousands. Žižka was the victor and, from that time on, he and his army of Hussites enjoyed the reputation of being invincible. In a later battle, the one-eyed Žižka lost his other eye, a fact which only served to increase his stature as a hero. The hill was named for him during his lifetime, and the district continues to bear the name today. He succumbed to the plague in 1424.

Upon the spot where the Hussites celebrated their victory in battle, a **national**

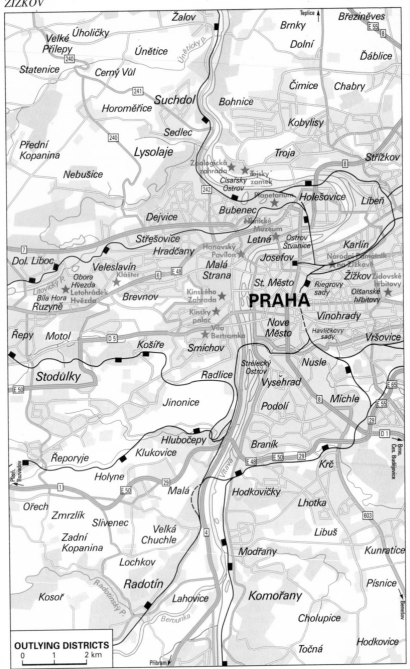

Žalov

Brnky

Březiněves

Velké
Přílepy

Úholičky

Únětice

Dolní

Statenice

Cerný Vůl

Únětický p.

Ďáblice

Suchdol

Bohnice

Čimice

Chabry

Horoměřice

Sedlec

Kobylisy

Přední
Kopanina

Lysolaje

Troja

Střížkov

Nebušice

Zoologická
zahrada

Trojský
zámek

Cisarský
Ostrov

Planetárium

Holešovice

Líbeň

Dejvice

Bubeneč

Střešovice

Hradčany

Hanavský
Pavilon

Technické
Muzeum

Letná

Ostrov
Stvanice

Karlín

Dol. Liboc

Veleslavín

Klášter

Josefov

Národní památník
na Žižkově

Žižkov

Obora
Hvezda

Litovický p.

Malá
Strana

St. Město

Riegrovy
sady

Židovské
hřbitovy

Bila Hora

Letohrádek
Hvězda

Brevnov

Kinského
Zahrada

PRAHA

Olšanské
hřbitovy

Ruzyně

Kinsky
pálac

Vinohrady

Řepy

Motol

Vila
Bertramka

Nove
Město

Havlíčkovy
sady

Vršovice

Košíře

Smíchov

Stodůlky

Radlice

Strělecký
Ostrov

Nusle

Jinonice

Vyšehrad

Vltava

Michle

Podolí

Brna,
Cás. Budějovice

Hlubočepy

Braník

Klukovice

Krč

Řeporyje

Holyne

Malá

Hodkovičky

Lhotka

Ořech

Zmrzlík

Slivenec

Libuš

Zadní
Kopanina

Velká
Chuchle

Modřany

Kunratice

Lochkov

Písnice

Radotín

Lahovice

Komořany

Kosoř

Radotínský p.

Berounka

Cholupice

Hodkovice

Točná

OUTLYING DISTRICTS

0   1   2 km

Příbram

monument (*Národní památník na Vit-kově*) was erected between 1929 and 1932; although it was not actually completed until after World War II. A terrace overlooking the city supports a 30-foot (9 m) equestrian statue of Jan Žižka, designed by Bohumil Kafka (1878-1942) though not cast and erected until 1950. It is reputed to be the largest bronze monument in the world. Behind this statue is a monumental **Mausoleum** which was also not finally completed until after World War II. This structure reflects the predominant aesthetics of the Socialist state. Below a hall of mourning, there's a columbarium, or hall of urns, with (now empty) sarcophagi of post-war politicians as well as a memorial hall for those who gave their lives in World War I. Anyone who wants a last look at the art of socialist realism had better make plans to visit this mausoleum soon, as no one is certain what's going to become of it in the future.

North of Žižkov, a narrow city district stretches along the Moldau to the east. This is **Karlín**, founded in 1817. After Napoleon's defeat was sealed and the industrial revolution had gotten underway in central Europe, factory owners began to view the area in the center of the city as too confined; and plans were accordingly drawn up for a residential and industrial district just outside the city gates. The neighborhood centered around a square with a church and administrative buildings; a harbor was constructed on the Moldau, and paper and textile plants were built at the edge of the district. Noteworthy sights here include the Art Nouveau buildings, unfortunately a bit run-down today, on Lyčkovo náměstí to the east. One of these is a richly-decorated elementary school named after Jan Amos Komenský (Comenius), built in 1905. Further to the east, in Invalidovna Park, is a home for invalids designed by the Baroque architect Kilian Ignaz Dientzenhofer.

LETNÁ, TROY AND THE NORTHERN DISTRICTS

North of Josefov, on the other side of the Moldau, is a hill which offers a view as lovely as that from Hrad Castle – a panorama of the entire city of Prague lying nestled in the bend of the river. The name of the hill is **Letná**, or Summerhill. Stretching along this elevation is a park which since its opening in 1858 has offered visitors an escape from the oppressive crowds, the noise and the smog of the city. To get to the park, cross the Svatoplus Čech Bridge, which is the continuation of Pařížská Street leading over the Moldau. Stairs here lead up to a monumental pedestal supporting a huge metronome which sometimes moves. It was erected after the "Velvet Revolution" and is intended to remind everyone who sees it of the fact that the times are continually changing. Originally, this was the site of a statue of Stalin nearly 100 feet (60 m) tall; but this was removed in 1962, after Khrushchev's speech at the 20th congress of the Soviet Communist Party in 1956 had ushered in his campaign of de-Stalinization.

If you're only up for a short walk and want to focus on a wonderful view of the city, head west to the **Hanau Pavilion** (*Hanavsk pavilón*), where you can drink in the view of Prague from the outdoor terrace along with your coffee or while eating a meal. The pavilion was created in the foundry of Prince Hanau in 1891, based on a design by Z.E. Fiala, for the National Exhibition, and set up on its present site in 1898. Recent renovations have brought out its full *fin-de-siècle* luster. From here, it's a pleasant stroll over to Hrad Castle, as the only heavily-trafficked street that might interfere with the pleasure of a walk, Chotkova, is bridged by a wide pedestrian overpass.

A second route through the park leads east to Ullmann Restaurant and its outdoor summer terrace. Just next to this

there's a quaint antique carousel, with wooden horses, for the enjoyment of younger visitors.

Behind the restaurant, on the other side of the street, is the **Technical Museum**, a must for those interested in technology of days gone by. Old motorcycles and bicycles, farcical limousines, luxurious train cars and airplanes from the earliest age of flight are on display here, as are optical and other precision instruments. Children are involved in the exhibits by the fact that you're allowed to push buttons on many of the displays to set them into motion.

If you'd like to seek out yet another park, which many consider to be the most beautiful in Prague, head to the north and traverse the city district east of the Sparta Prague Stadium. On a square shaded by chestnut trees, next to the Russian Embassy, is the entrance to the venerable park known as **Stromovka**, or the Royal

Above: Palace of Industry from the 1870s.
Right: Fountain in front of Troy Chateau.

Enclosure, which has been open to the public since 1804. The park's paths and bike trails make it a popular retreat for Prague residents. As early as the 13th century, these grounds were a royal game preserve containing a hunting palace and several small ponds commissioned by the Jagiello king Vladislav II; the hunting palace is still in evidence, albeit in another incarnation. After numerous renovations, including its transition into a Renaissance pleasure palace under Rudolph II, it was transformed into its present Tudor-style manifestation by A. Palliardi between 1804 and 1806. The palace was the residence of the Bohemian governors up until the end of the Habsburg monarchy. Today, it houses the periodicals department of the library of the National Museum. The park, which is in places somewhat overgrown, also contains a rose garden.

Adjacent to this park, on its eastern edge, is a cultural and recreational park which was originally created for the National Exhibition of 1891. Its designer was Antonín Wiehl, who was also responsible for the huge public cemetery of Slavín, and the arcades on Vyšehrad. Most impressive building here is the Palace of Industry, which housed exhibits of Bohemian manufacturers during the 1891 Exhibition. Created by Bedřich Muenzberger and echoing contemporary French designs of the time, this iron structure was intended to emphasize Bohemia's importance as a producer of iron through its very materials, even though parts of the building are admittedly of stone. The style is an eclectic blend of Art Nouveau and stylistic elements of bygone eras, as was popular during the 1870s. The wide promenade is flanked by two pavilions. The one on the right today houses the Lapidarium of the National Museum. In the round Lipany Pavilion, to the left of and behind the Palace of Industry, you can see a panorama painting by Luděk Marold dating from

1898, depicting the final defeat of the Hussites on May 30, 1434. Along its lower edge, the painting gives way to a realistic representation of a landscape strewn with actual instruments and tools of war.

In addition to these, the grounds include a number of sports facilities and other cultural institutions, including the huge covered sport hall of the Czech Republic which holds more than 18,000 fans, an indoor swimming pool, a number of buildings for exhibitions, an open-air theater, and the country's only cinerama. Another round building – although this is actually outside of the grounds, toward the Royal Enclosure – houses a planetarium with a two-ton Zeiss projector from Jena, Germany. It projects the constellations onto a dome measuring 77 feet (23.5 m) in diameter. A large folk festival, the Matthias Fair, is held in the cultural and recreational park beginning in mid-February and lasting six weeks. Some of the rides remain open throughout the year so that, particularly on holidays, the park has a bit of the atmosphere of Vienna's Prater, or of Coney Island.

If you still have the energy to keep walking, follow the signs to the zoological garden, which will lead you back to the banks of the Moldau; across a bridge onto Emperor's Island (*Císařsk ostrov*); and from there, on over a footbridge to the northern banks of the Moldau, where you'll find the zoo and Troy Chateau, side by side.

Troy Chateau is situated on a terraced hill behind a symmetrically-landscaped park. To the east there's a large orchard, still in the process of development, which seems to be laid out in a kind of diamond pattern. The palace itself was built in 1679/80 to serve as the summer residence of Count Wenzel Adalbert von Sternberg, according to plans by the French architect Jean Baptiste Mathey. The construction called for unusually large bricks, which were produced in a brick factory constructed especially for this purpose. The palace has a raised central wing, reached by a staircase which rises

from the ground in a graceful oval. The sculptures on the stairway represent the legendary battle of the gods against the giants; and indeed, there are a few fallen giants lying around within the oval. As you ascend the stairs, the figures change from reclining to sitting to standing, underlining the sense of the rise of the staircase. These clever carvings were the work of the Dresden sculptors Johann Georg and Paul Heermann. Busts on the outside of the steps represent the four continents known at that time, the four classical elements and four times of day; these sculptures are from the studio of Michael Johann and Ferdinand Maximilian Brockoff.

Beyond the stairs, a portal leads into the large and noteworthy Emperor's Hall, transformed into a grand Baroque eulogy to the greatness of the Habsburg dynasty through the paintings in oil and tempera

Above: Przewalski wild horse, bred in the Prague zoo. Right: The first all-male monastery in Bohemia – Břevnov Monastery.

by the brothers Abraham and Isaak Godin (Godyn) of Antwerp. At either end of the hall, royal portraits – one of the first German king of the Habsburg dynasty, Rudolf von Habsburg; the other depicting Leopold, the Emperor who conquered the Turks at Kahlenberg – dominated the room; while the other two walls bear artists' renderings of further high points of the Habsburg history. The images in the other rooms are frescoes by the Italian artist Francesco Marchetti who, with the help of his son Giovanni, also decorated the count's chapel. Particularly noteworthy, in some of the rooms, is the juxtaposition of allegorical ceiling frescoes and images of Chinese landscapes painted in a style derived from Chinese painting – a combination you don't often see.

The **Prague Zoo** next door dates from the early 1930s, and gained renown by successfully rebreeding the Przewalski wild horses. The zoo is home to more than 2,500 animals of 600 different species. If you'd like an overview before or after a detailed visit, take the cable car up a nearby hill which provides a panorama, not only of the zoo, but also of Prague and the Moldau Valley.

DISTRICTS WEST OF THE MOLDAU

Running west, past Hrad Castle and Strahov Monastery, streetcar line 22 facilitates a lovely excursion to the **White Mountain** (*Bílá Hora*). This is where, in 1620, it was decided that Bohemia would spend the following three centuries under the sovereignty of the Catholic emperors and kings of the Habsburg dynasty. But before you get there, stop off along the way to inspect the noteworthy Benedictine monastery of Břevnov.

Břevnov Monastery itself is only open to the public on weekends, although if you register in advance you can join a group for a weekday tour. When it was founded in 993 by Duke Boleslav II and Bishop Adalbert (Vojtěch) of Prague, it was the first monastery for men in Bohemia, and, after the Benedictine convent at Hrad Castle, only the second monastery in Bohemia of any kind. All that remains from the monastery's early days is the crypt of the former monastery church, which has only recently been discovered and excavated. It is thought that this pre-Romanesque relic dates from the 11th century. Because of its window openings, archaeologists have inferred that the crypt was not entirely underground.

Virtually all of the buildings on the site today, however, date from the Baroque era; construction was begun in 1708. One enters the monastery grounds through a portal by Christoph Dientzenhofer, above which a graceful statue of St. Benedict by Karl Josef Hiernle points gently but firmly in the direction of Christian heaven (this statue was temporarily removed in 1994 for the purposes of restoration). The central building is the single-nave St. Margaretha's Church,

completed in 1715 according to plans by Christoph Dientzenhofer. The basic geometric figure of its floor plan is an ellipse, or rather many ellipses, one merging into another, which made the construction of the ceiling notably complicated. This plan means the nave is divided into four zones. Engineers will be interested to note that the weight of the ceiling is borne, not by the walls, but rather by pillars with a 45° angle of rotation, which are made to seem less massive precisely by virtue of this rotation. The arched vaulting between the pillars forms convex ceiling surfaces, which were ornamented with religious frescoes by Johann Jakob Steinfels. The main altar was designed by the architect himself; while a painter named Johann Peter Brandl was responsible for the pictures over the side altars. The third altarpiece on the southern side of the church depicts the *Death of the Blessed Günter*. This 11th-century hermit, although he lived apart from the world in the Bohemian Woods, was nonetheless able, by virtue

of his royal blood, to serve as a mediator in the dispute between his cousin Henry II and Duke Břetislav of Bohemia. When Günter died at the age of 90 in his hermitage, Duke Břetislav ordered his remains brought to Břevnov. His tomb is near the altar, embedded in the southern wall. The altarpiece is especially impressive because of the artist's subtle yet effective use of light in illuminating the hermit's cave.

The hermit appears again in another part of the monastery. Cosmas Damian Asam captured a miraculous event from the life of Günter in a ceiling fresco in the Prelate's Hall. Invited by a duke to a feast on a day of fasting, Günter prays to God to get him out of this embarrassing dilemma, wanting, on the one hand, to observe Christian asceticism, but on the other hand not wishing to be impolite to his host. Heaven intercedes by means of a "peacock miracle." The peacock, which

Above: Wolfgang Amadeus Mozart was a guest in the Villa Bertramka.

has already been served, comes back to life and flees from the plate. Angels replace the meat of the bird with heavenly food, thus admonishing the host to follow a more modest way of life.

Two streetcar stops further on is the walled enclosure of a former game park, of which the main architectural attraction is the **Star Palace** (*Hvězda*). You can either get off the streetcar here and approach the palace on foot along a lengthy tree-lined road, or you can disembark at the last stop and enter the palace grounds via a side gate to the right. This route leads you through a woods made up mainly of beech trees, over a small stream in a kind of moat, and then up a short slope to the palace. This unique structure consists of six diamond-shaped halls linked to one another via a 12-cornered central room: its floor plan thus forms a six-pointed star (hence its name). Archduke Ferdinand of Tyrol came up himself with the idea for this Renaissance edifice, and commissioned the architects Juan Aostali and Giovanni Luchese to build it for him in 1555. The interior of the palace is just as interesting: the ceilings of the rooms on the ground floor are decorated with a wealth of stucco reliefs. Giovanni Campione and Andrea Avostalis created 334 images depicting scenes from Greek mythology and Roman history, including the flight of Aeneas from the burning city of Troy.

In the basement of the palace is a replica of the Battle on the White Mountain, while the ground floor houses an exhibition about Alois Jirásek, and, on the second floor, drawings and graphic works by Mikoláš Aleš are on display. The park around the palace is a lovely spot for a picnic.

Smíchov

Our next stop is the district of Smíchov and the neighboring districts to the south. Smíchov can be loosely translated as

"Laughing Meadow"; but the laughter has long since stopped with the advent of unattractive industrial sites. Still, there are two little gems here which hold considerable interest to visitors. One is the Kinský Palace with its English Garden, the other is the Villa Bertramka.

Kinský Palace, built in the Empire style, is part of the National Museum, although its collections are not to be open to the public in the foreseeable future. The palace is located on a small mound in a park (*Kinského zahrada*) graced by trees planted in the last century. The upper regions of this park are wonderfully wild; and the grounds are also dotted with such attractions as a Carpatho-Ukrainian wooden church, a wooden bell tower from Walachia, and a number of sculptures, including a bronze statue by Karl Dvořák entitled *The Fourteen-Year-Old*.

While the simple bell tower, located behind the palace to the left, is easy to find, the tiny church is somewhat tucked away, slightly above the palace, behind a stand of trees, and just next to a playground.

A bit of the illusion of the "Laughing Meadow" is preserved in the street Na Václavce, where two or three lovely Art Nouveau houses can still be found. From Fráni Šrámka, a dead-end street, a path leads up to Villa Bertramka. Walking along this path, it's easy to imagine the attractions this area once held. In Mozart's day, this villa belonged to the composer and piano teacher František Xaver Dušek and his wife Josefine, a renowned singer. When Mozart visited the city of Prague – his last visit was in 1791 – he was a welcome guest in the home of this musical family.

Today the villa houses a Mozart Museum, with exhibits including a piano designed by Ignatz Kober and a harpsichord on which it is said that the composer himself played. It also serves as a venue for festive concerts.

Accommodations

With only a few exceptions, these lodgings are all located within easy access of the excellent public transportation network to the city center. If you're likely to be out late, however, you should find out from the hotel what you should expect to pay for a taxi, and/or ask about the night bus schedule. These remarks, by the way, also hold true for the information listed after the chapters dealing with the city center.

VYŠEHRAD AND SOUTHERN PRAGUE

LUXURY: **Forum**, P-4, Kongresová 1, Tel: 6119 1111, Fax:: 42 06 84. **Panorama**, P-4 (Pankrác), Milevská 7, Tel: 6116 1111, Fax: 42 62 63. **Club Hotel Praha**, Praha-západ (Průhonice 400), Tel/Fax: 6775 0868. *MODERATE:* **Oáza**, P-4, Jeremenkova 106, Tel: 692 70 90, Fax: 692 71 85. *BOTEL:* **Racek**, P-4, Dvorecká louka, Tel: 6121 4109, Fax: 6121 4390.

VINOHRADY, ŽIŽKOV, KARLÍN AND EASTERN PRAGUE

LUXURY: **Hilton Atrium**, P-8 (Karlín), Pobřežní 1, Tel: 2484 1111, Fax: 2481 1932. **Olympik**, P-8 (Karlín), Sokolovská 138, Tel: 6618 1111, Fax: 6631 0559. Don Giovanni, P-3, Vinohradská 157a, Tel: 6703 1603, Fax: 6703 6704. *MODERATE:* **Karl-Inn**, P-8 (Karlín), Šaldova 54, Tel: 2481 1718, Fax: 2481 2681. **Luník-Garni**, P-2, Londýnská 50, Tel: 25 27 01, Fax: 25 66 17. **Velodrom**, P-10, Nad Třebešínem III. 3070/2, Tel: 77 07 37, Fax: 781 67 40. *BUDGET:* **Libeň**, P-8 (Libeň), Zenklova 37/2, Tel: 683 40 09, Fax: 683 40 14. **City**, P-2, Belgická 10, Tel: 691 13 34, Fax: 691 09 77.

LETNÁ AND NORTHERN PRAGUE

LUXURY: **Praha**, P-6 (Dejvice), Sušická 20, Tel: 2434 1111, Fax: 2431 1218. **Holiday Inn Praha**, P-6 (Bubeneč), Koulova 15, Tel: 2439 3111, Fax: 2431 0616. **Parkhotel**, P-7, Veletržní 20, Tel: 2013 1111, Fax: 2431 6180. *MODERATE:* **Belvedere**, P-7, Milady Horákové 19, Tel:2010 6111, Fax: 37 03 55. **Splendid**, P-7, Ovenecká 33, Tel: 37 33 51-9, Fax: 38 23 12. **Kozlovka**, P-6, Kozlovská 24, Tel: 32 58 82, 311 33 73, Fax: 311 33 73.

SMÍCHOV AND WESTERN PRAGUE

LUXURY: **Club Hotel Bohemia**, P-6, Ruzyňská 197, Tel: 316 24 01, Fax: 316 34 42. **Vaníček**, P-5, Na Hřebenkách 60, Tel: 35 07 14, 35 28 90, Fax: 35 06 19. *MODERATE:* **Coubertin**, P-6, Atletická 4, Tel: 35 28 51-3, Fax: 2051 3208. **Pyramida**, P-6, Bělohorská 24, Tel: 311 32 96, Fax: 311 32 91. **U Blaženky**, P-5 (Smíchov), U Blaženky 1, Tel: 55732 0953, 5732 0924. *BUDGET:* **Vila Maria**, P-6, Čistovická 37, Tel: 302 18 21, Fax: 302 23 26. *BOTEL:* **Admirál**, P-5, Hořejší nábřeží, Tel: 2451 1697, Fax: 54 96 16.

CENTRAL BOHEMIA

KARLŠTEJN
KŘIVOKLÁT / SLANÝ
NELAHOZEVES / VELTRUSY
MĚLNÍK
PODĚBRADY / KOLÍN
KUTNÁ HORA / KONOPIŠTĚ

KARLŠTEJN

Of all the objects and places that bear Charles IV's name, Karlštejn is historically the most important. Charles, or Karl, as he is known in Bohemian, has given his name to Karlsbad (Karlovy Vary), Charles Bridge (*Karlův Most*) and most recently to an elegant new hotel called *U Krále Karle*. There is even a Charlie Pub. But for many tourists Karlštejn remains the best-known symbol of the Czech Republic to be found outside of the capital city of Prague.

Charles IV built the castle Karlštejn on top of the 1,128-foot (345 m) high limestone cliff that dominates the landscape of rolling hills. It was to be a refuge for himself and his personal belongings; not until much later was it also considered worthy of holding the Royal and Imperial Crown Jewels, which are now housed in Prague's St. Vitus's Cathedral.

"Karlštejn is a monument to Charles' self-sanctification," wrote Ferdinand Seibt in his biography of the emperor, "with all the holy relics from whose magical proximity he drew his strength; and it reflects his image of himself as a

Preceding pages: Spring landscape. Promenade and changing hall in Marienbad. Left: Křiovklát Castle.

successor to Christ. The architecture therefore progresses through separate stations of those saints in whom Charles had a personal interest, and culminates in the Chapel of the Holy Rood, where Charles himself, with crucifix and jewels, sits aspiring to act as a symbolic image of the suffering of Christ, or of heaven itself. Karlštejn in its unattainable woodland solitude is Charles' spiritual pleasure palace..." Charles, born in 1316 in Prague and raised in Paris, was destined to become a King and Holy Roman Emperor. He mastered five languages and is the only German king to have written an autobiography. On his father's side he descended from the German-French house of Luxembourg; on his mother's side, he was a Přemyslid. With his far-seeing constitution, set out in the "Golden Bull" of 1356 and in effect until 1806, he brought new life to the German Empire.

It took nearly a decade (1348-1357) to build the Gothic castle. By the end of the 15th century the lower fortifications were finished. In the 1530s it became the seat of the Counts of Karlštejn. Half a century later, a Renaissance addition and sgraffito decoration were added to the complex. The castle was completely restored between 1887 and 1899. Today, it is one of the most-visited historical attractions in the country. Because of its many pre-

157

historic sites and small caves with stalag-
mites and stalactites, the surrounding
area has long a protected nature preserve.

The National Cultural Monument of
Karlštejn consists of three distinct parts:
the former burgrave's palace; the Small
Tower (*Malá věž*) with its church of the
Virgin Mary (sometimes referred to as
the Lady Chapel) and chapel of St. Catherine along with the Červenka jail; and
the Great Tower with the Chapel of the
Holy Rood.

Pass the palace and go through the 3rd
courtyard to get to the **Chapel svatého
Mikuláše**. The statue of the patron saint,
dating from the second half of the 14th
century, is now on display in the exhibition hall. The Emperor's bedroom, study
and state rooms were in the **Palác**.
Today, you can see two real gems here: a
Madonna from 1350 and a traveling altar
by Tomasso da Modena (1370).

The **Small Tower** with its **Lady Chapel** dominates the second terrace. The
magnificent frescoes of the Apocalypse
cycle are especially valuable; although
those along the north wall were unfortunately destroyed when the building was
enlarged in the 16th century. The Emperor is portrayed on the south wall in the
company of two male figures identified
by some as the French Dauphin and
Louis I of Hungary. The paintings are
thought to be the work of Master Wurm-
ser from the Alsatian city of Strasbourg.
A statue of St. Catherine from about 1400
stands on the neo-Gothic altar.

From here, it's not far to the chapel of
this saint herself: the **kapel svaté
Kateřiny** was consecrated in 1357 during the Emperor's reign. A double portrait depicts the ruler with his second wife,
Anna von Schweidnitz; another scene
shows him adoring the Madonna. The
walls are richly arrayed with precious
and semi-precious stones, a medieval
fairy tale right out of a central European
version of *The Arabian Nights*. The
statues of St. Peter and St. Paul are also

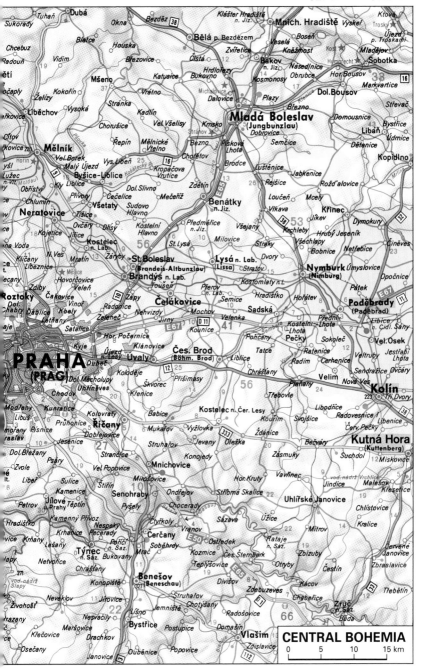

CENTRAL BOHEMIA

0   5   10   15 km

159

worth noting. The sacristy has a coffered ceiling. The frescoes in the stairwell, painted in 1360, were painted over in the last century, and restoration efforts have been only partially successful. There's also a marvelous collection of embroidered late Gothic vestments from around 1500.

The **Chapel of the Holy Rood** (*Kaple svatého Kříže*), also richly decorated with precious and semi-precious gems, is on the second floor of the Great Tower. It served as the private chapel of Charles IV until his death in 1378. Master Theodoric and his assistants painted the 130 panels depicting saints, prophets and angels around 1360 (they were restored in 1959-60); to them are also ascribed the five frescoes. Art historians point in particular to the paintings of the *Crucifixion* and the *Sufferings of Christ*. Because of their his-

toric importance to the entire country, a couple of the paintings are exhibited in the National Gallery in Prague and have been replaced in the chapel by copies. Above the altar is a medieval masterpiece: a triptych painted by Tomasso da Modena in the late 14th century. As if this rich display were not enough, the windows are also adorned with gems.

Zbraslav

Zbraslav in *Praha 5* is still within the city limits of Prague, some six miles (4 km) south of the city center. A documented settlement since the 13th century, the town's spiritual center was, in its day, a Cistercian abbey founded there in 1291. Partially destroyed by fire during the Hussite wars, the monastery was rebuilt by the prominent Baroque architects Giovanni Santini and Franciscus Maximilian Kanka. After the secularization of the monastery in 1785, the splendid rooms served for a time as a sugar refinery; fortunately, the frescoes by Wenzel

Above: Karlštejn, the personal castle of Emperor Charles IV. Right: The Chapel of the Holy Rood. Far right: On the bastion of Karlštejn Castle.

Lorenz Reiner and Franz Xaver Palko survived.

After the founding of the Republic, the monastery was renovated into a palace between 1924 and 1932, under the direction of architect Dušan Jurkovič. The palace now houses the National Gallery's collection of Czech sculptures from the last two centuries.

KŘIVOKLÁT / LÁNY
SLANÝ / TŘEBÍZ

Sitting high over a valley, **Castle Křivoklát** first enters recorded history in the middle of the 13th century under its German name Burglin or Burgleis. Initially, it was a hunting lodge to which its early occupants invited traveling minstrels. This late Romanesque building, later adorned with Gothic elements, originally only had room enough for the King's most intimate entourage. Wenzeslas I and his son, Přemysl Otakar II (King from 1253-78), enlarged the New Castle (*Castellum novum*); following Otakar's death, however, the castle fell into disuse and remained deserted for 200 years. Vladislav II of the Polish Jagiello dynasty, King of Bohemia (1471-1516), revived Křivoklát's court life. He had the palace and attached chapel rebuilt in late Gothic style with cruciform and stellar vaulting in the state rooms and chancel. Benedikt Ried, the court architect who built Vladislav Hall in the Old Palace in Prague, created Křivoklát's dazzling throne room. The Gothic passage in the upper castle and fragments of doors and windows have also survived.

In the 16th century, the castle was expanded with fortifications and a protective wall; but the complex was again deserted after 1526, and remained uninhabited until the 18th century, when the Fuerstenbergs took over. The decrepit castle was rebuilt in the 1880s, and restored anew in a neo-Gothic style in 1906. It currently houses a marvelous collection of Gothic and Renaissance panel paintings, as well as a notable collection of weapons from the 16th-18th

161

centuries, and some amusing Baroque sleds. Note the two lovely altars with depictions of the Holy Trinity, the Virgin Mary in the castle chapel, and the four patron saints of Bohemia.

Castle **Lány**, 8 miles (13 km) west of Kladno, became a royal residence at the end of the 16th century. The Fuerstenbergs acquired the property the following century and enlarged it in the 1830s; yet another addition was built at the beginning of this century. Since 1918, the castle has been used by the leaders of Czechoslovakia, and now of the Czech Republic, as a summer or weekend residence. The "Friday gatherings" of author Karel Čapek, attended by President Masaryk, have become legendary. Parts of the surrounding grounds, laid out in 1770, are open to the public.

The next destination, **Slaný**, also calls itself a "royal city," but the damage

Above: Country girl. Right: More than two centuries old: a farm in Třebíz.

caused during the Communist era makes it very difficult for a casual observer to find any connection between this city of 16,000 inhabitants and its 700 years of history. As so often happens in the absence of written record, the history of Slaný begins with a legend: a salt-water spring was believed to have had its source on the slope of a nearby mountain in the 8th century, until an earthquake buried it. Today, all that's left of the legendary spring is the name Slaný, meaning "the salty" or "the salted." The hill about half a mile (1 km) from town is called *Slánská hora*. In fact, water found in the coal mines of the region actually contains even more salt than sea water.

At the beginning of the 14th century King Wenceslas II granted royal status to the town; other privileges soon followed. The oldest building still extant is the **Deanery Church of St. Gotthard** (*děkanský chrám svatého Gotharda*). The earliest part of this former Romanesque basilica dates from 1130-50; the church later received a Gothic facelift, with the addition of such elements as the west portal. The three-aisle basilica with its pentagonal presbytery was frequently expanded and embellished, and was completely renovated at the turn of the century. The frescoes (Christ giving his blessing, the four evangelists and angels) in the cruciform vault above the altar date from the 16th century but have seen frequent subsequent restoration. Overall, the interior is Baroque, but some elements were not added until the last century.

Little else has survived from the Middle Ages. One of the four original city gates, the *Velvarská brána* dating from 1460, still remains, although the city wall is gone. Coats of arms and guild symbols decorate the gate, which was restored in the 1990s.

In the 15th century, Slaný was a Hussite stronghold, which then fell to the radical Protestants. After the defeat of the Protestant army at the Battle of the White

Mountain in 1620, Slaný was re-Catho-licized. It lost its royal status and was demoted to a vassal city. By that time the Franciscan **Church of the Holy Trinity** (*Kostel Nejvatější Trojici*, 1581) with its wonderful Renaissance altar had already been built, but the monastery wasn't added until after 1655.

Built in 1660, the **Piarist College** on the main square has served as a city mu-seum since 1886. Dominating the square called *Masarykovo náměstí* is the 140-foot (43 m) tower of the City Hall, which was begun in 1751. Many patrician homes from the 17th through 19th cen-turies have survived into the present but are urgently in need of restoration.

There is a wonderful example of suc-cessful restoration in the neighboring town of **Třebíz**, where a group of peas-ants' houses and a farm built between the 17th and 19th centuries have been res-cued just in time. The photos in the mod-est folklore museum at Trebiz document the desolate condition of the buildings before their recent restoration.

NELAHOZEVES

The composer Antonín Dvořák was born in Nelahozeves in 1841. The small museum that's been set up in his **birth house** may have fewer objects than the Villa America, as the Dvořák museum in Prague is known; however, the carefully and lovingly assembled assortment set up in the four modest rooms of this branch of the National Museum in Prague does the composer full justice. Even foreign visitors are astonished to learn that American astronaut Edwin Aldrin had a copy of Dvořák's last symphonic work, the *New World Symphony*, in his luggage aboard the Apollo II mission that landed on the moon in July, 1969. The *New World Symphony* is a musical memoir of Dvořák's stay in New York, where he was artistic director of the US National Conservatory from 1892-95. His other major works include a *Stabat Mater* and ten operas.

Dvořák, who dedicated his famous *Slavonic Dances* to his homeland, spent

163

the last years of his life in the land of his birth and directed an orchestra in Prague. Every year, his hometown celebrates his birthday on September 8 with a music festival called "Dvořák's Nelahozeves." Zdeněk Hošek's larger-than-life statue of Dvořák from 1988, entitled "Return" or "Concentration," shows the composer conducting.

In the Gothic **Church of St. Andreas** (*kostel svatého Ondřeje*), you can see, next to the font where Dvořák was baptized, the organ on which the talented student used to practice.

Although this spot on the left bank of the Moldau has been inhabited since the 14th century, only a nobleman's castle remains to attest to its distant past. It's not certain who first built this Renaissance structure; but old records do show that Florian Griesbeck von Griesbach, a Bavarian court official, acquired it in

Above: The castle in Veltrusy. Right: Arcade on the city square in Mělník.

1544, and had rebuilt it and given it its present appearance by 1553. A number of well-preserved sgraffito frescoes on the outer walls of this fortified structure date from this period. Later, ownership passed to a branch of the Lobkowicz family, who were to lose it when Czechoslovakia nationalized private property in 1945 (it was restored to them in 1990). After undergoing extensive reconstruction through most of the last century (the most comprehensive between 1910-12), the castle now houses several art collections. There's a respectable group of Spanish paintings (including a Velázquez), once the property of the wealthy Lobkowicz family, in the Castle gallery; Italian and Dutch painters from the 16th-18th centuries are also represented. There are also valuable faience collections from Holland (Bruegel) and Italy (Canaletto, Bellotto), as well as 17th-century weapons that were once a part of the family armory.

At **Zlonice**, not far from Nelahozeves, is yet another monument to Antonín Dvořák along with an impressive Baroque church designed by Kilian Ignaz Dientzenhofer.

VELTRUSY

A different and exotic world awaits visitors to the vast castle complex of **Veltrusy**. An English garden, laid out in the 18th century by Richard van der Schott for Count Wenceslas Anton Chotek, extends along the Moldau; this park is dotted with whimsical, fanciful structures including a **Chinese aviary** and an **Egyptian pavilion**. In the court of honor, a number of Baroque statues (restored in 1960) represent the twelve months and four seasons. The building, designed by either Franciscus M. Kaňka or Giovanni B. Alliprandi, dates from the second half of the 18th century. In addition to the exceptional stucco work, the palace is worth visiting for its noteworthy porce-

lain and faience collections, as well as the furniture. Originally Gothic, later remodeled as Baroque, the **Church of St. John the Baptist** (*kostel svatého Jana Křtitele*) is also worth seeing.

MĚLNÍK

The rivers Elbe and Moldau (Labe and Vlatva) are to the Czechs what the Rhine is to the Germans or the Volga and Don are to the Russians. And it may be precisely because of the exaggerated mythical and mystical importance given these two rivers that Mělník's origins are enveloped in legend. Local wisdom has it that a Slavic people had already settled here in prehistoric times, although there's no documentation or archaeological evidence to support this claim. And it was in Mělník in the 9th century, so the story continues, that Ludmila, youngest daughter of Prince Slavibor, married the Czech prince Bořivoj. Ludmila, who is one of the region's patron saints, has lent her name to three Mělník sites: the 16th-

century cemetery church, the chapel of Mělník's castle, and a popular local wine.

The scenery is right out of a picture book. At the confluence of the Elbe and Moldau rivers, above the vineyards which climb the hills, next to the originally Romanesque church of Sts. Peter and Paul, a castle was built some time around the 13th century: its majestic silhouette against the sky is one of the hallmark sights of the Czech Republic. The name of the town has its roots in *mělniti*, a common Czech word that means to mill, grind, crush, or sometimes also to press (as, for example, grapes are pressed). Viticulture here is a tradition that goes back to the 14th century, when Burgundy grapes were first grown in the region. Even older are the walls of the part of the castle now used as a wine cellar; they date from the 13th century. The current owner and lord of the manor, Jiří z Lobkowicz, uses this ancient cellar to age the wine he currently produces. Wine-tastings in the castle's elegantly furnished rooms are an unforgettable experience,

165

and can be specially organized for tour groups. In addition, the castle hosts not only wine festivals, but also concerts, balls and weddings. The traditional grape harvest takes on new meaning here, in a castle that has long housed a professional vintner's school. An 18th-century painting by Karel Škréta in the Lobkowicz Gallery illustrates the importance of viticulture to the area: St. Wenceslas himself is depicted pressing grapes to produce the communion wine. The Lobkowicz coat-of-arms mingles a royal crown with a stylized "L" and a bunch of grapes.

If you're unable or unwilling to travel to Mělník, you can sample the treasures of the noble cellars of this most important wine center of Bohemia at the **Lobkovická vinárna** on Vlašská ulice in Prague's Lesser City.

The Romanesque-Gothic **Castle** was built around the middle of the 16th cen-

Above: Wine, women, and song... Right: Picturesque spot: Mělník Castle on the Moldau and the Elbe.

tury and extensively enlarged in the century that followed. The tower is from an earlier period, around the end of the 15th century. The most significant renovations took place during the Renaissance, particularly with the addition of the arched colonnade with its two wings decorated with sgraffito. This part of the castle offers an example of the style of the waning 17th century; the side facing the river, however, underwent reconstruction and additions which made it unmistakably Baroque. All of this combines to provide the ideal space for one of the country's best museums, which the Lobkowicz family opened to the public at the end of the last century. Among the exhibits is a comprehensive collection of furniture that spans several centuries. Another superb collection, even by international standards, are the paintings of the Bohemian Baroque period. Among the best are works by Peter Brandl, Johann (Jan) Kupetzky, Wenzel Lorenz Reiner and Karel Škréta. Time and again, anyone traveling through the Czech Republic

will encounter works by these artists in historic churches, other museums and palaces throughout the land. The altarpiece in the castle's chapel is often attributed to Karel Škréta but was, in fact, painted by F.M. Schieffers at the end of the 17th century; it depicts the baptism of St. Ludmila. One of the more curious exhibits is a collection of baby carriages, production of which has a long tradition in Mělník.

The neighboring church of **Sts. Peter and Paul** (*kostel svatého Petra a Pavla*) was originally Romanesque; its 42-foot (13 m) tower dates from that period. Gothic renovations and additions ensued until the end of the 15th century, as you can see from the architecture of this three-aisled building. The net vaulting of the ceiling is very well preserved. Most of the church's furnishings date from the 18th century.

Mělník's other churches are pure Baroque: the **Protestant Church** in the *Mělnícké vtělno* section of the city and the **Church of the Archangel Michael** (*kostel svatého arhanděle Michaela*). In the district called **Chloumek**, there are two more Baroque churches: the Church of the Holy Trinity (*kostel Nejsvatější Trojice*) and the Chapel of St. John Nepomuk (*kapel svatého Jana Nepomuckého*). Also worth a visit is the Augustine church, *kostel svatého Vavřince*, in **Psovka**. There are two monasteries in the city: one Augustine (founded in 1263), one Capuchin (1752). The most interesting non-religious building is the Gothic City Hall, which was reconstructed after a fire at the end of the 18th century, but received its present appearance between 1939-41. The city center also contains a number of interesting structures built during the 1930s.

PODĚBRADY / KOLÍN

Poděbrady, 31 miles (50 km) east of Prague, is among the prettiest of the Czech Republic's many spa resorts. Part of its charm comes from the natural way that the spa, founded in 1907/8, expanded and grew into the landscape. The sur-

(Labe), is significant as the birthplace of George (Jiří, 1420-1471), commonly known as the "Hussite King," one of Bohemia's most important rulers. His election to King in 1458 was a triumph, a victory over the Emperor, the Pope, a number of aristocrats, and other candidates from Poland and Hungary. Although he had promised to lead Bohemia's Hussites back to the Roman Catholic faith, George changed his mind and lent his sword to the Hussite cause. As a result he was declared a heretic in 1466, and his son-in-law Matthias I Corvinus was chosen to replace him. The new "opposition" King challenged George and unleashed a bitter armed conflict that eventually cost George his life; he was killed in the second Hussite war in 1471. Historians regard his short reign as the acme of Bohemia's struggle for independence. His historical importance is shown, among other things, by his attempt to organize a union of the European countries for joint defense against the powerful Ottoman Empire. In Poděbrady, the main square is named for Jiří, and guarded by his equestrian statue.

rounding park, dotted with sculptures, is beautifully groomed; the sanatorium and villa-like hotels, architecturally pleasing in themselves – most were built in the 1930s – are conveniently located near the center of the spa and the city. Because of the well-developed infrastructure, even Western guests can enjoy a cure here, taking waters from mineral springs which, with their alkaline, iron and carbon content, are said to benefit patients suffering from heart and vascular disease and circulatory problems. The altitude, 611 feet (187 m) above sea level, is also considered beneficial. Some art historians have praised the proportions of V. Kerhart's colonnade from 1938. Poděbrady is also famous for its flower sundial, in bloom from early spring to autumn, unique in the Czech Republic.

Historically, Poděbrady, founded in the 15th century on the banks of the Elbe

Poděbrady's 13th-century Gothic fortress was expanded in several stages by a number of leading architects and builders in the course of the 16th century, resulting in the **Castle** of today. But Baroque additions followed, and its present appearance is actually the result of yet another facelift at the turn of this century.

Notable religious structures in Poděbrady include the **Provost's Church of the Holy Cross** (*proboštský kostel svatého Kříže*) with a valuable baptismal font (1563) and the **Miners' Church** of the Assumption of Mary (*havířský kostel Nanebevzetí Panny Marie*). Art Nouveau fans should look around the cemetery (*hřbitov*) on the road leading to Prague.

A Jewish cemetery is indicative of the diverse culture that awaits you in **Kolín**, not far from Prague. Some of the graves date from the 15th century; the syna-

Above: The park of Poděbrady. Right: Poděbrady's mineral springs have turned the town into a spa.

gogue, which houses a display of liturgical garments, was built in the 17th century. Much older is the **Miners' Church of All Saints** (*hornický kostel Všech svatých*), consecrated in 1292.

The center of Kolín, an industrial city of 33,000 inhabitants, is a protected landmark district, and contains some notable buildings. Most important of these is the Gothic **Church of St. Bartholomew** (*chrám svatého Bartoloměje*), dating from the second half of the 13th century, when Přemysl Otakar II was having Kolín laid out as a royal city. One artist who worked on the church's construction between 1358 and 1360 was the Swabian architect Peter Parler, master builder of Charles IV and architect of St. Vitus's Cathedral in Prague. A more unusual sight is the Baroque charnel house (*kostnice*) behind the church.

In the former **Hospice Church of St. John the Baptist** (*špitální kostel svateho Jana Křtitele*) there's a depiction of the crusade of 1759. Many statues are scattered about the city, including one of Jan Hus. A famous local son is composer František Kmoch (1848-1912), known throughout the country for his marches and polkas.

KUTNÁ HORA

The economic pressures that we experience worldwide today were also familiar in the waning days of the Middle Ages. The discovery of the New World had created a crisis for Bohemia's mines. Were the conquistadors who conquered Mexico responsible for the closure of silver mines around Prague? Indirectly, yes, because the output of mines in Nueva Espana was so great that neither Kuttenberg (Kutná Hora) nor Iglau (Jihlava) could keep up with their American competitors. Until then the mining town of Kuttenberg, founded by Germans in the second half of the 13th century, had supplied most of Europe with precious metal. Kuttenberg grew rapidly in importance: the settlement was already fortified by 1300; the Foreign Court (*Vlašský dvůr*) dates

from around this time, and the town even had its own mint. In 1318 the settlement was made a royal city, and was then systematically developed. One of the first three churches here was the **Deanery Church** (*kostel svatého Jakuba*); there is documentary mention of a city hall in 1375. The influence of the wealthy patrician families went unchallenged until the rise of the Hussites; after 1424, however, the mines began to decline. The introduction of new drilling techniques at the end of the 15th century ushered in a brief period of reflowering before Bohemia finally stopped supplying the world market forever a century later. Today, you can visit some of the former mine shafts.

The religious and secular structures that survive bear witness to the high level of urban culture that once flourished here. For a time Kuttenberg was second

only to Prague in importance among the Bohemian cities. Kuttenberg also played an important role in German cultural history: after the 1409 Decree of Kuttenberg, German professors and students made a gesture of protest against the growing spirit of Bohemian nationalism at Prague's Charles University, resigning from the university altogether and going off to found the University of Leipzig.

There's such a wealth of sights in Kutná Hora that you'll need at least a full day to see them all. The former **mint** in Vlašský Dvůr, originally Gothic but altered and enlarged through the centuries, received a palace and a chapel, dedicated to Sts. Wenceslas and Vladislav, around 1390. Today this chapel is regarded as one of Kutná Hora's architectural gems. Especially notable are an *Ecce homo* sculpture from 1511 by an unknown artist (the work is signed with his initials, H.E.) and a carved wooden bench of the same period. The chapel in the **Little Castle** (*Hrádek*) is also dedicated to St. Wenceslas (Václav). Hrádek was built in

Above: Fresco depicting the minting of coins in the Middle Ages. Right: St. Barbara's Church in Kutná Hora.

the 14th century as a manor house, which after 1620, as Catholicism was back on the rise, was expanded and served as a Jesuit college after 1686. Since the 1960s this historic building has been regarded as one of the most important and most beautiful Czech museums.

Among the earliest churches of Kutná Hora is the Gothic **Church of St. Jacob**, built between 1330 and 1420 under the influence of Peter Parler. As well as the interior, Charles IV's master building executed the frescoes, which can be seen today as fragments. Besides two Rococo carved confessionals and two choir stalls, the church contains various Renaissance and Baroque paintings, including a *Last Supper* from 1515 and the *Trinity* painted by Peter Brandl in 1734 (main altar).

The **Church of St. Barbara** (*kostel svaté Barbory*) is one of the grandest and most beautiful churches in Bohemia. Built by wealthy patrician families for the miners, it is dedicated to St. Barbara, the patron saint of miners. Construction took place in three phases: 1380-1420,

1481-99 and 1512-58. One of Parler's sons, Henry, was in charge of the first phase of building; Benedikt Ried added two further aisles in the early 16th century. The soaring vault with its complicated ribbing still astounds the visitor. Several of the chapels are noteworthy: *Smiškovská kaple* (1485) contains Stations of the Cross, the sibyls, and the Queen of Sheba; *Hašplířská kaple* (1493) has a painting of Christ's passion and the city's coat-of-arms; the *Mincířská kaple* depicts the mint master and a mint worker (1463). Particularly notable in the interior are a Gothic Madonna from 1380 and two carved choir stalls from 1490.

The church *kostel Panny Marie na Náměti*, begun in 1360, was largely finished by the end of the 15th century. The interior has survived the half a millennium since virtually unharmed. Note the late Gothic main altar, based on a design by Albert Dürer, as well as the side altars. Another impressive detail is the stone pulpit carved with figures of the church fathers (1520).

Around 1520, the **Church of the Most Holy Trinity** (*kostel Nejsvatější Trojice*), was constructed in the old cemetery a little ways outside the city center. The church with three naves was enlarged around 1600. In 1870, the art historian Franti_ek Rint redid the **charnel house**, known as the "bone chapel" using the bones of about 40,000 people, even the chandelier is a bony work of art.

The Baroque Ursuline convent (*Klášter voršilek*) belonged to the Catholic order until it was transferred to the state in 1950. Four wings were originally planned, but only two were actually built between 1733 and 1743. Kilian Ignaz Dientzenhofer designed the octagonal plan with its interesting winding staircase. Another religious building of note is the former Jesuit College next to St. Barbara's Church, an early Baroque building, designed by Domenico Orsi and built between 1667 and 1700. The

elegant promenade in front of the building was later embellished with Baroque statues of saints (1703-16; St. John of Nepomuk, 1740). The interior is remarkable for its high-relief stucco. But perhaps the most impressive Baroque sculpture group in Kutná Hora is the **Plague Column** honoring the Virgin Mary (F. Baugut, 1713-15), thought to be based on a design by Giovanni Santini.

Kamenný dům, **Stone House**, is the name given a late Gothic town hall built at the end of the 15th century and restored at the turn of the 19th century. Matthias Reiseck, who was also largely responsible for St. Barbara's, is thought to have directed work on the 12-sided stone fountain. This elegantly detailed work, dating from 1493-95, was reconstructed at the end of the 19th century.

KONOPIŠTĚ

"So, they've murdered our Ferdinand." – "Which Ferdinand, Mrs. Müller?" Josef Švejk, a dog trainer from Prague, asked

Above: Sunning on the grass is enough to make even a dog smile.

his landlady. "But, sir, the Archduke Ferdinand, the one from Konopiště, the fat bigot. – They shot him with a revolver in Sarajevo; he was traveling with his Archduchess in an automobile." This is the opening dialogue of what is probably the most important Czech novel of the 20th century, *The Adventures of the Good Soldier Švejk* by Jaroslav Hašek. With irony and wit Hašek describes the situation in Europe on June 28, 1914, the day Austrian Archduke Ferdinand, heir to the throne, fell victim to an assassin's bullet in Sarajevo.

Ferdinand had been director of the Imperial defense ministry at **Castle Konopiště**, a palace that had been enlarged especially for him 20 years earlier. Space had to be made to house one of Europe's most extensive weapons collections, comprised of more than 6,000 examples from several centuries. One of its strengths are 16th- and 17th-century guns. The castle also contains thousands of hunting trophies and hundreds of preserved and mounted animals, reflecting Ferdinand d'Este's considerable ability as a hunter and his fanatical love of the sport.

The original Gothic fortress, converted into a palace in the 17th and 18th centuries, displays what is perhaps Europe's largest collection of artifacts pertaining to the cult of St. George: more than 1,500 objects spanning a millennium. The Lobkowicz Hall (the palace belonged to this ubiquitous princely family until 1887) contains an impressive mural depicting the four seasons, painted in 1741 by Franciscus Julius Lux. The monumental gate in front of the palace was based on a design by Franciscus Maximilian Kaňka and embellished with figures from the workshop of Matthias Bernhard Braun. Many of the sculptures on the palace grounds, laid out in 1900, are originals; the Baroque statues, however, are casts. The palace now houses a restaurant; an added attraction is a pond in the park.

Ticket reservations for Karlštein, Veltrusy, Kutná Hora and Konopiště can be made in writing or by telephone at **Or-Fea**, 110 01 Prag 1, Dlouhá 10, Tel: 232 19 19, Fax: 232 31 00.

KARLŠTEJN
Visits are only possible on a tour. Open daily except Mon: Nov through March: 9 a.m.-12 p.m. and 1 p.m.-3 p.m.; April and Oct: 9 a.m.-12 p.m. and 12:30 p.m.-4 p.m.; May, June and Sept: 9 a.m.-12 p.m. and 12:30 p.m.-5 p.m.; July and Aug: 9 a.m.-12 p.m. and 12:30 p.m.-6 p.m. As a rule, during holidays and high tourist season the ticket counter is crowded. Departing from Prague: 17 miles (28 km) southwest over Radotín, Černošice and Dobřichovice. By train to Smíchov station.

VELTRUSY
Open daily except Mon: April and Oct through Dec: 9 a.m.-4 p.m., May through August: 8 a.m.-5 p.m.; Sept 9 a.m.-5 p.m. From Prague: 17 miles north on the E55 direction Kobylisy.By train to Masarykovo nádraží station in P-1, Havlíčkova, until Kralupy nad Vltavou. Then continue by local bus.

KUTNÁ HORA
Opening hours: **St.-Barbara-Kirche**: Open daily except Mon: Oct through March from 9 a.m.-12 p.m. and from 1 p.m.-4 p.m. and April through Sept from 8 a.m.-12 p.m. and from 1 p.m.-5 p.m.. **Welsch Courtyard**: Daily from 9 a.m.-5 p.m., Oct-March from 10 a.m.-4 p.m.. **Small Castle**: Daily except Mon: April-Oct from 9 a.m.-12 p.m. and from 1 p.m.-5 p.m., May throug-til 6 p.m.. **Stone House**: check opening hours due to renovation, Tel: 0327/51 23 78. Departing from Prague: 43 miles east on the 333 over Říčany. By train to the main train station of Masarykovo nádraží or Holešovice, with the bus from Florenc.

KONOPIŠTĚ
Visiting hours: daily except Mon: May through Aug from 9 a.m.-5 p.m., April and Oct from 9 a.m.-3 p.m., September from 9 a.m.-4 p.m.. Departing from Prague: 25 miles southeast on the E50/65 direction Průhonice until Mirošovice. Then to Benešov. By train to the main station of Benešov.

KŘIVOKLÁT
Visiting hours daily except Mon: Oct through April: 9 a.m.-12 p.m. and 1 p.m.-3 p.m.; May and Sept: 9 a.m.-12 p.m. and 12:30 p.m.-4 p.m.; June through Aug daily: 9 a.m.-12 p.m. and 12:30-5 p.m. Departure from Prague: 19 miles west on the E50 direction Beroun. From Beroun on small roads along the river Berounka in northwest direction. By train to the main station in Smíchov.

NELAHOZEVES
Castle gallery daily except Mon from 9 a.m.-5 p.m.. Antonín-Dvořák birth home daily except Mon from 9 a.m.-12 p.m. and from 2 p.m.-5 p.m.

NORTHERN BOHEMIA

DĚČÍN

TEPLICE

LITOMĚŘICE / TEREZÍN

JIČÍN

KADAŇ / LOUNY

ŽATEC

LIBEREC / FRÝDLANT

Since the loss of the upper and lower Tatra mountains, which became part of Slovakia after the division of Czechoslovakia, Northern Bohemia, with its Ore Mountains (*Krušně hory*) and Giant Mountains (*Krknoše*), was suddenly the foremost winter vacation spot in the Czech Republic. But that is only one aspect of this varied region. How else to the North, which also includes fertile plains? A quotation out of a picture book published in 1980 in Ústí nad Labem to commemorate the "35th anniversary of the liberation of Czechoslovakia by the Soviet army" may shed some light on a region that has become synonymous with trauma for millions of people on both sides of the border, in eastern Germany and Poland.

"The district of Northern Bohemia stretches from the mountainous north to the fertile plains of České středohoří, through coal fields and industrial regions; from the mighty transportation artery of the Labe (Elbe) river to the foothills of Český Ráj (Bohemian Paradise). It is the smallest region of the Czechoslovakian Socialist Republic in area, but it is of great political and economic significance

Left: A typically 18th-century Baroque Trinity Column, here in Žatec.

to the entire country. It is the major source of the country's fuel and energy. The brown coal mines of Northern Bohemia supply three-quarters of the inhabitants with brown coal, and their output is steadily increasing. The region supplies more than one-third of the ČSSR's electrical energy. The petrochemical industry and mechanical engineering are both highly developed. The glass and textile industries are also extensive. The People's Severočeské papírny (Northern Bohemian Paper Works) supplies almost all the paper needed by the Republic's newspapers. The uranium supply is steadily increasing in importance, and significant exploitation of tin, tungsten and fluoride and barytes is imminent. More than one-third of the nation's gasoline and the same proportion of nitrogen and phosphate fertilizer are produced here..."

For all that, a trip to Northern Bohemia also means encounters with castles and palaces, historic marketplaces, churches and museums.

DĚČÍN

Děčín, the district capital on the banks of the Elbe (Labe) river, received its city charter in 1283. Its coat-of-arms shows the Bohemian lion grasping a fish of al-

most equal size; but chemical pollution has taken care of fish in the Elbe. The river is a link to such cities as Dresden.

For decades, the castle of Thun-Hohenstein was headquarters of a Soviet army command. It would be perfect for the collection of Gothic art housed in the *Okresní muzeum*. The castle's well-tended **rose garden** (*Růžova zahrada*) is a beloved oasis for Děčín residents. At the end of the 17th century, the **Church of the Holy Rood** was added, along with an early Baroque calvary. The Gothic parish church of St. Wenceslas (*farní kostel svatého Václava*) was remodeled in Baroque in the 18th century.

TEPLICE

Once a pretty spa town on the Elbe, Teplice has turned into a sprawling industrial giant. Its fame stems from the many hot (40°C) mineral springs that at-

Above: Memorials to victims of the Nazis at Theresienstadt (Terezín).

tracted visitors from all of Europe in its heyday which began in the 18th century and lasted until the 1930s. Famous guests in the past have included such cultural luminaries as Goethe, Beethoven, Chopin, Wagner and Liszt. The largest sanatorium even bears Beethoven's name. Nowadays, visitors are more likely to be Austrian or German patients whose medical insurance subsidizes their visit.

The Renaissance palace, much altered since its construction in the 16th century, now houses a regional **museum** with a variety of exhibits ranging from ethnography and natural history to painting and sculpture. The Gothic palace church was reconstructed in the last century in neo-gothic style. The **Deanery Church of John the Baptist** (*děkanský kostel svatého Jana Křtitele*) was originally built in the Gothic style, later remodeled to Renaissance and finally rebuilt in Baroque style. It contains paintings by Peter Brandl and Wenzel Lorenz Reiner. Matthias B. Braun created the Baroque **Trinity Column** in 1718/1719.

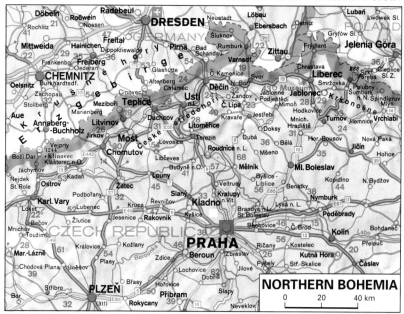

NORTHERN BOHEMIA

0   20   40 km

LITOMĚŘICE AND TEREZÍN

Now a historical landmark, the town of Litoměřice looks back on more than 900 years of history. First mentioned in 1057, it was a royal city by 1228 and a bishopric by 1655. One impressive church here is the Baroque **St. Jacob's** (1730-40). Even older is the **Deanery Church of All Saints** (*děkanský kostel Všech svatých*), begun in 1235, enlarged in 1480. More history is shown in the *Severočeská galerie* (Northern Bohemian Gallery), with works of art spanning 7 centuries. There's another museum in the 16th-century Old Town Hall. Lucas Cranach the Elder's *St. Anthony as a Hermit* hangs in the Cathedral of St. Stephan.

The former garrison town of Terezín was named in honor of Queen Maria Theresia, who died in 1780. Yet what's stamped indelibly on the town is the mark of more recent history. During World War II Terezín was better known by its German name, **Theresienstadt**. Although Theresienstadt was held up by the Nazis as a "model camp" where Jews supposedly lived happily and autonomously, the facts were quite different. For at least 160,000 Jews, this was a station on the way to the death camp of Auschwitz; others died as a result of living conditions within the camp itself. Today, a memorial here is a poignant reminder of the horrors of the Nazi regime.

JIČÍN

1,200 linden trees line a mile-long avenue near Jičín. The town, now a landmark, received its city charter in 1300, and was fortified in the 16th century. Center of town is the **castle** (now a museum). Tree-shaded arcades front the houses around the enclosed marketplace. Some original Gothic elements were preserved in the Baroque renovation of the Jesuit **St. Ignatius Church**. The **Plague Column** was erected in 1702, the **Coronation Fountain** (*Korunovační kašna*) in 1836. Jičín was also the birthplace of writer/critic Karl Kraus in 1874.

177

Above: At Klášterec Castle.

KADAŇ AND KLÁŠTEREC NAD OHŘÍ

Within sight of the electrical power plant of Tušimice, the center of the historically protected town of Kadaň has both beauty and centuries of culture to offer. Many of the pretty town houses date from the 16th century: a few are Gothic; some have undergone Baroque remodeling. During the Hussite wars in the 15th century, this royal city fortified itself; a few towers and bastions have survived. The popular *barbakán* dates from 1458. The Gothic town hall has a helmet-shaped tower that is unique in Bohemia. The Gothic **Franciscan monastery** (on Mount Strážiště outside of town) is notable, as is its Church of Fourteen Saints. The **Deanery Church** *Povýšení svatého Kríze* (Raising of the Holy Cross) underwent numerous renovations up to and into the 19th century. The Romanesque

Hospice Church of the Beheading of St. John the Baptist (*Stětí svatého Jana Křtitele*) was converted to Baroque in 1820. But the **Convent Church of St. Elizabeth** (*kostel svaté Alžběty*) and the **plague column** retain their original style. Both were erected between 1735-55 by local artists.

The **Thun-Hohenstein porcelain factory** in **Klášterec nad Ohří** celebrated its 200th anniversary in 1993. In 1590 the Counts of Thun-Hohenstein also built the fortified castle that now exhibits products of this, the second-oldest porcelain factory in Bohemia. A beautifully groomed English garden surrounds the castle. Trinity Church (1670) and the Cemetery Church (1760) merit a visit.

LOUNY

Founded around 1260 by King Otakar Přemysl II on the banks of the river Ohře (Eger), Louny has gone down in Czech history as an important Hussite stronghold; most of its fortifications date from this time. The only surviving city gate, *Žatecká brána*, built in 1500, was restored in 1842. The houses in the town center range from Gothic through to Classical. The **Column of Mary** created by Johann Bendl in 1673 is Baroque. The **Church of St. Peter** and the parish church of **St. Nicholas** were both built in the 15/16th centuries. The studio of Benedict Ried succeeded in constructing the church with its three-aisled nave and tripartite choir between 1520 and 1538. The richly decorated main portal and the chancel (1540) merit special attention.

ŽATEC

The fortified castle of this landmarked city has been renovated and converted into a brewery. Not surprising considering that Žatec – known for several centuries by its German name, Saaz – is the center of Bohemia's hop-producing region. It's this crop which is associated with the annual harvest festival; this crop which made the town prosperous in the past. Žatec is full of fine merchants' houses, some with tree-shaded arcades. Its most interesting sights include two city gates and a town hall which is Baroque in appearance but Gothic in origin. A religious highlight is the once-Gothic **Parish Church of the Ascension** (*farní kostel Nanebevzetí Panny Marie*) which was "Baroque-ized" in the 18th century.

LIBEREC AND FRÝDLANT

More than the Czech name of **Liberec**, the German name Reichenberg reflects the centuries of history of this textile center. The first linen weavers and cloth makers here are mentioned as early as the 15th century. The town continued to flourish in the industrialized 19th century. Demonstrating this are the **theater** built by Vienna's star architects Helmer and Fellner (1881-83), as well as the **town hall**, a neo-Renaissance edifice modeled on Flemish originals, built between 1888-92 by Franz Neumann. The same style was used for the **Northern Bohemian Museum**, which has an excellent collection of glass. Liberec **Castle**, a fitting home for the District Gallery, dates from the 17th century. Some of the town's monuments are Baroque, such as Matthias B. Braun's **Column of Mary**, erected in 1720, or the richly-decorated cemetery church of the Holy Rood (1753-56).

The castle that was once the favorite residence of Duke Albrecht von Waldstein (1583-1634), **Frýdlant**, (deriving from the German *Friedland*, peaceful country) is first mentioned in the 13th century. In 1801 it was made into a museum and opened to the public. Several dozen rooms dazzle the visitor with a grandeur that corresponds to the castle's position of dominance in the surrounding countryside.

NORTHERN BOHEMIA

Today, there are plenty of different options for hotels, pensions, and private accommodations in virtually every area. You can get more detailed information at the information office of every town (*Městský úřad*). You can also get information free of charge from the Chambers of Commerce in the main city of every county (*Okresní hospodářská komora*). Central office for the Czech Republic: *Česká obchodní komora*; Argentinská 38, 17005 Praha 7, Tel: 00420/2/6679 4111, Fax: 00420/2/66710253.

Museums, Galleries, Theaters, and Sights

All museums are closed on Monday. Otherwise, they're generally open from 9 a.m.-5 p.m.; some of them may be closed during lunch hour. Signs on some smaller museums tell you where you can pick up the key to let yourself in.

Děčín: Okresní muzeum - Muzeum labské plavby (Museum of Elbe Shipping).

Frýdlant: Státní zámek (Castle Museum), Zámecká kaple.

Jičín: Okresní muzeum (County Museum), Valdštejnovo náměstí 1, Okresní galerie (County Gallery), Zámek (Castle).

Kadaň: Okresní muzeum (County Museum) with lapidarium.

Klášterec nad Ohří: Zámek (Castle).

Liberec: Severočeské muzeum (Northern Bohemian Museum), Masarykova 11, Oblastní galerie, U Tiskárny 1. Divadlo F. X. Šaldy (Šalda Theater) - Naivní divadlo (Marionette Theater as well).

Litoměřice: Okresní vlastivědné muzeum (Country Museum), Stará radnice. Galerie výtvarného umění (Gallery of Fine Art), Michalská ulice 7.

Louny: Okresní muzeum (County Museum), Pivovarská 28. Galerie Benedikta Rejta (Benedikt Ried Gallery), Pivovarská 29.

Mladá Boleslav: Okresní muzeum (County Museum), Hrad (Castle).

Osek: Cisterciácký klášter (Monastery).

Teplice: Krajské muzeum (State Museum), Zámecké náměstí 14. Annual music festival *Ludvík-van-Beethoven*.

Terezín (Theresienstadt): Národní hřbitov (National Cemetery) - Concentration Camp Memorial. Malá pevnost (Small Fortress).

Žatec: Městské vlastivědné muzeum (State Folk Museum), Husova 678. Hops harvest in the autumn is accompanied by folklore festivals.

WESTERN BOHEMIA

KLATOVY / DOMAŽLICE
SUŠICE / PŘÍBRAM
STŘÍBRO / PLZEŇ
CHEB / JÁCHYMOV
MARIÁNSKÉ LÁZNĚ
FRANTIŠKOVY LÁZNĚ
KARLOVY VARY

KLATOVY

From either one of the nearly 260-foot (80 m) Renaissance towers on the town church, the **Black Tower** (*Černá věž*, 1557) or the more recent **White Tower** (*Bila věž*), you can make out the original Gothic layout of Klatovy's old town, like a chessboard set within an oval. But the true flowering of the city planning of Klatovy, often referred to in old history books by its German name, Klattaus, took place in the Baroque period.

Earlier – early Gothic, in fact – is the **city church, notable for its ribbed vaulting**. There was a Late Gothic restoration in the 16th century, and a course of radical renovation between 1898-1908. Of artistic interest is the ornate Rococo pulpit, carved in 1700. The **Jesuit Church of the Immaculate Conception** (*kostel Neposkvrněného početi Panny Marie*) stands out among Klatovy's other sacred buildings. Many famous builders and artists participated in its construction between 1656 and 1679. Domenico Orsi designed the church, assisted by Carlo Lurago. In 1730 another great architect, Kilian Ignaz Dientzenhofer, took charge of its Baroque rebuilding. Johann Hiebl's

Left: In the nature reserve of Soos.

frescoes in the dome are a high point of Bohemian Baroque illusionist painting. There are two towers atop the Baroque **St. Lawrence Church** (*kostel svatého Vavřince*) of the Dominican order.

The mid-16th century saw the building of the Town Hall, with its notable cruciform ribbed vaulting. Most of the town's residential and commercial houses were originally built between the 14th and 17th centuries. There are a number of Gothic sculptures in the District Museum; while the Baroque pharmacy of the White Unicorn (*U bilého jednorožce*) still has its original interior furnishings.

DOMAŽLICE

Every schoolchild in the Czech Republic knows the historical novel *Psohlavci* by Alois Jirásek (1851-1930). "Dog's Heads" would be the English term for the border guards and freedom fighters of the Chods, a South Bohemian tribe entrusted in the Middle Ages with patrolling the country's borders along a vital trade route between Bavaria and Bohemia, and rewarded, in turn, with special privileges. When these privileges were revoked at the end of the 17th century, the Chods revolted. The Chod capital Domažlice, founded in the 13th century, was once the westernmost royal city in Bohemia. Kil-

181

ian Ignaz Dientzenhofer oversaw the renovation of Chod Castle, which has an exhibit devoted to these historic events.

Dientzenhofer is also believed to have been involved in the reconstruction of the **Parish Church of the Birth of Mary** (*Narození Panny Marie*) from 1751-56. The Deanery Church's striking tower was built in the 13th century; note, too, the Late Gothic (1520) woodcarving *The Assumption of the Virgin*. The town also has two interesting cemetery chapels; yet even more interesting are the uniformity and coherence of its main square. Most of the buildings have shaded arcades. Originally Gothic or Renaissance, the houses were later given Baroque facelifts.

RABI

If there ever was a photogenic, romantic castle ruin, it is the one in Rabi. The

Late Gothic historic monument – completed in 1500 and abandoned in the 17th century – is the largest castle ruin in the Czech Republic. Even in its ruined state, this monumental complex is a vivid reminder of bygone power.

SUŠICE

Not far from Klatovy is the tiny town of Sušice whose **parish church** (*farní kostel svatého Václava*) and **cemetery church** (*hřbitovní kostel Panny Marie*), as well as the main square's residential and merchant houses, are Gothic. Beloved of pilgrims is the Baroque **chapel of the Guardian Angel** (*kaple Anděla Strážce*) above the town. Sušice was once known as Schüttenhofen. After the mid-19th century, matches produced here took over the world market, until Ivar Kreuger invented his Swedish matches. The history of this industry, as well as glass, tin, and Gothic sculptures, are displayed in the **Bohemian Forest Museum** (*Muzeum Šumavy*).

Above: Daily costume in Domažlice. Right: The main square of Domažlice. Far right: Sgraffitoed façade in Sušice.

PŘÍBRAM

Silver is still mined at Příbram, and now uranium has also been discovered. During the early years of the Communist regime, prisoners were sentenced to hard labor in the mine. The true history of the former Royal City of Příbram (1230) lies between the extremes of the dreaded mine and the rustic piety seen on the Holy Mountain (*Svatá Hora*). The pilgrimage church of the **Assumption of Mary** (*poutní kostel Nanebevzetí Panny Marie*) was consecrated in 1709; and pilgrims from Austria, Bavaria and other parts of Bohemia have been coming ever since. Art lovers who make the trip are also rewarded: Carlo Lurago built a marvelous Baroque edifice for the Jesuits, which was largely completed by 1772.

STŘÍBRO

Stříbro means silver. This sums up in one word the history of this town, founded in 1240 on the important trade route from Eger (Cheb) to Prague. Original 13th-century Gothic fragments were incorporated into the Baroque buildings of the **Minorite Convent**. As prosperity lasted well into the 16th century, the town boasts some imposing Renaissance structures: two churches (All Saints parish church, later remodeled in Baroque style, and the cemetery church of the Assumption of Mary) and a splendid Renaissance town hall built between 1543-1588. The sgraffito decoration was restored in the 19th century. An exhibition in the local history museum (*Vlastivědné muzeum*) commemorates silver mining.

PLZEŇ (PILSEN)

If a television game show posed a question about three things most often associated with the Czechs, one of the answers would have to be Pilsner beer. Certainly Pilsner Source, with 11% malt content, is this Western Bohemian city's most important export. However, this beer (*prazdroj* in Czech) was in fact the

idea of a Bavarian farmer. In the middle of the 19th century in Plzeň, he was the first to brew this wholesome, slightly bitter beer, and launch it on the road toward international success. "Lightly fermented, very light beer with a strong component of hops," is the way proper beer experts describe it.

The city was laid out at the end of the 13th century at the confluence of the rivers Mže and Radbuza, 4.5 miles (7 km) from a prince's estate now called *Starý Plzenec*. You can still make out the generous ground plan of the original town in modern Plzeň. The town prospered and developed close relations with Nuremberg and Regensburg. By the 15th century, Plzeň was even more active than Prague in some areas: the first Czech book, for example, was printed here in 1468. Even today, there are still a few landmark buildings from the Renaiss-

Right: Ornate Renaissance building on Cheb marketplace.

ance. The industrialization that set in around the middle of the 19th century ushered in a new burst of prosperity. The brewery was built in 1842 (guided tours are available); the Škoda factory followed in 1859. This upswing was reflected in concrete form in the city's architecture, in, for example, the sgraffito decoration on the Renaissance-style City Hall, or the elegant theater, built in 1902.

Significantly older is the Gothic church of **St. Bartholomew**, which sports the highest tower in the country (337 feet/103 m); its cornerstone was laid in the early 14th century. Experts laud its *Pilsner Madonna* (circa 1400); other art treasures are the Late Gothic sculptures of St. Barbara and St. Catherine. The Calvary Altar, with sculptures by L. Widmanns, dates from 1765. The former **Minorite monastery,** to which the Church of the Assumption of Mary belonged, now houses the excellent **Western Bohemian Museum** (*Západočeské muzeum*) with a collection of prehistoric artifacts from the region. The **Western Bohe-**

mian **Gallery** is set up in a Late Gothic building that was restored in 1850 and nicknamed Masné krámy, "butcher's block." Originally a Gothic house of worship, the building has a wonderful 14th-century cloister. **St. Anna Church** and its Dominican convent were built around the end of the 15th century and altered to Baroque. The Archdeanery with its valuable stucco work is built in a similar style.

The internationally known creator of animated films for young and old, Jiří Trnka (1912-1969), was born in Plzeň. Other famous "native sons" include Bohemia's best-known marionette figures, the erudite father Špejbl and his cheeky son Hurvínek, both creations of the famous puppeteer Josef Skupa.

CHEB

Cheb, known formerly by its German name Eger, has gone down in European history by virtue of a murder. In 1634 Duke Albrecht von Waldstein, a general in the Thirty Years' War, made his officers swear their allegiance, not to the Emperor, but to himself. The Duke then tried to negotiate with the Saxons and Swedes. However, a traitor revealed his plans to the Kaiser. When Waldstein returned from a trip to Plzeň on the night of February 25, he was murdered. Two dozen of his officers were later tried in an Imperial court and condemned to death.

Because of its strategic location between Bohemia and Bavaria, Cheb had already been cast in an historically important role. A defensive wall was built around the city center (now a landmark) in the 13th century. The privileged town continued to prosper until into the 18th century. Cheb's rich and varied history is written on the façades of its many old residential and commercial houses. Some of the buildings are Gothic, others were built during the Renaissance. Since the Romanesque-Gothic fortress was de-

stroyed by fire in 1743, it has been a ruin; only the **Black Tower** (*Černá věž*) has survived. Part of the castle has, however, been restored, and one section is used as a museum. Among Cheb's non-religious edifices, two buildings deserve mention: the old and new **town halls**. The old town hall dates back to the Middle Ages; the new one was built in 1716. *Špaliček* (building blocks) is the name given to a charming group of buildings that once housed shops. Two fountains, one dedicated to Roland and the other to Hercules, are a reminder of the splendors of the Renaissance.

Most of the sacred architecture dates from Gothic times. This is true of the **parish church** and the **Minorite Church** that was later taken over by the Benedictine order. It has a beautiful cloister. The Church of **St. Bartholomew** is another Gothic structure, as is the **Church of the Poor Clares**, consecrated in 1273 and later remodeled by Dientzenhofer in Baroque style. Also dating from the 13th century is the **Dominican monastery**; its

church is named after its patron saint, Wenceslas II (*kostel svatého Václava*).

JÁCHYMOV

For many citizens of the former Czechoslovakian Republic in the 20th century – condemned criminals or simply opponents of the Communists – Jáchymov was synonymous forced labor. Its uranium mines were the dreaded last stop on many resumes. In the days when it was called Joachimsthal, Jáchymov was famous for its silver mines. Since the Middle Ages, the town's silver coin, the Joachimsthaler, has given its name to many other currencies: taler, tolar and dollar. Then, silver ore was the source of the town's wealth; today, this is based on the radioactive water used in medical treatments in modern sanatoriums. The **Radium Palace** is an Art Nouveau gem that reflects a turn-of-the-century flair.

Above: Going to Karlovy Vary means following in the footsteps of the rich and famous.

MARIÁNSKÉ LÁZNĚ

Mariánské Lázně, or Marienbad, is the youngest of Western Bohemia's four most important spas. In 1812 the town could only claim 13 buildings. Since then, this spa resort has been expanded and fitted out with amenities of a sort that enable the country's second-largest spa to meet Western European standards. Its three dozen curative mineral springs are thought to be beneficial to patients with urinary tract problems. Classical revival and Art Nouveau style predominate in the spa's architecture. Concerts and festivals liven up the cultural life, while there's golf for the more active guests.

FRANTIŠKOVY LÁZNĚ

Františkovy Lázně, once Franzenbad, is an architectural gem. It was laid out in 1791 to cover an area measuring only 703 x 735 feet (215 x 225 m); and this spa, with its two dozen curative springs, has changed little since then. The city's classical architecture, painted "Kaiser yellow," along with its well-groomed parks and leisure activities, make it an ideal place for rest and relaxation.

KARLOVY VARY

German tourists come to Karlovy Vary, or Carlsbad, to follow in the footsteps of Goethe. The famous German writer spent many a holiday taking the waters in Western Bohemia's fashionable spas. Karlovy Vary is the largest and boasts 60 curative mineral springs. The "drinking cures" offered here are said to have a positive effect on metabolism and help patients suffering from glandular disorders, circulatory problems, and motor impairment. Goethe credited Carlsbad for granting him a "new lease on life."

The list of prominent guests reads like a Who's Who of European cultural history: Bismarck, Brahms, Chopin, Gogol, Goncharov, Leibniz, Lenin, Marx, Paganini, Rousseau, Schiller, Schumann, Leo Tolstoy, Tchaikovsky, Turgenev, Wagner. With so many Russian visitors, it's no wonder that a **Russian Orthodox Church** was built in 1893. Culture and politics ruled the day: important Jewish congresses took place here; it was here that Dvořák's *"New World" Symphony* had its premiere. Two casinos provided entertainment. One center of Carlsbad's social life was the **Grand Hotel Pupp**, going strong for almost 300 years, and thus among the world's oldest hotels. Another was the **theater**, built by the famous Viennese architects Helmer and Fellner. The neoclassical Sprudel Spring Colonnade built by Josef Zitek in 1881 is worth noting. Part of the cure, of course, is strolling through the pedestrian area. At **Vřídlo**, the hottest (salt-water) mineral spring in the country at 72°C (161°F). is a jewel of High Baroque architecture: Kilian Ignaz Dientzenhofer's **parish church of Mary Magdalene**.

WESTERN BOHEMIA

Today, there are plenty of different options for hotels, pensions, and private accommodations in virtually every area. You can get more detailed information at the information office of every town (*Městský úřad*). You can also get information free of charge from the Chambers of Commerce in the main city of every county (*Okresní hospodářská komora*). Central office for the Czech Republic: *Česká obchodní komora*; Argentinská 38, 17005 Praha 7, Tel: 00420/2/66794111, Fax: 00420/2/66710253.

Museums, Galleries, Theaters, and Sights

All museums are closed on Monday. Otherwise, they're generally open from 9 am-5 pm; some of them may be closed during lunch hour. Signs on some smaller museums tell you where you can pick up the key to let yourself in.

Cheb: Chebské muzeum, náměstí Krále Jiřího z Poděbrad. Galerie výtvarného umění, náměstí Krále Jiřího z Poděbrad.

Domažlice: Muzeum Chodska, Chodské náměstí 96 (Chodský hrad - *Choden castle*). *Branch*: Muzeum Jindřicha Jindřicha, náměstí Svobody 61.

Frantiskovy Lázně: Městské muzeum, dr. Pohořeckého 8. Excursion to the Soos nature preserve.

Jáchymov: Muzeum, Hornické náměstí 37.

Karlovy Vary: Karlovarské muzeum, Lámecký vrch 22. Sklářské muzeum (Moser Co.), Dvory. Muzeum karlovarského porcelánu, Březová. Divadlo Vítězslava Nezvala (Theater), Divadelní náměstí. Mezinárodní filmový festival (annual Int. Film Festival). Grand Hotel Pupp. Golf course.

Klatovy: Okresní muzeum a galerie, Hostašova 1. Baroque apothecary (*lékárna*) U bílého jednorožce, náměstí Míru.

Kynžvart: Státní zámek (*State castle*). Lázně - traditional mineral pool.

Mariánské Lázně: Městské muzeum, Goethovo náměstí 11. Golf.

Plzeň: Západočeské muzeum, náměstí Republiky 13. Západočeská galerie, *Masné krámy* - Pražská 35. Pivovarské muzeum (*Brewery Museum*), Veleslavínova 6.

Příbram: Okresní muzeum, Březové Hory. Pilgrimage Church of the Ascension on Svatá Hora, or sacred mountain.

Rábí: The country's largest castle ruin.

Stříbro: Muzeum, Masarykovo náměstí.

Sušice: Muzeum Šumavy, náměstí Svobody.

Teplá: monastery with marvelous monastic library dating from 1666.

SOUTHERN BOHEMIA

ČESKÝ KRUMLOV

JINDŘICHŮV HRADEC

PÍSEK

STRAKONICE / ROŽMBERK

BECHYNĚ / TŘEBOŇ / TÁBOR

ČESKÉ BUDĚJOVICE

PRACHATICE

ČESKÝ KRUMLOV

The German term *die krumme Au,* the crooked valley, aptly describes the meandering course of the Moldau (Vlatva). Hence the "Krumlov" of the town's name, while *český,* or Czech, is a way of distancing the town from its Krumlov in Moravia. Today under landmark protection, the town was founded in the 13th century by the Vítkovci dynasty and later passed on to the Rožmberks, one of the wealthiest families of Bohemian aristocrats. Thereafter the town had three more landlords: the Eggenbergers, the Schwarzenbergs, and the state. Since 1993, Český Krumlov has been on the UNESCO list of world cultural monuments.

The town, which has evolved since 1302 around the stout fortress, later converted into a **castle**, has retained – at least at its center – much of its look from the 17th and 18th centuries. Of course, however picturesque it may be, there had to be renovations, and many buildings received a Renaissance or Baroque facelift. The richly furnished castle has a Rococo chapel (1750-53); outstanding among its secular rooms is the **Hall of Masks** with its beautifully preserved fre-

Left: Fresco in the castle chapel at Zvíkov.

scoes. Its most famous attraction is probably the Late Baroque **theater**. While the city boasts 250 buildings under landmark protection, and is therefore often used as a setting for films, the **Deanery church of St. Vitus** (*svatého Víta*), built in 1309, is the city's oldest. The impressive Baroque building of the former **Jesuit seminary** dominates a hill above the Latrán district of town. Now used as a museum, it houses a valuable collection of Gothic and Renaissance art. Recently, the town has started to attract art lovers who make the pilgrimage to Český Krumlov to see the permanent display of works by Austrian artist Egon Schiele.

Zlatá Koruna

Near Český Krumlov is Zlatá Koruna, which is among the country's most complete **monastery** complexes. The 13th-century Cistercian monastery, partially destroyed by fire in the 15th century, was rebuilt and retains a series of fine buildings that have earned it protection as an historical monument. As well as old farm buildings, these include a basilica built at the turn of the 13th and 14th centuries, which was later enlarged and remodeled in the Baroque style. The convent is Gothic. The chapel *Andělů Strážných* (the **Chapel of the Guardian Angel**) with its

189

extraordinary portal was built in 1290. Secularized in 1785, the convent still boasts a beautiful cloister.

Hluboká nad Vltavou

The elegant Tudor-style, white-painted **castle** complex crowning the hill is visible from far and wide. Frauenberg, the Gothic castle's German name, is first documented in the 13th century. Until 1939, Hluboká belonged to the noble Schwarzenberg family, after 1947 to the state. Innumerable treasures fill the castle, furnished with valuable objects. The library has 12,000 books which came from a Frankish monastery. There are dozens of tapestries, some of which are displayed in the large dining room; as well as valuable examples of faience pottery from Delft. The former riding hall now houses the **Southern Bohemian Aleš Gallery** (*Alšova Jihočeská galerie*;

Above: On UNESCO's list of international cultural sites: the town of Český Krumlov.

Mikoláš Ales, 1852-1913), a worthy space for a superb collection of Gothic sculpture and paintings.

JINDŘICHŮV HRADEC / ORLÍK

Since it was founded by the Wittigons, the **fortress** of Jindřichův Hradec has been the center of a town which was known for centuries – since its charter of 1255 – as Neuhaus. *Jindřich* is Czech for Henry; *hradec* means fortress. Because of their extensive land holdings, the lords of Neuhaus were among the country's most powerful and feared princes. During a brief pause in the Thirty Years' War, the counts of Czernin acquired the property, now converted into a castle; they retained it until 1945. Restored in 1993, the castle again reflects the glory of its centuries-long history with its carefully preserved interiors and objects. Among the town's noteworthy sights are a number of bourgeois houses that are sadly in need of restoration. The 14th-century **Provost Church** of the Virgin

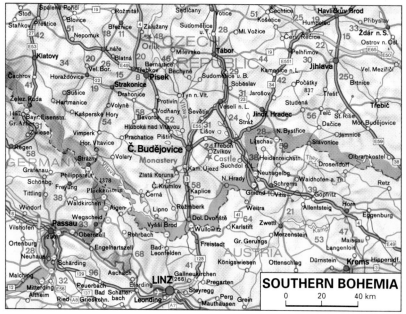

SOUTHERN BOHEMIA
0   20   40 km

Mary was refurbished at the beginning of the 16th century in Late Gothic style. Badly damaged in a violent fire in 1801, the church was restored during the 19th century in neo-Gothic style. The convent of the Minorites with its church of **St. John the Baptist** (*kostel svatého Jana Křtitele*) was begun in the 13th century. Construction continued into the 15th century. Medieval frescoes from 1350 depicting the Legend of St. George cover several walls; they are considered among the country's best examples of Gothic art. Four other religious buildings from the Gothic or Baroque periods vie for your attention. The **local history museum** has found a perfect home for its exhibits in the former Jesuit college (1615).

Orlík, or "little eagle," is the name of a 13th-century fortress on the Moldau, which has belonged to the Schwarzenberg family since the 18th century, and was converted into a castle in the 19th. A dam on the Moldau has turned the three-story building into a water castle. Although the castle was returned to Prince Karl Schwarzenberg, Václav Havel's former chancellor, in 1992 and is thus privately owned, part of it is open to the public. In addition to its elegant interior, the castle holds an extensive collection of arms, hunting weapons and trophies.

Zvíkov

The national cultural monument of Zvíkov, formerly known as Klingenberg, is considered to be among the country's best examples of the architecture of royal **fortresses** in the Přemysl period. It was built around 1230 at the confluence of the Vlatva and Orava rivers. Otakar II had it enlarged, and construction of various sorts continued into the 16th century. Because of its strategic position, Klingenberg was considered impregnable. But the castle fell victim to centuries of slow decay, until the Schwarzenbergs had it extensively restored at the end of the 19th century. The castle complex includes a **chapel** containing valuable frescoes from the late Middle Ages.

191

PÍSEK

What most travel guides about Prague don't tell you is that Charles Bridge (*Karlův most*) was often repaired and restored in the course of its 650-year history, before it finally achieved its present form. By contrast, the **stone bridge** over the river Otava in Písek (*písek* means sand), built in 1265, is one of the oldest original stone bridges in Central Europe. Písek, founded in the 13th century, lay on the once-famous trade route between Bavaria and Bohemia known as the "Golden Path;" its wealth derived from gold mining in the Middle Ages. This period also saw the building of Písek's **fortress**, now serving as a regional museum. Bohemia's five most important architectural styles are reflected in the houses here: Gothic, Renaissance, Baroque, Classical and Art Nouveau. The **parish church of**

Above: Písek boasts one of the country's oldest stone bridges. Right: Invitation to the Fire-Fighters' Museum in Bechyně.

the **Nativity of Mary** (*farní kostel Narození Panny Marie*), consecrated in 1250, is notable, as is the Gothic **Church of the Raising of the Cross** (*Povýšení svatého Kříže*), "Baroque-ized" in the 18th century. The Renaissance cemetery church of the Holy Trinity (*Nejsvatější Trojice*) is also recommendable.

STRAKONICE

In the 13th century, the **fortress** of Strakonice came into the hands of the Knights of St. John, who soon took over the land surrounding the castle, expanded the Gothic fortress, and made it the residence of their Grand Prior. There's been no major construction since the 16th century. As well as a section devoted to local history, the *Muzeum středního Pootaví* features a show about the bagpipers for which Strakonice is famous. The two houses of worship, *kostel svatého Prokopa* and the parish church of St. Margaret (*farní kostel svaté Markéty*) date from the 13th and 14th centuries respectively. A Baroque merchant's house in the town center is decorated with a relief called *Cattle Butchering* (1759).

ROŽMBERK

Many Czech place names, especially those ending in "berk," have their origins in German names: and Rožmberk was formerly Rosenberg. In the 13th century, a member of this large and wealthy family of aristocrats built the **Upper Fortress**, of which, after a fire in 1522, only a single round tower was left. The **Lower Fortress** was completed in the 14th century and fell to the Habsburg General Buquoy in the Thirty Years' War. The Buquoy family, of French descent, owned the castle until it was nationalized in 1948. The complex is in excellent condition; the interiors beautifully preserved; and the whole thing is open to the public.

BECHYNĚ

In the second half of the 16th century, Prince Rosenberg built a grandiose **Renaissance palace** on an exposed site where a 13th-century castle had once stood. Although it was expanded and rebuilt throughout the ensuing centuries, the palace retained much of its original shape. In 1715 Leopold Count Paar inherited Bechyně; and it remained in the possession of his family until its expropriation by the Communists. In 1994, however, the property was restored to the family intact – if you overlook the loss of its contents.

Bechyně is also well-known for its mud baths, or for the local porcelain factory, which enjoys a good reputation. A **Ceramics Museum** documents details of porcelain manufacture and production.

Another point of interest is the **Fire-Fighters' Museum**, housed in the former synagogue. The town's main square is lined with Renaissance and Baroque houses.

The dome of the 15th-century **Franciscan Church of Mary's Ascension** (*kostel Nanebevzetí Panny Marie*) is the most imposing of the town's religious structures. Also Gothic, later "Baroqueized," is the deanery church of **St. Matthew** (*děkanský kostel svatého Matěje*).

TŘEBOŇ

Currently under landmark protection, the town center of Třeboň is remarkable for having managed to preserve not only its Renaissance appearance, but also the air of quiet introspection of a bygone era. Central building here is the 16th-century **Renaissance palace**, within its beautifully groomed park; parts of it are used as a museum. In the convent church of **St. Aegidus** (*kostel svatého Jiljí*) there's a marvelous altar with an image of the Crucifixion dating from 1380, one of the most important examples of Gothic art in Bohemia.

The secular architecture is mostly Renaissance or Gothic in style. Notable is

the town hall built in 1566 and restored in 1820. In 1832 it was converted into a **theater**, one of the oldest in the Czech Republic. The fishponds, which the Rosenbergs laid out on the outskirts of Třeboň (formerly Wittingau) in the 16th century, are in use to this day. The fish caught here are one of the Republic's most important exports.

TÁBOR

The name of this historic city is inseparably linked with the Hussites. Tábor (*tábor* means warehouse) was built up into a Protestant stronghold in the 15th century, and withstood all attacks until 1434. The city did sustain serious damage in the Thirty Years' War. Nonetheless, many Gothic and Renaissance buildings survived, including a number of residential houses and, above all, the 1515 **Town Hall**. Among Tábor's chur-

Above: České Budějovice's central square with renovated arcade houses.

ches, two deserve special mention: the **Church of the Transubstantiation** (*děkanský kostel Proměnění Páne*) and the **Church of the Nativity of Mary** (*kostel Narození Panny Marie*). The first, dating from 1440, has remarkable vaulting. The second, the monastic church of the Augustines, consecrated in 1666, is embellished with Baroque glitter. The monument to Jan Žižkas by Josef Strachovsky dates from 1884. The **Muzeum husitského revolučního hnutí** tells the story of the Hussite movement in Europe.

ČESKÉ BUDĚJOVICE

Budějovice is known for beer; the German name of this Czech city, Budweis, is familiar through Budweiser beer, a name that greets us at all important US sporting events. The American-based company Anheuser-Busch, the world's largest brewery, has long used the name Budweiser for its product. But České Budějovice is famous for its own Budweiser beer, and the state-owned brewery has been wrangling with the American giant for decades over legal rights to the name. During the monarchy, a historically protected carriage route ran from here to the Austrian city of Linz (1832), and even today, the *lingua franca* of the town's tourist industry is Austrian-flavored German.

The Dominican church of the **Sacrifice of Mary** (*kostel Obětování Panny Marie*, 13th century) contains, among other treasures, a 14th-century cloister. Most important religious structure, however, is **St. Nicholas Cathedral**, rebuilt in the 16th century, but incorporating many of its original Gothic elements. The Rococo chancel is a true gem. Totally restored, the town's main square, a literal square measuring 425 feet (130 m) on a side, is unique not only the Czech Republic but in Europe as well. Virtually all the houses and shops (except the City Hall, built in 1730) have arcades. Most of the buildings date from the Gothic or Renaissance. The **Samson Fountain** (1720-27) is the largest stone fountain in the country. The 235-foot (72 m) high **Black Tower** (*Černá věž*) dominates the historic heart of the old city, and affords a wonderful panorama. Anything that remains hidden from view is revealed in the exhibits of the **Southern Bohemian Museum** (*Jihočeské muzeum*).

PRACHATICE

Since the 14th century, this town in the shadow of **St. Jacob's Church** has flourished. The house of worship displays a number of rare Gothic and Renaissance art works. Hans Holbein made the sketches used for the frescoes that decorate the **Old Town Hall** (completed in 1572). Most of the residential houses in the town center also date from the 16th and 17th centuries, and hint at the now-forgotten wealth and grandeur of towns along the so-called Golden Path that linked Bohemia and Bavaria.

SOUTHERN BOHEMIA

Today, there are plenty of different options for hotels, pensions, and private accommodations in virtually every area. You can get more detailed information at the information office of every town (*Městský úřad*).

You can also get information free of charge from the Chambers of Commerce in the main city of every county (*Okresní hospodářská komora*). Central office for the Czech Republic: *Česká obchodní komora*; Argentinská 38, 17005 Praha 7, Tel: 00420/2/66794111; Fax: 00420/2/66710253.

Museums, Galleries, Theaters, and Sights

All museums are closed on Monday. Otherwise, they're generally open from 9 am-5 pm; some of them may be closed during lunch hour.

Signs on some smaller museums tell you where you can pick up the key to let yourself in.

Bechyně: Muzeum keramiky (Ceramics Museum), náměstí (central square).

Muzeum požárnictví (Fire-Fighters' Museum) in the former synagogue.

České Budějovice: Jihočeské muzeum (Southern Bohemian Museum), Dukelská ulice 1.

Divadelni soubor J. K. Tyla (a theatrical ensemble).

Český Krumlov: Zámek (Castle).

Rococo palace theater, *Zámecké divadlo* , dating from 1767.

Okresní vlastivědné muzeum (Museum of Regional History), Horní 152.

Hluboká nad Vltavou: Alšova jihočeská galerie (Aleš-Southern Bohemian Gallery).

Zámek (castle).

Jindřichův Hradec: Okresní vlastivědné muzeum (regional museum of local history), Balbínovo náměstí 19.

Písek: Okresní muzeum (district museum).

Hrad (castle).

Prachatice: Okresní vlastivědné muzeum (regional museum of local history), Žďárský dům.

Branch: City history - Sytrův dům.

Rožmberk: Muzeum

Dolní hrad (Lower Fortress).

Strakonice: Muzeum středního Pootaví, Hrad (*Castle*).

Tábor: Muzeum husitského revolučního hnutí (Museum of the Hussite Movement).

Stará radnice (Town Hall).

Třeboň: Muzeum, Zámek (castle).

Vyšší Brod: Monastery library.

Zvíkov: Hrad (castle).

195

EASTERN BOHEMIA

HRADEC KRÁLOVÉ
DVŮR KRÁLOVÉ
NÁCHOD / BROUMOV
NOVÉ MĚSTO
PARDUBICE / CHRUDIM
LITOMYŠL

HRADEC KRÁLOVÉ

Hradec Králové, known for centuries by the name of Königgrätz, was never more intact than in the year 1916. It was the year that Josef Žaloudek, curator of the municipal museum, finished eight years of work on a project that was to capture the old town center forever in its mid-19th-century image. What he made was a model measuring 15.5 square yards (13 sq. m), which is still on display in the regional **Eastern Bohemian Museum** (Muzeum východnich Čech). Allowances must now be made, unfortunately, when comparing this idealized model to reality. Hradec Králové has not fared well, a victim of neglect and of the architectural sins of the last 50 years. Today, there's no longer anything royal about the city; but it is one of the most important industrial centers in the country. This city between the Labe and the Orlice produces the world-famous Petrof pianos; the manufacturer regularly sponsors a Smetana piano competition.

For historical orientation, a few milestones: in 1337, Hradec Králové became a royal city, 1660 a bishopric. The Habsburgs fortified and extended Königgrätz

Left: Architecture of the 1920s in Hradec Krá-lové.

in the second half of the 18th century. Prussia defeated Austria in 1866 in nearby Chlum. The "losses including prisoners" were toted up with embarrassing exactness: the Austrian Army lost 1,313 officers and 41,490 soldiers, their Saxon allies 55 officers and 1,446 enlisted men, the Prussians 360 officers and 8,812 soldiers.

What's notable here, architecturally speaking, are several Cubist structures from the 1920s (schools, a church, museum, banks and apartment buildings) by the important architects Jan Kotěra, Dušan Jurkovič and Josef Gočár. The city center, which enjoys landmark protection, has a number of historical sites to lure the visitor. Today's **Cathedral of the Holy Ghost** (*katedrální Kostel svatého ducha*) retains many of the characteristics of the original building from the 13th and 14th centuries, including the cross-ribbed vaulting or the frescoes. Inside is a pewter baptismal font from 1406 and a triptych from 1494. Peter Brandl painted the altarpiece; Josef V. Myslbek created the chancel with evangelists (1869). The Church of **St. Clement** (*svatého Klimenta*) is older still. Giovanni Santini is thought to have drawn up the plans for rebuilding this former Romanesque church. Next to it is the **White Tower** (*Bílá věž*), constructed between

1574-85. Also worth mentioning is the former Jesuit church of the **Assumption of Mary** (*kostel Nanebevzetí Panny Marie*) by Carlo Lurago (1654-66). Santini was responsible for parts of the adjacent convent. Marco Antonio Canevalle is believed to have built the **Bishop's Residence**; Santini may also have contributed. The **Column of Mary** dates from between 1714-16. The park called *Žižkovy sady* is beloved of locals as well as visitors. Even on the outskirts of town, you can find some interesting Baroque religious buildings: in **Kukleny**, the classical Convent church of St. Anna; in **Nový Hradec Králové**, the Late Baroque church of St. Anthony.

In neighboring **Třebechovice pod Orebem**, the local museum has a crèche (*Proboštův betlém*), carved in 1890, consisting of hundreds of figures.

Within day-trip distance of Hradec Králové are two castles, Opočno and

Above: Horsepower has not yet replaced the horse.

Rychnov nad Kněžnou, with beautiful art collections. The Renaissance castle of **Opočno** was rebuilt in the Baroque style by Giovanni B. Alliprandi; its gallery exhibits Italian paintings. Other attractions are a venerable old library, and a weapons collection from several centuries.

Giovanni Santini is thought to have worked on the Baroque reconstruction of Castle **Rychnov**. For decades, it's been used to exhibit a painting collection started in the 17th century by the aristocratic Kolowrat family, who were among the wealthiest of Bohemia's nobility. But the landscape around the castle and its church is equally lovely.

DVŮR KRÁLOVÉ AND KUKS

Dvůr Králové translates as Queen's Court; for this spot on the Elbe was once a royal residence. The **deanery church of St. John the Baptist** (*děkanský kostel svatého Jana Křtitele*) is Romanesque, but received a Gothic renovation in 1480. The Baroque buildings of the central

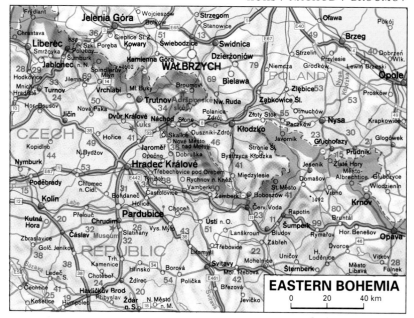

EASTERN BOHEMIA

0   20   40 km

square are lovely; many of them sport arcades. The popular castle **Kuks** is only 2 miles (3 km) away. Here, sculptor Matthias Bernhard Braun created a veritable monument to himself with the countless allegorical statues he created in the 1720s for Count Sporck. Kuk was also known as a curative spa in its day. A pharmacy with its original Rococo furnishings is a reminder of the town's former glory.

NÁCHOD AND BROUMOV

Since the opening of the borders of the Czech Republic, Náchod has steadily gained in importance throughout the post-Socialist states as a transit town. It's a role the town has played for centuries. Some of this past history is evident in the town's makeup. Dating from the turn of the century is the neo-Renaissance town hall, ornated with frescoes based on drawings by the beloved painter Mikoláš Aleš. There is a lovely 19th-century theater in the sgraffito-decorated Renaissance **castle** which crowns a hilltop above the town. The sights here include a collection of tapestries, a valuable library, and the castle chapel, designed by Carlo Lurago. Originally Gothic church of **St. Lawrence** (*kostel svatého Vavřince*) received its current appearance in the 16th century.

An excursion from Náchod takes you to **Broumov**; which has enough sights to reward the trip in full. The wooden **cemetery church** (1449) is one of the oldest religious buildings of its kind in all of Central Europe. **St. Wenceslas Church** (*kostel svatého Václava*) was built in 1729 from designs by Kilian Ignaz Dientzenhofer, who was also responsible for the Benedictine monastery; its richly-decorated buildings are now under landmark protection. The same is true of the **Church of St. Adalbert** (*klášterní kostel svatého Vojtěcha*), the work of a number of renowned Baroque artists. In addition to frescoes and paintings, the church displays rich figurative decoration along its exterior, although these could use some restoration.

199

Adršpašské skály is a jewel of nature not far from Broumov. This nature reserve is known for its unusual stone formations.

NOVÉ MĚSTO NAD METUJÍ

In 1501, a Nové Město, or new city, was founded on the banks of the Metuje: a closed settlement virtually unique in Bohemia. Most of the historically protected residences here were built during the Renaissance; although there was a bit of an effort made to impose a new, uniform look in the 1950s. Still, the 16th-century arcades were left largely undisturbed. The parish church of the **Holy Trinity** (*farní kostel Nejsvatější Trojice*) also dates from this time, which you can recognize from the helmet-shaped roof of its tower. The **Castle**, dating from the early 16th century, was often rebuilt and extended. Its radical, and controversial,

Above: Cute little statuettes by Matthias B. Braun in Nové Město.

reconstruction into a rustic form of Art Nouveau was carried out by the prominent architect Dušan Jurkovič. The castle is open to the public, as is the surrounding park, dotted with statuettes by Matthias B. Braun.

PARDUBICE AND CHRUDIM

The city center of **Paradubice** enjoys the status of a historic landmark. But animal lovers and animal protectionists know the town for another reason: the annual **steeplechase** held here since 1856. Fans rave about the event; opponents point to the many horses every year who injure themselves so badly in this, the world's most difficult race (there are 32 obstacles along the 4.5 mile course), that they have to be put down.

In the late 13th century, a small settlement began to grow up around the monastery and water castle; this was expanded considerably after the 16th century. Among the earliest buildings is the church of **St. Bartholomew**, enlarged in

1514 and restored at the beginning of our century. In 1912/3, architect Boža Dvořák added a striking and unusual nave in the then-contemporary style of Bohemian Art Nouveau. An interesting presbytery has survived the centuries at the Late Gothic **Church of the Annunciation** (*kostel Zvěstování Panny Marie*). The castle fortress once belonged to Ernst von Pardubitz, the first Bohemian Bishop of Prague. Virtually every century has seen additions to the complex. Since 1892, the **castle** (*zámek*) has served as a museum. It is surrounded by a pleasant urban area. Houses on the main square of this big city demonstrate a plethora of architectural styles; The plague column was erected in 1777.

A popular marionette museum in the so-called "Soap Boilers" house (*Mydlářův dům*) in **Chrudim** is dedicated to the memory of puppeteer Prof. Josef Skupa. Even in the Gothic age, this town already had five churches, all of which have seen various renovations. This former royal city is also known as the birthplace of Joseph Ressel, inventor of the ship's propeller.

LITOMYŠL

This town's main claim to fame, apart from its architectural treasures, is that it is the birthplace of Bedřich Smetana (1824-84) who, with Antonín Dvořák, is one of Bohemia's most important composers. The son of a beer brewer came into the world in the servants quarters of the Renaissance palace, ornate with rich sgraffito decoration. In addition to a music museum, the palace's chief attraction is its **court theater** (1797), which is one of the oldest preserved theaters in Europe. Under protection as a historic landmark, the town has a few fine buildings: the town hall, a Benedictine monastery founded in 1098, and the Baroque church of the Discovery of the Holy Cross (*kostel Nalezení svatého Kříže*).

EASTERN BOHEMIA

Today, there are plenty of different options for hotels, pensions, and private accommodations in virtually every area. You can get more detailed information at the information office of every town (*Městský úřad*). You can also get information free of charge from the Chambers of Commerce in the main city of every county (*Okresní hospodářská komora*).

Central office for the Czech Republic: *Česká obchodní komora*; Argentinská 38, 17005 Praha 7, Tel: 00420/2/66794111; Fax: 00420/2/66710253.

Museums, Galleries, Theaters, and Sights

All museums are closed on Monday. Otherwise, they're generally open from 9 am-5 pm; some of them may be closed during lunch hour. Signs on some smaller museums tell you where you can pick up the key to let yourself in.

Broumov: Monastery, monastery library. Nature reserve Broumovské stěny. Adršpach-Teplice: rock formations Adršpašsko-teplické skály.

Chrudim: Okresní muzeum, Široka 86, closed for renovations (1998). Muzeum loutkářských kultur (Marionette Museum), Brtislavova 74.

Dvůr Králové nad Labem: Městské muzeum (City Museum), Kohoutův dvůr.

Hradec Králové: Krajské muzeum východních Čech (District Museum of Eastern Bohemia), Eliščino nábřeží 465.

Krajská galerie moderného umení (gallery of modern art), Velké náměstí 139.

Kuks: Baroque statuettes by Matthias Bernhard Braun in the palace gardens.

Litomyšl: Music Museum, Bedřich Smetana Memorial, Státní zámek (State Castle).

Opera festival *Smetanova Litomyšl*.

Náchod: Okresní muzeum (District Museum), Státní zámek (State Castle).

Galerie vytvarného umění (Gallery of Fine Arts), Státní zámek (State Castle).

Nové Město nad Metují: Zámek (Castle).

Opočno: Zámecká obrazárna (Castle Picture Gallery), Státní zámek (State Castle).

Pardubice: Východočeské muzeum, Státní zámek (State Castle) 1; Východočeská galerie, Státní zámek (State Castle) 3; annual steeplechase *Velká pardubická steeplechase* (autumn).

Rychnov nad Kněžnou: Okresní muzeum Orlických hor, Javornická 12.

Orlická galerie, Státní zámek (State Castle).

Třebechovice pod Orebem: Muzeum betlémů, Masarykovo náměstí 24.

SOUTHERN MORAVIA

BRNO
MIKULOV / LEDNICE
ZNOJMO / VRANOV
TŘEBÍČ / TELČ
JIHLAVA / ŽĎÁR

BRNO (BRÜNN)

Highlights of the city of Brno are a church and an infamous dungeon. The **Cathedral of Peter and Paul** and **Špilberk Fortress** (from the German Spielberg) are both holdovers from the days of the monarchy. Between these two poles, symbols of spiritual and of secular power, is the whole spectrum of the life of this urban center, stretching back more than 700 years.

Brno first became the capital of Moravia in the 14th century; today, it's a center for trade conventions and a vital industrial, commercial, cultural and sport center. Despite its growth, the city has preserved its historic center and increased its value by turning it into a large pedestrian zone. There seems to be a striking number of churches and monasteries here: understandable when you learn that Brno was made a bishopric in 1777. Notable sights include the Gothic **Church of Our Lady** on *Mendlovo náměstí*. The early Baroque Dominican church of **St. Michael** (1655-79) and the church of the **Discovery of the Holy Cross** (*Nalezení svatého Kříže*) also

Preceding pages: There's not much visible difference between towns (here: Telč in Bohemia and Moravia. Left: Moravian beauty.

merit attention; while the Capuchin church has some enchanting paintings by Johann Lukas Kracker. The Minorite church of St. John, the monastery church of St. Thomas and the parish church of St. Jacob were all founded in the 13th century and remodeled in the Baroque period. It was in the garden of the **Augustine monastery** that Father Gregor, better known as Gregor Johann Mendel, carried out his genetic and biological experiments with plants. Mendel's Law of genetics still holds true to this day.

Composer Leoš Janáček (1854-1928) also lived and worked in Brno, first as director of the organists' school, later of the conservatory. Today the music academy is named after him. One of the architectural jewels of this university city is the **theater** built by Viennese architects Helmer and Fellner in 1882. With the regional **Moravian Museum** (*Moravské muzeum*), the city museum, and the Ethnographic Museum, Brno is a significant museum city. Both **city halls** merit a visit: the Old City Hall dates from the 13th century; the new one from the 16th. Fans of car racing will be familiar with Masaryk Ring, where auto races have been held for several decades.

Not far from Brno, in **Tišnov**, is Moravia's finest Romanesque portal, the *Porta coeli* (Heaven's Gate) on the front

of a monastery church consecrated in 1239. Nature lovers should not miss the stalagmite- and stalactite-filled caves of the Moravian Karst (*Moravský kras*).

Further south, between Brno and Znojmo, is a rare treat for fans of Czech Art Nouveau painting. Alfons Mucha (1860-1939), who was born in the area and became a popular figure in the salons of Munich, Paris and New York, painted a giant cycle of paintings in the Renaissance castle of **Moravský Krumlov**. Called *Slavic Epos*, the work is a pastel-colored hymn to pan-Slavism, executed in the spirit of the growing tide of nationalism that was then sweeping the country.

MIKULOV AND LEDNICE

A Iron Age settlement was uncovered near Mikulove, a historic landmark that has had strategic importance since the late Middle Ages. Here, in a town then

Above: "Heaven's Gate" on the monastery church of Tišnov.

known as Nikolsburg, a treaty was signed in 1662 negotiating religious peace between Hungarian Protestants, led by Gábor Bethlén, and the Habsburgs.

Along with a synagogue built in the 17th century, the parish church of **St. Wenceslas** (*farní kostel svatého Václava*) is noteworthy. This Piarist church contains, among other works of art, frescoes by Franz Anton Maulbertsch and sculptures by Paul Troger.

The castle of **Lednice** is also worth a visit. Its main attraction is a 196-foot (60 m) high **minaret** built in 1802. The romantic castle is set in a beautiful English park and contains a lovely museum.

ZNOJMO AND VRANOV NAD DYJÍ

Today a protected landmark, **Znojmo** recorded as a royal city as early as the 13th century, has played a significant role in history. In 1628, the council of Znaim (its German name) accepted the Treaty of Succession according to which the Bohe-

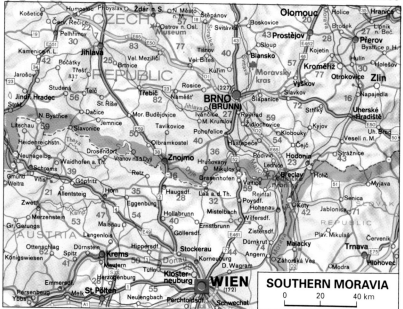

mian throne was to be occupied by the Habsburg dynasty, a state of affairs that held until 1918.

This wine-producing area blossomed during the Baroque period. Johann Lucas Hildebrandt designed the huge **Premonstratensian monastery** in the district of Louka. The Baroque **Church of the Holy Rood** (*kostel svatého Kříže*) contains fine frescoes by Johann Lukas Kracker and a painting by F. A. Maulbertsch. **St. Nicholas Church** (*kostel svatého Mikuláše*) is much older. A national cultural monument is the Romanesque **Rotunda**, dedicated to St. Catherine, with some fairly well-preserved medieval frescoes. Parts of the former castle (*Hradiště svatého Hypolita*) also date from the Middle Ages; F. A. Maulbertsch decorated the dome of its church in 1765. One of the most popular sights is the old **City Hall** with its soaring tower (1448). This also contains the entrance to underground passages, built between the 15th and 17th centuries, which used to connect the cellars of residential houses.

The photogenic **Vranov** is virtually identical to the Gothic fortress which originally stood on the outcropping of stone over the river Dyje, and was later remodeled into a more comfortable castle. Today it houses a museum with a collection of ceramics from the local factory, which ceased production in 1882.

TŘEBÍČ

In the 12th century, a town began to grow up around a Benedictine monastery, which today houses the Western Moravian Museum; the town received its city charter in 1335. Its greatest period of prosperity was the 16th century when cloth produced in Třebíč's looms was exported to all of Europe. After looms became passé, the city managed to build up a modern textiles industry.

The late Romanesque basilica of **St. Procopius** (1240-60) was rebuilt in the Baroque period; it's dedicated to the Assumption of the Virgin (*Nanebevzetí Panny Marie*). The church is also evi-

207

Above: A climber braves the Moravian chalk formations of the Hřebenac cliffs.

dence of the city's former wealth. The Gothic church of St. Martin also got a Baroque facelift in the 17th century, about the same time that the Baroque Capuchin church was built. The city retains some residences in Baroque and Renaissance style; some of these are remodelings of Gothic originals.

TELČ

Disney Studios couldn't have invented a more picturesque setting than this lovely little town of brick and stone built among the foothills of the Bohemian-Moravian Plateau. Telč, population 6,100, is often used as a location for films, and is one of the Czech towns listed on UNESCO's World Culture Heritage status. Lining the triangular **Marketplace**, which looks as if it were enclosed, are dozens of fine Renaissance and Baroque houses, with a Column of

Mary in the middle: truly a gem of Czech town planning. A special touch of charm is conferred by the arcades running around the square. Underlining the significance of this historic little town are the **castle** with the Zrzavy art gallery (20th century), and several Romanesque and Gothic churches. The **Church of the Holy Ghost** (*kostel svatého Ducha*) has a Romanesque tower; the Gothic Church of the Virgin Mary was expanded into a Baroque basilica in the 18th century. Also Gothic is the church of St. Jacob, whose towers can be seen far and wide.

JIHLAVA

Together with Kutná Hora (Kuttenberg), Jihlava (Iglau), founded by German miners toward the end of the Middle Ages, was one of the most significant suppliers of silver to the courts of Europe. As early as the 13th century the town, now under landmark protection, enjoyed royal privileges; later, the mine owners even wrote their own set of laws, the so-called Iglau Code. The discovery of the New World, with its seemingly inexhaustible supply of silver from the mines of Mexico, was the death toll for Iglau, much as it had been for Kuttenberg. The city switched to weaving cloth. You can still visit a former mine shaft beneath the town.

Traces of former wealth are Jihlava's abundance of beautiful Renaissance (some with sgraffito decoration) and Baroque buildings; although the overall image is a bit skewed by an unsightly modern department store. The parish church of **St. Jacob** and the **Church of the Holy Rood** (*kostel svatého Kříže*) are both from the 14th century; while the **Jesuit church** of St. Ignatius of Loyola is Baroque. The secularized Capuchin monastery was turned into a theater in 1850; Somewhat later, Moravian-born composer Gustav Mahler came to Iglau. Jihlava is known to ice hockey fans for having produced some excellent players who have even been successful in the North American Hockey League (NHL).

ŽĎÁR NAD SÁZAVOU

Even if you are not a Slavic student, it's worth detouring to visit the *Muzeum knihy* (**book museum**). Although the collection cannot compare with the Strahov Monastery Library in Prague or the Clementinium, its fine presentation of several centuries of printing ranges from medieval block printing to manuscripts of modern writers, all housed in a former Cistercian monastery adjacent to a Gothic church. It was radically renovated by Giovanni Santini after fire destroyed much of the original building at the beginning of the 18th century. On nearby **Green Mountain** (*Zelená hora*) is Santini's masterpiece, the Church of St. John of Nepomuk (*kostel svatého Jana Nepomuchkého*) built in 1719-22 on a star-shaped lot, a Baroque church of exquisite proportions.

SOUTHERN MORAVIA

Today, there are plenty of different options for hotels, pensions, and private accommodations in virtually every area. You can get more detailed information at the information office of every town (*Městský úřad*).

You can also get accommodation information free of charge from the Chambers of Commerce in the main city of every county (*Okresní hospodářská komora*).

Central office for the Czech Republic: *Česká obchodní komora*; Argentinská 38, 17005 Praha 7, Tel: 00420/2/66794111, Fax: 00420/2/ 66710253.

Museums, Galleries, Theaters, and Sights

All museums in this region are closed on Monday. Otherwise, they're generally open from 9 am-5 pm; some of them may be closed during lunch hour. Signs on some smaller museums tell you where you can pick up the key to let yourself in.

Brno: Moravské zemské muzeum (Moravian County Museum), Zelný trh 6.
Diecézní muzeum (Diocesan Museum), Mendlovo náměstí 1 a.
Technické muzeum, Orlí ulice 20.
Moravská galerie (Moravian Gallery), Husova 14.
Muzeum města Brna. Hrad (Castle) Špilberk.
3 theaters: Janáčkovo divadlo - Mahenovo divadlo - Divadlo bratří Mrštíků.
Mezinárodní brněnský veletrh (International Trade Convention of Brno).
Motorcycle races (Grand Prix). Excursion: chalk formations at Moravský kras.
Jihlava: Muzeum Vysočiny, Masarykovo náměstí 55.
Oblastní galerie Vysočiny, Komenského 10.
Lednice: Zámek (Castle) with its signature minaret and gardens.
Mikulov: Regionální muzeum, Zámek (Castle).
Telč: Muzeum, Zámek (Castle).
Tišnov: Klášter cisterciáku, Kloster *Porta coeli*, Předklášterí.
Třebíč: Západomoravské muzeum (Western Moravian Museum).
Podklášteří, Zámek (Castle).
Vranov nad Dyjí: Státní zámek (State Castle).
Znojmo: Jihomoravské muzeum (Southern Moravian Museum), Přemyslovců 6.
Žďár nad Sázavou: Muzeum knihy (Book Museum).
Church of St. John of Nepomuk by Giovanni Santini on Zelená hora, the Green Mountain.

NORTHERN MORAVIA

KROMĚŘÍŽ
OLOMOUC
MORAVSKÁ TŘEBOVÁ
OSTRAVA
OPAVA

KROMĚŘÍŽ

In its "invitation to Kroměříž," the tourist bureau writes: "The city has preserved its historic tradition of culture and education into the present." Between the lines: even under the Communists, Kroměříž's citizens upheld their values. As the residence of the Bishops of Olomouc, Kroměříž, which now numbers 30,000 inhabitants, developed into a jewel of Moravian Baroque architecture. The city was founded by a ford across the river Morava (March). Prehistoric artifacts, exhibited in the Regional Museum, are evidence of an even earlier settlement.

Badly damaged during the Thirty Years' War, the **Fortress** was rebuilt as a castle. Today, it houses one of the best collections of paintings in the country (*zámecká obrazárna*), including such artists as Cranach, Titian, Bassano, Veronese, van Dyck, Bruegel. The palace garden is extraordinarily well-tended. Likewise, the public park *Květná zahrada* echoes some of the glory of the Baroque period.

As well as the library of the Archbishop's Palace (containing frescoes by

Left: Olomouc's astronomical clock was rede-signed in 1955.

Josef Stern), the Late Gothic Church of **St. Maurice** (*kostel svatého Mořice*) is worth a look. While the Gothic **Parish Church of the Assumption of Mary** (*farní kostel Nanebevzetí Panny Marie*) was rebuilt in Baroque style, the **Piarist Church of St. John the Baptist** (*kostel svatého Jana Křtitele*) is an original Baroque work. The Trinity Column was erected in 1725; the mill tower dates from 1585; and the town hall was last rebuilt in the 17th century.

OLOMOUC

One deed characterizes the spirit of this city. As soon as the "Velvet Revolution" of 1989 swept away Communist power, the University, named after historian František Palacký, moved to rehabilitate professors and students who had been suspended, mostly for political reasons, between 1948 and 1989. Václav Havel was the first to be awarded a doctorate. It goes without saying that liberalism didn't always characterize the city's rulers. Even when it was the seat of important Moravian rulers, the one-time royal city of Olomouc was always dependent on the clergy. Olmütz, as it was formerly known in German, was a bastion of Catholicism during the Hussite wars. In the process of re-Catholicizing

211

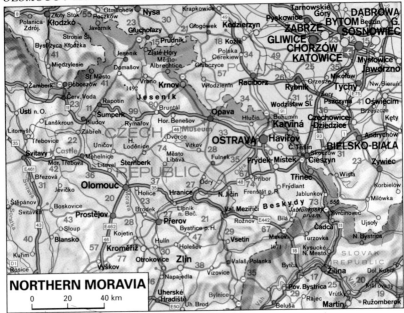

NORTHERN MORAVIA

0   20   40 km

that followed, the Jesuits were particularly active; as a reward, their seminary was elevated to the status of a university, the *Universitas Olomucensis*, in 1573. Today this large city – which was, with Brno, long one of Moravia's most important urban centers – remains the seat of the Archbishop.

The historic city center has many buildings of note. Romanesque fragments are in evidence both in the *Bazilika svatého Václava* (Wenceslas) and the chapel of St. Barbara. Excavation at the **Přemyslid Palace** has brought to light remains of a 13th-century Romanesque fortress, incorporated into the later Gothic and Renaissance additions to the structure. It was here that seven-year old King Wenceslas III was murdered in 1306, bringing the powerful Přemysl dynasty to a close. Both **St. Michael's** and the **parish church** *svatého Mořice* are Gothic; the latter has the largest organ (1745) in the country. The church of the **Immaculate Conception** (*Nejsvatější Početí Panny Marie*), has largely re-

tained its Gothic character. Note the fresco of the *Rosary Festival* from around 1500. The city hall is also from this period. For years Olomouc has hosted a popular flower festival, *Flora*.

The astronomical clock, damaged in World War II, got a new look in 1955. As well as the Trinity column, several churches represent the Baroque period, including **Mary of the Snows** (*chrám Panny Marie Sněžné*). The six Baroque fountains, constructed between 1683 and 1735, have no equal in the Czech Republic. From the same period is the Premonstratensian monastery, Hradisko, thought to be the largest in Europe, and nicknamed the Moravian Escorial.

MORAVSKÁ TŘEBOVÁ

Although the old center of this town of 12,000 inhabitants was officially declared a historic landmark in 1950, most of its buildings are, 40 years later, in a shocking state of disrepair. Still, it is well worth a visit. The dilapidated **castle** possesses some wonderful reliefs by master 17th-century Italian stonemasons. In the Baroque parish church of Mary, some frescoes have survived or been restored. In addition to its 16th-century town hall, the town center has a number of Renaissance and even Gothic houses with marvelous vaulting, hidden, often as not, behind crumbling façades.

OSTRAVA

Smoking chimneys, steel mills, towering cranes and decades' worth of rusting scrap iron turned Ostrava into a model socialist city after 1945. This region, once favored by the Communist party, is actually a conglomeration of several independent towns. Despite the industrial development it has several noteworthy sights: the 13th-century **Church of St. Wenceslas** (*kostel svatého Václava*), or the 16th-century wooden parish church in the center of the **Hrabová** district. The town hall has an exhibit of Silesian folklore. For recreation there are the nearby mountains Beskides and Jeseník. The **Darkov** district has a spa which is popular for the iodine content of its water.

OPAVA

Once the royal city of Troppau, Opava looks back on an 800-year history. In 1849 it was the capital of Austrian Silesia. The impressive **Silesian museum** (*Slezské muzeum*) displays a portrait of the Austrian Empress Elizabeth near the entrance. Noteworthy, too, are a number of religious structures dating back to the 13th century: the **Church of the Holy Ghost** (*kostel svatého Ducha*), **St. Wenceslas Church** (*kostel svatého Václava*) and the **Church of the Assumption of the Virgin** (*kostel Nanebevzetí Panny Marie*). By contrast, the churches of **St. John the Baptist** (*kostel svatého Jana Křtitele*) and **St. George** are from the Baroque period.

NORTHERN MORAVIA

Today, there are plenty of options for hotels, pensions, and private accommodations in virtually every area. You can get more detailed information at the information office of every town (*Městský úřad*). You can also get information free of charge from the Chambers of Commerce in the main city of every county (*Okresní hospodářská komora*). Central office for the Czech Republic: *Česká obchodní komora*; Argentinská 38, 17005 Praha 7, Tel: 00420/2/66794111, Fax: 00420/2/ 66710253.

Museums, Galleries, Theaters, and Sights

All museums in this region are closed on Monday. Otherwise, they're generally open from 9 am-5 pm; some of them may be closed during lunch hour. Signs on some smaller museums tell you where you can pick up the key to let yourself in.

Kroměříž: Muzeum Kroměřížska (District Museum), Velké náměstí 38.
Zámecká obrazárna (Castle picture gallery).
Státní zámek (State Castle).
Summer Music Festival *Kroměřížské hudební léto* (June-September). Castle gardens, flower gardens.
Excursion to the interesting stalactite and stalamite caves of Hranice-Zbrašov.

Moravská Třebová: Městské muzeum (City Museum), Svitavská 18.

Olomouc: Krajské vlastivědné muzeum (District History Museum), náměstí Republiky 5.
Muzeum umění, Denisova 47.
Moravské divadlo (Moravian theater), Horní náměstí 22.
Russian Orthodox Church.
Pilgrimage church of **Svatý Kopeček** (7 km).

Opava: Slezské muzeum (Silesian Museum), Tyršova 1.
Excursion to the castle **Hradec** nad Moravicí.

Ostrava: Ostravské muzeum, Masarykovo náměstí 1.
Galerie výtvarného umění (Gallery of Fine Arts), Jurečkova 9 (*Dům umění*).
Divadlo Antonína Dvořáka (Theater).
Iodine-bromine springs in **Darkov** near Karviná.
In the Černá louka area are the so-called Wandering Rocks (*Rovinské balvany*) from the Ice Age.
You can hike through the mountains of the Beskides and Jeseník.

THE FAMILY OF ŠVEJK
Czech Thinkers from Hus to Havel

"In moving times, people say *We* in moving voices; it is a companionable, social, strengthening word, while *I* is anti-social, personal, self-loving and egoistic. Anyone can say, 'Jan Hus's great legacy lives on in *us*' – but who of you can say, 'Jan Hus's great legacy lives on in *me*?'" Karel Čapek asked, or sermonized, ironically. "*We* have shed blood and sacrificed freedom for our national cause, but, excuse me, *I* have sacrificed nothing; and when *we* had to endure this or that, *I* was sitting at home. *We* are all heroes, martyrs and brothers through and through; *we* are the epitome of generosity and self-sacrifice; *we* fight, *we* demand; certainly, I can present to you a very wonderful *we*, a courageous, famous, and active *we*; but

Preceding pages: Fashion show in front of Troy Chateau. Pantomimes en route. Above: A collection of Czech thinkers. Right: In memory of the 100th birthday of Karel Čapek.

beware, lest *I* possess none, absolutely none, of *our* wonderful attributes! In this country, we like to say *we*, the people of Hus, Žižka, Smetana; *we*, the people of Comenius. It doesn't matter so much whose people we are, but rather to whom you feel allegiance. The nation itself needs more people than names," Čapek wrote to his countrymen in 1918.

"We are all heroes, martyrs and brothers through and through" – are we? Čapek was right. *We* are world champions in ice hockey, *we* have won the Olympics in boxing and swimming, *we* have Karlštejn Castle... Have we? are we?

Karel Čapek (1890-1938), a linguistic virtuoso, liked – affectionately – to hold up a mirror to his compatriots. Čapek was himself a powerful *homo politicus*, who for years presided over a select "Friday gathering" which included writers, philosophers, historians, lawyers, politicians, scientists, civil servants, artists, and journalists – as well, often as not, as State President Tomáš G. Masaryk. Čapek, author of countless novels and well-known short stories, was regarded, nationally and internationally, as the dominant literary figure of Czechoslovakia. His brother Josef (1887-1945) also produced works of subtle social criticism. Because of his critical articles against Fascism, this popular artist, draughtsman and author was arrested by the Gestapo and killed, shortly before the end of the war, in a German concentration camp.

The Čapek brothers were welcome guests at President Masaryk's – and indeed, this President was himself a respected philosopher who dared to explode a concept that had existed for centuries: the Habsburg Monarchy. Tomáš Garrigue Masaryk (1850-1937) – he took the surname of his American wife, Garrigue, as a part of his own, which was absolutely unheard-of at that time – tried to gain more independence for the Czech and Slovak regions throughout his career, from his days as a professor at the university in Prague to his work as a representative of the Young Czechs and finally as an elected official of the liberal Czech Progressive Party in the Federal Council of Vienna.

When World War I broke out in 1914, Masaryk emigrated to London, there to found, together with Edvard Beneš, a Czech National Council. In 1917, Masaryk organized a Czech Foreign Legion in Russia. After the United States entered the war, he became the undisputed leader in developing a national concept for the peoples whose interests he represented: the Czechs and the Slovaks. As a result of this, the Pittsburgh Treaty included provisions for the founding of a Czechoslovakian Republic. After Austria's capitulation, the new country was officially proclaimed on October 28, 1918: a Slavic triumph. Masaryk – by then 68 years old – was the integral figure in all of this, a beloved *tatíček* (a kind of Big Daddy), a head of state respected on every side. 13 years after Masaryk's death, Jan Masa-

ryk, his son and the Foreign Minister of what was by then the Communist Czechoslovakian Republic – fell – or perhaps was made to fall – out of a window of the Cernín Palace in 1948. From then on, until 1968, the name Masaryk was completely taboo.

In the Prague Spring, instigated by a Slovak named Alexander Dubček, T. G. Masaryk's role was discussed anew; but when the movement was put down he disappeared again into the archives, not to be aired again until 1989. Since then, however, statues of the founder of the Republic have been springing up all over the place, even if his work to create a unified state was undone by the power calculations of a handful of Czech and Slovak politicians in the early 1990s. Many main squares and streets in Czech villages and towns now bear Masaryk's name. A historical figure who under the Communists was *persona non grata* is now undergoing an unusual renaissance. Do *we* long for the union of Czechs and Slovaks? No referendum was ever held to

answer this question; the voice of the people was drowned out by the static noise of political demagoguery.

Is it, perhaps, the Prague dog-seller Josef Švejk who gives utterance to the voice of the people? Is he, as depicted by the Prague Bohemian Jaroslav Hašek (1883-1923) in the seminal novel *The Good Soldier Švejk*, a Czech prototype? Are *we* really like that? Bourgeois critics saw Hašek as a disturber of the peace, an anarchist, a talented writer who shipwrecked on the shoals of his failings (including alcoholism, which led to his tragic early death at the age of 40). We encounter Hašek in 1917, when Masaryk founded the Czech Legion in Russia; we know that he stopped drinking for five years during this period, but no other stories about this section of his life have survived. Later, however, after the catastrophe of World War I, Hašek completed his portrait of the ingenious but seemingly simple-minded Švejk, one of the great figures of world literature. The word *žvejkat* has even been adopted into the language as a slangy term for chat, chew, mull over. Unlike such other luminaries as Don Quixote, however, Švejk survives, getting around all dangers in the field of battle, or in bed. Švejk manages things, he figures out how to get by. Are the Czechs like that? Do they adapt, get around things? Would they rather offer passive resistance than get mixed up in a jam? Are *we* the people of Švejk?

How different, by contrast, is another literary figure who was born in the same city as Hašek, and in the same year, 1883, although into a German-speaking family: the lawyer-official Franz Kafka, a man plagued by doubts, a great skeptic, but a talented satirist. To echo Čapek's line of questioning: are the Czechs the people of Kafka, the Prague Jews?

One figure who refused to adapt to circumstances was Master Jan Hus (1370-1415), professor of theology at the (German) university founded by Charles IV. This scholar from southern Bohemia, a reformer of Czech language as well as religion, a rebel against bigotry and the cult of the Pope, dared to revolt against the leaders of tradition, and as a preacher, succeeded in mobilizing (as far as this was possible in the 15th century) the masses. At first, the King was on his side, but to dare to speak out against the mighty Emperor and against Rome was to ask for spectacular defeat. Jan Hus believed too much in the safe-conduct guaranteed his freedom of movement at the Council of Constance. The democratic Czech Republic has introduced July 6 as a national holiday to commemorate Hus's death by burning at the stake.

Had he not emigrated from Bohemia, the Moravian reformer Jan Amos Comenius (1592-1670) might well have met with a similarly gruesome fate. The wanderings of this theologian and teacher

Above: Švejk in souvenir form. Right: Poet and protest singer Karel Kryl.

led him through Germany and Poland, Hungary, Stockholm and London to the Netherlands, where he found his final resting-place in Naarden. "My whole life has been one long journey," stated this virtually omniscient man, author of the *Orbis pictus*. It was a great expatriate career; and Comenius (also known as Komenský) left several documents in his native language, as well as writings in Latin, German, and Hungarian, which still have current relevance even 300 years later.

A leading protester of modern times, who unceasingly fought the ruling regime with his words, rejected the option of exile. Vaclav Havel, a respected playwright throughout Europe as early as the 1970s, decided not to emigrate; he wanted to criticize the system from within his own country. He thus had a chance to discover that prison, where he spent many years, was a suitable forum in which to formulate his protests against the regime and demand respect for human rights. His petitions to the people in power, and his letters to his wife, Olga, published in the Western media, were right on the mark – and the effects can be seen today. Havel has become a symbol of post-Communist Czechoslovakia, a hero in spite of himself. The restrained, generally somewhat shy author has been forced to abandon his desk for a time; a year after the 1989 "Velvet Revolution," he became the internationally-renowned president of a country united in its protest and resistance to the rule of the Communist Party. But the philosophical intellectual wasn't able to save the republic: the Federal Republic of Czechoslovakia dissolved. Havel's radio broadcasts from Lány, where Masaryk once had his summer home, are now only intended for the ears of his Czech compatriots.

"But why?" These two words were printed in a German newspaper as the obituary of Karel Kryl (April 4, 1944 - March 3, 1994). In the autumn of 1969,

Kryl saw no other answer to the current situation than to leave his occupied homeland, armed with a used guitar and a notebook full of protest songs and poems, and seek political asylum in Germany. For Kryl, a bard in the tradition of Bellman and Villon, Heinrich Heine and Vladimir Vyssotski, a gifted poet who was also able to set his grief to music, the decision to emigrate was far from easy. "Half-heretic" was the title of his book in interview form, published in Prague in 1992. In it, the emigrant, who remained in Bavaria even after 1989, noted bitterly just how far the reality of his country had distanced itself from his ideals.

Resigned, Karel Kryl cried out his protest one last time – but in vain.

What would everyone say
who's applauding you here
if the people in power suppressed
> *your voice?*

They would dance again
would play you like others
they would hop and leap
until they broke their necks.

221

JEWISH LIFE IN PRAGUE

"Prague is a lover you take for life. You never leave her entirely, even if you're physically unfaithful. And you love her even if you're married to her."

This declaration of love for Prague was written by Gabriel Laub, a Czech Jew. In 1968, after the Russian tanks had put an abrupt end to the dreams of the Prague Spring, Gabriel Laub left his beloved city, a part of the most recent wave of Jewish emigration from Prague. Laub settled down in Hamburg, learned German, and soon became one of the most popular satirists of his new, adoptive country.

Praises of the Golden City on the Moldau have been sung by many poets through her history, but particularly often by Jewish ones, writing in German or Czech. In this city, where so many cultures intersect, combine, and cross-pollinate, Jewish life has deep roots. It's no longer certain when the first Jews settled here; according to legend, Nezarnysl, the son of the city's founder, Princess Libussa, took in a group of Jewish refugees from Lithuania. The first Jewish settlements were located under the two castles, Hrad and Vyšehrad. Because they stood by the Christians in their battle against the "heathen," the Jews were allowed to build a synagogue in the Lesser City, below the castle.

Eventually, however, they were driven out of their original settlement to the other bank of the river. After the stone Judith Bridge was built (a forerunner of Charles Bridge), the only new territory left open to them was the bend of the Moldau at the edge of the Old City. Early on, chroniclers tell of the first pogroms and attacks on Jewish residents, led by Christian fanatics, priests, and crusaders, but in fact incited by hate and envy at the prosperity and financial security of the Jewish community. The source of much of this wealth, money-lending, a trade regarded with social disdain, was in fact the only trade which the Church allowed the Jews to practice.

Only the King could afford the persecuted Jews a measure of protection, and he provided this only at a price. Every conceivable occasion was used as a pretext to require the protected ones to pay up; and if no occasion seemed to present itself, rulers tended not to shrink from downright robbery. The patience of the Jews, who endured this and the pogroms with hardly any open resistance, can be explained by the fact of their powerlessness as a small minority of the population.

At times, certainly, the Jewish population could behave in quite a different manner. When, in 1150, members of a Christian sect whom the king had turned out of the country wanted to stop overnight in the Jewish settlement, the Kosher

Above: The grave of Rabbi Loew. Right: In the Old-New Synagogue.

butchers ran out to drive off the offenders with their cleavers and knives. After that, Prince Vladislav I awarded to the guild the privilege of bearing the Bohemian lion on its coat-of-arms; at the same time, he allowed Prague's Jews to surround their neighborhood with a wall. While this served defensive purposes, it also hemmed in the growing community; the settlement became, in effect, a ghetto.

Shutting out the Jews was just fine by the Church, which wanted to prevent any kind of Jewish influence from reaching Christians, and therefore forbade all contact with them, even in the context of purely business transactions. The Jews had to wear special clothing, or a yellow spot on their chests. Men of the cloth were almost always involved in inciting pogroms, such as the one on Easter Sunday, 1389. When a priest bearing a monstrance cut through the ghetto on his way to the bed of a dying parishioner, a Jewish boy threw a stone at him and hit him. That evening, a mob overran the ghetto. Three thousand Jews, nearly half the population, were killed; houses plundered; and the graves of the cemetery violated and robbed.

In 1541, under Emperor Ferdinand I, the entire Jewish population was turned out of the country on the pretext that they had been spying for the Turks. The order to expel them, however, was quickly retracted, as they were invaluable to the country's economy and the State's coffers. The Czech Jews saw a relatively easy time under Rudolph II von Habsburg (1576-1611). The Emperor trafficked regularly with the High Rabbi Jehuda Bezalel, called Rabbi Loew, and with Mordechai Maisel, the wealthy financier and constructor of the synagogue that bears his name. In 1591, he graced the ghetto with the extraordinary (at that time) honor of a royal visit, accompanied by his wife and a large retinue.

Rabbi Loew, known as a miracle-worker and cabalist, is also remembered as the ostensible creator of the legendary "golem," an artificial man made of clay who was said to protect the ghetto from

foreign attackers: a concrete manifestation, in short, of the Jewish community's constant fear of persecution and expulsion, a fear which was proved time and again to be all too grounded in reality. However, as the Jews hadn't participated in the Estates Revolt in 1618 which unleashed the Thirty Years' War, they remained protected from expulsion for the time being. They were even permitted to take part in markets outside of the ghetto, and to buy a whole row of houses outside the ghetto walls. When Prague, however, was beaten in the Battle of the White Mountain, the Jews had to pay 240,000 guilders over to the state, even though they had remained loyal throughout the conflict.

In 1725, authorities established a ceiling for the number of Jewish families in Bohemia and Moravia. No more than 8,541 families were allowed, which

Above: Joseph II issued the Tolerance Edict to protect Prague's Jewish residents. Right: Kafka has become a cult figure.

meant that only first-born sons had the right to marry within their own country; the others were faced with the choice between remaining single or emigrating. When Maria Theresa ascended the throne in 1740, the Jews were required to pay half a million guilders as a "coronation subsidy." This didn't stop the Empress from expelling Prague's entire Jewish population five years later, masking the personal hatred which was her true motivation with the pretext of an accusation of treason. But protests from the rest of the population, the aristocracy, Prague's Archbishop and most of the guilds, forced her to rescind her order – a concession which the Jews had to buy with a "residence permit fee" of 211,000 guilders a year.

The change came in 1781, when Joseph II passed the Tolerance Edict. Jews now had the normal rights of vassals: they were allowed to purchase country estates and farms and even to study in universities. The complete rights of citizens followed with the revolution of 1848 and the National Constitution of 1867. An unfortunate appendix to these signal improvements was that the Jews were also required to decide in favor of one of the two national groups in Bohemia. Most of Prague's Jews came out on the side of the Germans, while the poorer, country Jews supported the Czechs and their culture.

The ghetto walls had already been torn down in 1781: in 1885, Prague's municipal administration decided to tear down and renovate the ghetto itself. In its place, residential Art Nouveau houses went up; of the old buildings, only the Jewish Town Hall, a few synagogues, and the Old Jewish Cemetery survived. Around the turn of the century, Jewish life in Prague began fully to bloom. Authors and artists met in the city's coffee houses: "it's Werfeling and Brodeling, it's Kafkaing and Kisching," ran a satiric poem of the period attributed to Karl

Kraus, referring to the most famous German-speaking Jewish Prague authors. In addition to these, there were also Czech Jewish literati such as Jaroslav Vrchlický, who mourned the waning of the ghetto in his poem *Old Prague*. In addition to their own literary activities, many authors also worked as Czech or German translators, an expression of their view of themselves as a communicative force between several cultures.

But Prague's literary flowering came to an abrupt and tragic end when the city was occupied by German troops in March, 1939. Many people had acted on their informed premonition and left the city; nonetheless, more than 200,000 Jews fell victim to the atrocities of the Nazis. Theresienstadt was set up as a concentration camp housing mainly Jews from the former Czechoslovakia; they generally stopped off here on their way to the extermination camps in German-occupied Poland. Even before deportation, many people died in Theresienstadt itself of malnutrition, epidemics or maltreat-

ment by the guards. And yet the Nazis attempted to present Theresienstadt to the international media as a model ghetto, an enclave run by an autonomous Jewish administration, in which people were able to work and live and survive World War II. In fact, by 1945 only 40,000 of the Jewish prisoners from Bohemia and Moravia were still alive. Only a few of these returned to Prague after the liberation, and many of those who did quickly found themselves in new concentration camps as Nazi terrorism gave way seamlessly into Stalinist pogroms. The show trials of the late 1940s bore clear traces of anti-Semitism, and a number of prominent Czech Jews were sentenced to death. Only a few of the imprisoned Jews survived to see their rehabilitation in the post-Stalinist era. And the Soviet invasion of 1968 sparked a new wave of Jewish emigration from the country.

Still, some of these, such as the author Karol Sidon, returned, after the Velvet Revolution, to their city, their "lover for life" (Gabriel Laub): Prague.

THE NEW ECONOMY

"A market economy without adjectives:" this was the goal of Minister President Václav Klaus as he set about restructuring the Czech economy. After 40 years of Communist "command economy," the free play of the forces of supply and demand were now suddenly to govern the country's economic future. This route, a conscious attempt to play down the power of the state – a route, indeed, which calls into question the extent of the state's responsibility for those who can't keep up with the pace of the game – is the subject of considerable debate among the Czechs.

The most significant objection came from the top: President Václav Havel, a self-styled opponent of any form of dogmatism, included in his criticism a blanket put-down of the "cult of the purity of

Above: The Škoda plants (now VW) have long been a cornerstone of the Czech economy. Right: International selection.

the market economy system." In such a situation of transformation and upheaval, Havel believes, the republic can't afford what he terms the "luxury of a purely market-oriented economy."

In the first phase of "small-scale" privatization, which involved auctioning off more than 100,000 mid-sized firms, only Czechs were permitted to purchase. And even in "large-scale" privatization, which involved handing out non-transferable coupons for the acquisition of shares of stock to every adult citizen, actual practice did not exactly conform to the doctrines of a purely market economy.

At the beginning of 1993, two-thirds of the Czech Republic's entire production was manufactured by private companies. Before that, certainly, the Czechs had had to brazen out some tough times: in 1991, the gross national product shrank by 14%, and another 7% in 1992. In response, drastic measures were taken, starting in 1990 with three massive devaluations of the krone. Yet in comparison to nearly every other country of the former East Bloc, the Czechs managed to stabilize their currency with astonishing speed.

This didn't alter the fact that the prices for nearly every product exploded throughout 1991. In that year alone, the rate of inflation lay at nearly 60%. Display windows were once again filled with quality products, but the citizens didn't have anything like enough money to dream of paying the exorbitant prices. In 1992, however, the government was able to implement a restrictive financial policy to get the currency problem under control: in that year, inflation was kept down to around 11%.

What's truly sensational in comparison to other Eastern European countries is the rate of unemployment. At its highest point, in 1991, it reached a level of 4.1%, and swung back down to 2.6% in the following year: a remarkable result. This has been bought, certainly, by relatively low salaries: a Czech worker's minimum wage is approximately 200 dollars a month. In terms of buying power within the country, however, this is considerably more than the money appears to be worth on the international exchange scale: herein lies the secret of the Czech "economic miracle" and its success.

While wages in the Asian countries traditionally known for providing cheap labor are still lower than in the Czech Republic, the latter has the advantage of its location at the center of Europe, a plus which is reflected in lower transportation costs, as well as cheaper costs of retraining workers or communication. The neighboring German Federal Republic has become the Czech Republic's largest trade partner: 33% of the country's imports come from Germany, and 26% of its exports go in the other direction. A close second are the countries of the former Soviet Union (20%). The Czech Republic, in short, seems predestined to serve as a kind of "bridge" in East-West trade relations.

One blow for the development of the Czech economy came in the form of the separation from Slovakia. In the first half of 1993, the gross national product fell by 1%. But the Czechs quickly managed to make up this difference once again. More than 90% of all direct investments from abroad before the separation had gone to the western, or Czech, section of the country. In fact, the government's coffers stood to gain from the move, as subventions and financial transfers to Slovakia to the tune of more than 700 million dollars a year were now no longer necessary.

To demonstrate how solid the Czech economy has become, one need only mention that in 1993, the country was able to afford to take out a loan from the International Monetary Fund to the tune of 200 million dollars. The huge leap in tourism has also helped the economy along, enabling the Czech Republic to show a budget surplus of 150 million dollars in 1992, and to have built up, since the Velvet Revolution, a currency reserve amounting to nearly 5 billion dollars.

227

CZECH MUSIC

Bohemia was once (erroneously) thought of as the original home of the gypsies; and the French form of its name, Bohème, has become synonymous with unconventional artists who transcend their modest surroundings and aspire to greatness in the great cities of the world. And this sense of the word does, in fact, apply perfectly to the musicians of the real Bohemia. In the 18th century, attracted by the wealth of Vienna and the German courts, as well as by ambition and sheer artistic curiosity, hundreds of performers and composers deployed to the west. With the resilience of cats and chameleon-like adaptability – extending even to changing their names – they became profoundly influential, albeit often in a subtle way. Antonín Rejcha (1760-1836), for example, lived in Paris and taught at the Conservatoire, where he became the teacher of Berlioz and Gounod, among others.

Other examples abound. The horn player Giovanni Punto (1746-1803), born Jan Václav Stich, was the source of Mozart's inspiration for the horn part of the *Sinfonia Concertante* K.V. 297b; Beethoven later wrote his Sonata Opus 17 for him and even accompanied him in concert. Georg (Jiří) Benda (1722-1795), who worked in Gotha, was one of the first to shape the melodrama as a link between opera and theater; he inspired Mozart to his Singspiel *Zaide*. Pianist Jan Ladislav Dusík (1760-1812), meanwhile, became known for his active use of the sustaining pedal, and he initiated the custom of sitting sideways on stage, rather than facing the audience; this was not for artistic reasons, however, but merely so that the vain artist could show off his wonderful profile. In Italy the composer Giuseppe Venatorini was known as "il Boemo," for he was born Josef Mysliveček (1737-81).

Above: Music lesson. Right: Smetana is a revered, and well-tended, figure.

The bulk of the Czechs naturally went to the capital of the Habsburg Empire, Vienna, where they had a subtle but profound on musical life. In 1785 Pavel Vranický, a good friend of Mozart, Haydn and Beethoven, became director of the National Theater – his opera *Oberon* is considered a forerunner of Romantic opera. Simon Sechter (1788-1867) taught counterpoint at the Conservatory to Bruckner, among others. Leopold Koželuh (1752-1818) succeeded Mozart as Chamber Composer to the Imperial Court. And the Moravian Anton Schindler (1798-1864), a conductor in Vienna, became Beethoven's first biographer.

Perhaps the most important branch of the Czech musical mafia, as it were, settled in the German town of Mannheim. Under the aegis of Jan Václav Stamitz (1717-1757), his son Carl (1745-1801), Franz Xaver Richter (1709-1789), and Anton Filtz (1730-1760), the local orchestra developed into the epitome of technical brilliance. Furthermore they experimented daringly with new stylistic elements, notably long crescendi (the so-called "Mannheim steamroller"), daring melodic climbs (the "Mannheim rocket"), and great dynamic variations, all of which fit in well with the fashionable *galant* style and charged the music with a new level of emotion.

The Czechs, in short, were everywhere. They acquitted themselves well, sometimes even brilliantly, as composers, judging from, say, Kalivoda's *Symphony in F minor*, or the piano music of Jan Hugo Voříšek, which still remains to be discovered by our contemporary public. Meanwhile, however, music in Bohemia, and Czech music itself, was withering. "The whole country seemed to be musical, serenades and nocturnes rang out in every street on lively summer nights," wrote Carl Maria von Weber. "But this wonderful era passed, the excellent musicians became fewer and the performers ever more mediocre."

Two events changed this state of affairs. The first was the founding of the national conservatory in Prague in 1810. The second was the development of a national consciousness. František Škroup's (1801-1862) *Dráteník (The Tinker)* in 1826 was among the first operas based on popular Czech stories; Škroup also wrote the music to the country's national anthem. There followed a spate of similar attempts by composers who are largely forgotten today, such as Skuherský, Bradský, or Hřímalý. It was Bedřich Smetana (1824-1884), who started out as a pianist, who molded these inchoate beginnings into something of a school, inspired and incited by Franz Liszt, who had done much the same for Hungarian music. *Braniboři v Čechách (The Brandenburgers in Bohemia)* was a serious opera on Czech themes, but it was the 1866 *Prodaná nevěsta, The Bartered Bride,* that truly established a national style. For this opera united a "folksy" story that a wide public could identify with and skillfully stylized folk music.

Smetana's later operas failed to reach the level of the *Bartered Bride*, but in the 1870s, when he had already gone totally deaf, he succeeded in painting an impressive musical portrait of his country in a cycle of six entrancing symphonic poems under the general title *Má vlast, My Country*. The second of these, describing the course of the Moldau, has become an old chestnut of the concert repertoire.

Smetana's counterpart was Antonín Dvořák (1841-1904), the son of a butcher, who began his musical career playing violin and viola in inns. He was perhaps the first Czech composer whose music actually made its way into the world without the artist following. His first major success came in 1878 with the publication of the *Slavonic Dances*, an event he owed partially to the patronage of Johannes Brahms. Dvořák took up

Above: Street musicians. Right: Bohemian music is known for its brass.

where Smetana left off, plunging deeply into the world of Czech folk music, drawing heavily on its melodies and rhythms to color much of his output. Obvious examples are the use of the *dumka*, a melancholy piece with bright interludes, as a slow movement (notably in the *Dumki Trio*) or the lively *furiant* dance as a scherzo movement. Even his *Symphony Nr. 9*, "From the New World," sounds Czech in spite of the use of African American and Indian themes. His most famous opera, *Rusalka*, was based on a Czech fairy-tale by Jaroslav Kvapil.

Smetana and Dvořák represented the high point of Bohemian music in its pure form. Subsequent generations began to turn away from a strictly national expression, preferring to look beyond their borders toward new developments in the international music world. Josef Bohuslav Foerster (1859-1951) lived long enough to bridge the gap between the Romanticism espoused by Liszt and Wagner and the new musical trends. Joseph Suk (1874-1935), Dvořák's son-in-law, was a full-fledged Late Romantic, whose works, especially his grandiose tone poems, are yet to be discovered abroad. Oskar Nebdal (1874-1930), a student of Dvořák, remained true to the faith when it came to the use of Czech elements. The same applies to Jaromír Weinberger (1896-1967), who rejected modern idioms and was able to achieve popular fame especially with his opera *Schwanda the Bagpiper*.

A unique specimen, comparable perhaps to such individualists as Mussorgsky or Charles Ives, was Leoš Janáček (1854-1928), who spent much of his creative life working at the college of organists in Brno, where he also researched Moravian folk music. He achieved fame with the opera *Jenufa* in 1904. Particularly in his piano music, Janáček's musical language tends toward impressionism; and if there are any purely national concerns to be found, they are tied into a

more general expression of Slavism (*Glagolithic Mass*, the symphonic poem *Taras Bulba*, settings of Dostoevsky, etc.). His 1927 *Sinfonietta* is a frankly extroverted work, with a sensually dense texture, especially in the brasses. A far more fickle composer was the unusually prolific Bohuslav Martinů (1890-1959), who mixed folkloric elements with a streamlined neoclassical style.

The contemporary Czech music scene is just as rich and many-sided, even if the general public is seldom ready for the likes of Luboš Fišer, Miloš Štědroň or Jaroslav Krček.

And, last but not least, there's another important name that needs to be mentioned: that of Alois Hába (1893-1973). His research began with folk music, but he soon veered off to devote himself to the investigation of half-, quarter-, and even sixth-tone music. He later reverted to a more traditional expression, but his modern work opened the way for the latest, current generation of young composers.

ALL THAT JAZZ IN PRAHA

Old-timers who remember Prague in its previous incarnation rave about the nights they whiled away in the Sixties in jazz "Klubs" like *Reduta* or *Viola*. Today, these clubs both spell themselves with a "c," *très internationalement*, rather than the local "k," and the currencies of preference in both are the mark or the dollar: local jazz fans can no longer even dream of being able to afford either.

Once upon a time, both clubs were filled with a special kind of atmosphere that was not only inimitable, but specific to the city. The jam sessions just before midnight, long after the departure of the last metro, were so spontaneous that you felt you wanted to get up on the podium yourself – the word "stage" was still a foreign term – and get your fingers on the keys. Prague acted as a magnet for all of the talented musicians in Czechoslovakia. The trend was for tradition: modern jazz, free jazz, or any kind of experimentation tended to be looked down on. What

played in Prague was the good old New Orleans style, swing, or Dixieland, if the groups hadn't opted to present the dulcet tones of a trio or quartet.

And nonetheless, the Prague jazz fad represented a kind of pioneering spirit. Jazz, which radio stations had long been treating as something veritably exotic, began to flourish at the end of the Fifties. Two of the great trail-blazers were the orchestra of Karel Vlach in Prague and Gustav Brom's orchestra, featuring trumpeter Jaromír Hnilička, in Brno. One by one, a whole row of music stages opened in Prague (*Rokoko, Semafor*), while the jazz club *Viola* featured literary readings with a live jazz accompaniment.

One of the first popular bands was Zdeněk Čamrda's *Pražský dixieland*. In 1959, this was joined by the Traditional Jazz Studio, directed by Pavel Smetáček. Another orchestra of the 1970s that spe-

cialized in jazz of the 1920s, and enjoyed considerable public success in the West as well as at home, was the Original Prague Syncopated Orchestra (*Originální pražský synkopický orchestr*, directed by Pavel Klikar). Ferdinand Havlík's Swing Orchestra focused on a tried-and-true repertoire, which it continues to present at jazz festivals in Europe even today. The Prague Big Band (*Pražský big band*) under Milan Svoboda, who also appears on solo keyboards, also continues to guest at major jazz festivals. The Jazz Orchestra of the Czechoslovakian Radio in Prague, directed by Kamil Hála or Václav Zahradník and comprised of excellent jazz soloists, used to present fabulous big band music composed by local musicians. Soloists such as guitarist Rudolf Dašek, trumpeter Laco Déczi (who went on to found his own group, *Jazz celula*), Josef Audes (sax) and Felix Slováček (clarinet and sax), pianist Rudolf Rokl, and later the guitarist Radim Hladík or flautist Jiří Stivín, are only a few of the outstanding personalities of

Above: Jazz pianist Martin Kratochvil. Right: People are jazzing all over the city.

the past three decades. Stivín, an inventive and multi-talented musician, is one of the most popular guest soloists. Because of his versatility, he's perfectly able to assemble and present an entire solo evening. But this native of Prague, born in 1946, is particularly fond of playing duos: sometimes with a guitarist, sometimes with a percussionist.

The year 1962 proved to be a milestone in the development of Czech jazz: a whole group of musicians proved themselves to be of European and not merely local caliber. Most notable names are those of bass players Luděk Hulan and Jiří Mráz, the drummer Ivan Dominák and sax and vibraphone player Karel Velebný, who even composed music for a New York film company with his S & H Quartet (SHQ). And a group of 14- and 15-year-old musicians were on their way up: Jan Hammer Jr. on the piano, contrabass player Miroslav Vitouš and his drummer brother Alan. This Junior Trio was something of a musical sensation: Miroslav Vitouš and Jan Hammer each received scholarships to the prestigious Berklee College in Boston, as did, later, keyboards player Emil Viklický and Martin Kratochvíl. As a result, the Prague jazz community lost a certain amount of its life blood: Vitouš and Hammer remained abroad, as did bass players Milan Pilar and Jiří "George" Mráz, who played with Oscar Peterson, among others. In 1988, Alan and Miroslav Vitouš met for the first time in 22 years in a Prague music studio; Jan Hammer, meanwhile, had settled in Manhattan and conquered the world (as, among other things, the composer of the music for *Miami Vice*).

A name that's inextricably linked with the Prague jazz scene is that of one of the capital's busiest pianists: Karel Růžička. Růžička has made countless recordings both as a soloist and with various groups. Together with E. Viklický and M. Kratochvíl, who are also important com-

posers, he counts as one of the protagonists of Prague's jazz scene today.

The 1970s saw a number of attempts to produce a local version of jazz-rock: as well as Kratochvíl, the name of Lešek Semelka stands out in this connection. From the start, Jiří Cerha and Ladislav Kantor (C & K Vocal) sounded an individual note in concert halls and recording studios with their jazz-inspired compositions. Many attempts were abortive: the Barok Jazz Kvintet was short-lived; the Jazz Fragment Praha and the Jassfonický orchestra dazzled with a demanding repertoire. Many groups of (younger) musicians disbanded even before their own recordings had come out on the market.

Jana Koubková is, together with the unsteady Eva Olmerová, one of the few female vocalists who's managed to achieve success in this man's world. *Hot Breath* has long been her signature piece. Another luminary started her career with Jan Hammer's father at the end of the war, and is still s(w)inging today: Vlasta Průchová, born in 1926.

PANTOMIME, BLACK THEATER AND LATERNA MAGIKA

"The body," says Samy Molcho, "is the glove of the soul." Born in Israel in 1936, Molcho is one of the three lode stars in the international mime firmament. Leader of these is Marcel Marceau (b. 1923), whose solo character Bip has delighted generations. And the third, Prague native Ladislav Fialka (b. 1931), brought to perfection another form: the ensemble. In 1958, the graduate of Prague's Conservatory of Dance founded his own pantomime troupe in the Theater on the Balustrade (*Divadlo Na zábradlí*). What he produced were "straight" theater productions which presented evening-length dramas by means of pantomime, (*Caprichos*, based on Goya). Since then, Fialka has appeared in films and live performances around the world. He feels

Above: Marionettes for rather disrespectful productions. Right: Before the show.

himself the heir to a great tradition: the teacher of all Pierrots, Jean-Gaspard Deburau, was born in 1796 in Kolín (Central Bohemia). It was this artist whom Jean-Louis Barrault honored in the truly great classic film *Les Enfants du Paradis*.

Pantomime specialists refer to the "Czech School" of pantomime. Is there a Prague School, as well? There's certainly no lack of creative performers in Fialka's homeland. Yet this form of artistic expression is all too often used for mere showy effect, particularly now, in the commerce-oriented climate of the post-Socialist era. Rather than pantomime, one all too often sees mere revues that offer a pastiche of a number of different forms. In the Klub lávka, they're already presenting a pantomime evening called *Remember Ladislav Fialka*.

After Fialka, the most important Czech pantomime today is Boris Hybner. In his GAG Studio, *Laterna grotesca*, he clearly acknowledges his classical roots while ennobling such additional forms as clowning and slapstick comedy.

Viktor Hlobil is the director of the *Motion Theater 22* (in the Balustrade) on Anenské náměstí. One of his programs is called *The Castaways.*

Divadlo Image combines pantomime with stylistic elements of so-called Black Theater (*Černé divadlo*). The most important figure of this latter form, Jiří Srnec, is also a native of the Golden City. And he also started in the same year (b. 1931) as Fialka, and in the same theater (on the Balustrade): his *Černé divadlo* started there two years after Fialka's debut, in 1961. Srnec brought the "invisible art," one element of which are black-clad actors moving puppets against a black background, to near-perfection. His productions, like Fialka's, were poetic meanderings through the realm of the imagination. Today, his Black Theater presents *The Legends of Old Prague* in the Theater Za branou II (Národní třída). Nearby, on Reduta, František Kratochvíl's troupe performs a more humorous version of Black Theater with *The Anatomy of a Kiss.* Another

Prague stage (*Divadlo ACT – All Colors Theater*), which blends black theater, film, ballet, dance, musicals and colorful stage kitsch, presented its first revue in the Theater in Rytířská a total of 565 times. *Ta Fantastika & Pan Optikum* offers a blend of animation and puppet films, black theater, live action and erotica. The magical, wonderful Theater of the Baroque Age (*Zázračné divadlo barokního světa*) achieves an effective interplay between actors and marionettes.

Only a postscript, alas, on the famous *Laterna Magika*, which once dazzled with its unique mixture of live stage action, music, film, and multi-vision shows, all absolutely first-rate. Critics are unanimous that the light of Laterna Magika, which resides in an elegant abode by the National Theater, has been extinguished. The pressure of commerce to present effect-oriented, glitzy shows for the tourists has killed the fantasy of this once trail-blazing theater, a fantasy which led it to world-wide, and much-deserved, triumphs after its founding in 1958.

THE BRIEF FLOWERING OF PRAGUE SECESSION

In the second half of the 19th century, when the Czech people were seeking to give architectural substance to their new national self-awareness, the first results were, in line with the times, eclectic mixtures of past styles which were seen as having particular historical importance. The pinnacle of this effort toward worthy self-representation are the three neo-Renaissance buildings at the edge of the Old City: the National Theater, the National Museum and the Rudolfinum.

When, in the 1890s, a new style began to develop in the artistic centers of the United States and Europe, Prague was not unaffected, inasmuch as a Moravian artist, Alfons Mucha, was one of its protagonists. Mucha is today held to be one of the most successful Art Nouveau ar-

Above: Classic Art Nouveau (Jugendstil): the Hotel Evropa. Right: The city is rife with Art Nouveau details.

tists in the field of poster design. He became world-renowned for his advertisements for the divine Sarah Bernhardt.

While the French term "art nouveau" doesn't indicate anything about the content of this new artistic direction, and the German "Jugendstil" avoids mentioning the confrontation with previous traditions which it entailed, the term "Prague (or Vienna) Secession" clearly indicates a break from tradition. The point was to come up with a new formal vocabulary that corresponded to the spirit of the times. And indeed, the organically curving, often asymmetrical lines and forms of the style variously known as Jugendstil, Art Nouveau, or "Secession," with its stylization of selected, exotic natural forms – the filigree of a dragonfly's wing or the petals of lotus flower – were prominent, indeed, dominant elements in the decor of residential, business, and public buildings.

In Prague, you can still see countless examples of the Secession style. The clear leader in this style is the Municipal

Building on Republic Square, designed by Osvald Polívka and Antonín Balšánek. If you examine it closely, you can see that it clearly clings in certain respects to the old eclectic style, and simply enriches this with decorative elements characteristic of "Secession." The construction of the roof is notably similar to those of the above-mentioned Renaissance buildings.

One of the purest examples of Jugendstil in Prague is the Hotel Evropa on Wenceslas Square, a creation of the architect Friedrich Bendelmayer. Both its facade and its interior are some of the finest exponents of Prague Secession. The pure Secession style can also be seen in the appointments of Osvald Polívka's multi-purpose house "U Nováků" on Vodičkova. Similarly fine are two adjacent houses on Národní, originally built for the Praha Insurance Company and Topic Publishers. Particularly worthy of note is the ceramic work on the facades, executed by Ladislav Šaloun. Most monumental example of Art Nouveau in

Prague is the main train station by Josef Fanta, which has recently undergone a thorough renovation.

Countless other examples of Art Nouveau architecture can be found on Na příkopě and in Josefov. Even St. Vitus's Cathedral shelters a small Jugendstil gem: one of the stained-glass windows in the left-hand chapel is by Alfons Mucha.

Another major figure in the Prague Secession was Jan Kotěra, a student of the Viennese architect Otto Wagner. One of his first buildings was the Peterka House (12 Wenceslas Square). In his work, Art Nouveau decoration underlies even the basic construction of the building itself. He was, therefore, partly responsible for the next step past this style, as one of his maxims was that a new formal language had to develop out of the actual requirements of a building's construction, rather than being forced to develop into a new aesthetic through the will of the architect. As a result, he abandoned ornamentation, deriding it as superficial, in his subsequent building projects.

BOHEMIAN CUISINE

We've all heard that the way to a man's heart is through his stomach; and Bohemian mothers, too, armed their daughters with this home truth before sending them out into the world. But the benefits of these daughters' skills at cooking and baking were, and are, to be enjoyed by many more people than merely their spouses. Hospitality, and serving good food, are among the notable strengths of the Czech national character.

Bohemian – that is to say, Czech and Moravian – cuisine has developed from two different directions. One of these was a strong reliance on local products, which has especially characterized rural, peasant cooking: grains and fruits, milk and cheese, eggs and poultry, pork and bacon from home-butchered pigs all play a prominent role, joined, less frequently,

Above: Buchticky. Right: The national dish, vepřo-knedlo-zelo (roast pork, dumpling, and cabbage).

by fish and game. Also evident on the menu are mushrooms and other forest products, as well as fruit, both fresh and dried. When potatoes were introduced to Central Europe, they quickly came to feature as a main dish on farmers' tables.

But the other direction was from the castles and palaces. Such establishments employed first-rate chefs, who made use of game from the preserves, fish and fowl, and exotic ingredients and spices.

Middle-class kitchens in the 19th century saw the development of a symbiosis between these two schools of cooking. Evidencing this is the famous cookbook by Magdalena Dobromila Rettigová. For peasants, fish remained a dish eaten only on Sundays; soups were, and still are, the main staple of the daily diet.

Simplest and cheapest is the soup *oukrop*. Small, twice-baked pieces of bread are laid in a bowl, along with salt and grated or finely chopped garlic; then the whole is topped off with boiling water. *Bramboračka* (potato soup) takes more time and effort, as does *zelnačka* (sauerkraut soup). A filling soup of milk, sour cream, potatoes, and eggs or mushrooms is called *kyselo* in the Giant Mountains, *kuljada* in southern Bohemia. Pinnacle of the local cook's art is the traditional Christmas fish soup made with carp.

With cooked meat accompanied by potatoes, noodles or dumplings (and, more and more, rice), you need a good sauce. Some of the most common are made with tomatoes, horseradish, dill, mushrooms, paprika, mustard, or caraway.

In the popular dish *svíčková na smetaně*, sauce is the crowning glory. The recipe is as follows: spread larded beef with butter, margarine or sour cream (no oil!). Cover the meat with slices of onions, carrots, and celery root – the more the better – as well as parsley, pepper, and allspice, and let it sit for a few days. Then cover it with slices of bacon and simmer it with the vegetables. When the meat is done, puree the vegetables and bacon in a mixer, add sour cream, and bring to a boil. Serve it with Bohemian dumplings and cranberry sauce. The dishes *srničí na smetaně* (veal cream roast) and *zajíc na smetaně* (rabbit cream roast) are prepared in the same way. The beloved *bažant na slanině* (pheasant on a bed of bacon) is, because of the high price of the ingredients, an unheard-of luxury today. What you can get in its place is *kuře à la bažant* (chicken à la pheasant), prepared in the same manner.

Every tourist quickly learns that the most popular dish in the Czech Republic is in fact *vepřo-knedlo-zelo* (roast pork, dumpling, cabbage). Actually, people prefer roast goose, but pork is cheaper. The standard accompaniment to a good meal is good beer on tap (in Bohemia) or good table wine (in Moravia).

The manufacture of a true Czech dumpling requires a housewife's skill and special ingredients. One famous variety are fruit dumplings stuffed with plums, cherries, apricots, strawberries, or blueberries. Also deservedly famous are

buchticky, filled doughnuts, strudel, and other dough specialties. Bohemian *buchticky* are rectangular and stuffed with cottage cheese, pureed plums, or poppyseeds; Moravian ones are round, filled with a mixture of cottage cheese and raisins, and topped with plums or poppyseeds. And in southern Bohemia, the "filling" sits atop the dough, and each little pastry is a miniature masterpiece.

If these desserts remind the experienced traveler of something he's eaten in Vienna, he won't be far off the mark. During the Austro-Hungarian Empire, many Czech girls went to the capital to earn their dowries. Thanks to their cooking, they soon dominated Viennese kitchens, and – because the way to a man's heart is through his stomach – a number of Viennese men. Those who came back home brought not only money, but also the recipes for Sacher torte or cutlet. Thus, the characteristic breaded cutlet "Wiener Schnitzel" is featured on Prague menus, with one difference: instead of veal, the cutlet is generally pork.

TRAVEL PREPARATIONS

Information before you go
Czech Tourist Authority:

Canada, P.O.Box 198, Exchange Tower, 2 First Canadian Place 14th Floor, Toronto, Ontario M5X 1A6, Tel: +1 416 367 3432, Fax: +1 416 367 3492.

Great Britain: 95 Great Portland Str., London W1N 5RA, Tel: +44 171 291 99 20, Fax: +44 171 436 83 00.

USA, 1109-1111 Madison Avenue, New York, N.Y. 10028, Tel: +1 212 288 0830, Fax: +1 212 288 0971.

For more information about the country and visas, too, inquire at the **Czech embassies** abroad:

Australia: 38 Culgoa Circuit O'Maly, ACT 2606 Canberra, Tel: + 61 6 290 1386, Fax: + 61 6 290-0006.

Canada: 541 Sussex Drive, Ottawa, Tel: + 1 613 562 3875, Fax: + 1-613 562 3878.

Great Britain: 26 Kensington Palace Gardens, W8 4QY London, Tel: + 44 (0)171 243-1115, Fax: + 44 (0)171 727-9654.

USA: 3900 Spring of Freedom Street, N.W., Washington, D.C. 20008, Tel: +1 202 274-9173, Internet: http://www.czech.cz/washington/

Climate / When to Go

Prague and other popular spots in the Czech Republic are almost always in season. Only in January, February and November does the stream of visitors abate. The major sights are particularly crowded on long weekends or during German and Austrian school holidays.

The country has a mild, Continental climate, with warm, sometimes damp summers and cold, dry winters. In summer, the daytime temperatures average 75°F (24°C), but can get into the mid-80s (30°C); at night, however, it cools off to around about 60°F (15°C). In winter, the average daily temperature hovers around the freezing point, and falls at night into the 20s (around -4°C). In January and February, you can sometimes hit temperatures as low as -5°F (-20°C).

The period between April and August is the rainiest season: it rains an average of eight to ten days a month, where the monthly average during the rest of the year is five to seven days. In the mountains, there's often snow in winter; but snow is rare in Prague. Spring and summer, obviously, tend also to be the sunniest months, with six to eight hours of sun a day; and the gray winter-like smog, the product of exhaust pipes and the coal stoves which are still common, burns off into a somewhat more pleasant mist.

Clothing

Summer clothes are best from May – sometimes even Easter – until into autumn. But it's useful to come armed with a light raincoat and something warm to put on for long evenings outdoors. If you are planning to walk a lot in the city, wear comfortable shoes. If planning to go to the mountains, don't forget hiking boots.

Visas

If you're staying in the country for less than three months, all you need is a passport that's good for at least six months more. If you plan to stay longer, you'll need to get a visa from the Czech Embassy or Consulate in your home country (see Information before you go above).

Customs

Objects for personal use can be brought in without customs duty, as can gifts of up to 1000 Krone in value. You can also bring in 2 liters of wine, 1 liter of spirits, half a liter of perfume, and 250 cigarettes. Foreign currency can be brought in and out of the country at will; but the same does not hold true for Czech currency. To export genuine antiques, you'll need a special permit. For more customs information, contact the number (in Prague) 232 22 70 and 6133 1111.

TRAVELING TO, AND IN, THE CZECH REPUBLIC

By Plane

All of the major airline companies have regular, often daily, flights to Prague. The city airport, Praha-Ruzyně, is about 20 km northwest of the city center, and is administered by Air France. Amenities include a 24-hour money exchange office, rental car companies, restaurants, a post office, and a small duty-free shop. From there, you can get to the city by taxi; by bus 119, which connects to the A line of the subway; or the airport shuttle bus of ČSA (Czech Airlines), which runs every half hour in rush hour, hourly at other times, to náměstí Republiky in the center of Prague, with one stop along the way at the subway station Dejvická (line A). You can buy your ticket for this service on the bus.

Central Information Office of the Praha-Ruzyně airport: Tel: 36 78 14 and 36 77 60. The following offices also give flight information: **Vltava Travel Agency**, P-1, Revoluční 25, Tel: 231 73 95; **ČEDOK**, P-1, Na Příkopě 18, Tel: 2421 0351; **AC Tour**, P-1, Opletalova 29, Tel: 2422 1820, App. 277; **American Express**, P-1 Václavské náměstí 56, Tel: 2221 1136; **Atlantis Air Service**, P-1, Biskupská 6, Tel: 232 55 48, Fax: 2481 1573.

Ticket reservation for ČSA (the national airline): P-1, Valnici 5, Tel: 2010 4111 and 2010 4310.

By Train

The Czech Republic has an extensive railway network that reaches to just about every town of any size. Traveling in a regular local train (*osobní vlak*) can be a long undertaking, as the train stops at every station and travels slowly between them. You have to pay a supplement for express trains (*rychlík*); these travel considerably faster, and only stop at larger towns.

If the train is marked on the timetable with an "R," reservations are required. There are a number of daily connections to Prague from such major European cities as Vienna or Berlin.

Information about train schedules: Tel: 2422 4200 or 2421 7654.

By Car

If you're entering the Czech Republic by car, you'll need a valid driver's license, registration papers, and an insurance card. A highway sticker can be purchased at the border. You're required by law to have a first-aid kit, spare tire, warning sign, and an indication on the car of country of origin. Seatbelts are required, and children under 12 have to sit in the back seat. Driving is illegal if you've consumed any alcohol at all.

On country roads, the speed limit is 90 km/h (about 60 mph); on motorways, 110 km/h (75 mph); in towns, 60 km/h (40 mph). For motorcyclists, the speed limit outside of towns is 80 km/h (55 mph).

Drive especially carefully, as the pavement, particularly within towns, is always good for a surprise or two.

In Prague, it's not worth it to rely on a car, since it's almost impossible to find a parking place except in none-too-cheap parking garages. Furthermore, if you're not in a guarded parking lot, note that car break-ins and burglary are on the rise, with new or expensive cars as particularly vulnerable targets.

In the event of an accident, call the emergency service (see the section on "Emergencies") or the number 123.

In Prague, there's a 24-hour auto mechanic service: P-10, Limuzská 12, Tel: 77 27 70 or 0602/31 56 60. All of the big car companies have service representatives in Prague.

By Bus

The bus network in the Czech Republic is extensive. As a rule, it's used by students and workers; and the time-tables are set up accordingly. Central hub in Prague is the Florenc bus station (Tel: 2421 4990), which can be reached with subway lines B and C; if you're traveling West or South, use the Smíchov bus station (Tel: 54 00 08), which can be reached with subway line B (Anděl station).

For information about national and international bus connections, call: 2421 1060-4 (weekdays 6 am-8 pm).

For information about bus connections in Central Bohemia, call 54 31 13 or 54 08 50 (weekdays and Sundays 6 am-6 pm, Saturdays 6 am-3:30 pm).

The following travel agencies sell tickets and reservations for abroad: Bohemiatour, P-1, Zlatnická 7, Tel: 232 39 89, Fax: 231 38 06 and P-1, Jungmannova 4, Tel: 2421 6589, Fax: 2321 6264; Bohemia Euroexpress International, P-3, Koněvova 126, Tel: 74 79 63, Fax: 74 79 63; Bohemia Express, P-3, Koněvova 227, Tel: 684 21 48, Fax: 684 09 97; Eurolines, P-1, Opletalova 37, Tel: 2421 3420, Fax: 2421 0835.

Subways, Streetcars, and Buses in Prague

There are three subway lines (A, B and C), distinguished with the three colors green, yellow, and red. In the city center, these are supplemented with an extensive network of streetcars and buses. To destinations in the suburbs, there are buses either from the city center or from the nearest streetcar or subway stop. Between midnight and 5 am, there are regular (but infrequent) night buses.

The cable car to Petřín runs daily between 9:15 am and 8:45 pm. You can reach it on streetcar lines 9, 12, or 22.

The same ticket is used for all three forms of public transportation, as well as for the cable car to Petřín. You can buy it at machines in the subway stations or in specially marked kiosks, tobacconists, restaurants, hotel receptions, or even in some grocery stores. You then validate this ticket in a machine ticket-puncher

before you get to the subway platform, or when you get on a bus or streetcar, in a similar machine installed by the door. The ticket is good for one hour in the subway, even if you change your mode of transportation bus, tram, or subway. Or there are tickets valid for 15 minutes (bus, tram) or maximum three stations (subway) without changing. For tourists, there are day tickets as well as tickets good for several days. Children under six ride free.

PRACTICAL TIPS

Accommodations

Because the on-going privatization of what were once State- or community-run hotels and restaurants is still underway, and ownership is in many cases still uncertain, it's very difficult to make recommendations for a given region, or list certain addresses. But there are plenty of hotels, pensions and private accommodations available.

You can get information from any city tourist or administration office (*Městský úřad*). Information is also given out free of charge by the Chambers of Commerce in district or regional capitals (*Okresní hospodářská komora*).

Central Office for the Czech Republic: *Česká obchodní komora*; Argentinská 38, 17005 Praha 7, Tel: 00420/ 2/66794111, Fax: 00420/ 2/66710253.

Car Rental

Avanticar, P-5, Nádražní 54, Tel: 54 61 26, Fax: 54 93 05; **Hertz**, P-2, Karlovo náměstí 28, Tel: 29 18 51, Fax: 29 78 36, and in the Hotel Hilton Atrium, P-8, Pobřežní 3, Tel: 2484 1111, and in the Hotel Diplomat, P-6, Evropská 15, Tel: 2439 4155, and in the Hotel Forum, P-4, Kongresová 1, Tel: 6119 1111, and at the airport, P-6, Ruzyně, Tel: 312 07 17; **Europcar**, P-1, Pařížská 26, Tel: 2481 0515, Fax: 2481 0039, and at the airport, P-6, Ruzyně, Tel: 316 78 49; **Rent-a-car**,

P-1, Opletalova 33, Tel: 2421 1587, Fax: 2421 2032, and in the Hotel Atrium, P-8, Pobřežní 3, Tel: 2484 2043, and at the airport, P-6, Ruzyně, Tel: 2011 4370.

Crime

Since November 89, crime has risen, especially in the city center, owing mostly to the heavier influx of drugs, although the problem hasn't yet attained the dimensions it has in other major cities in western or eastern Europe. In crowds, keep close track of your wallet, as pickpockets are out and about, and don't exchange money on the street. If you come by car, only leave it in guarded parking lots or garages, and make sure you have insurance.

Currency / Money Exchange

The Czech unit of currency is the Krone (Kč), which is still divided into 100 Heller, which are practically worthless.

It's best only to exchange cash or travelers' checks in banks, as the countless money exchange offices (even the official ones) charge exhorbitant commissions of up to 12%. Even in banks, certainly, you should ask whether there's a charge for changing money; this shouldn't be any higher than 2%. If banks are closed, you can always change money in one of the big hotels; but rates here are usually worse than anywhere else. It's not a good idea to exchange money on the black market, as people may try to give you invalid banknotes, or, worse still, to steal your wallet.

Travelers' checks, still the safest form of payment, are not accepted as cash in restaurants or shops; you have to change them at a bank first. At many banks and exchange offices you can cash Eurocheques of up to 6,500 Kč per cheque.

Credit cards are only been accepted in the more expensive restaurants and shops, though their use is on the rise. In the city center, however, there are many ATMs, so that you can withdraw cash at any time if your card is authorized to do so internationally.

Disabled Facilities

Disabled travelers requiring help and information should contact the group founded by Mrs. Havel, the **Good Will Committee** (Výbor dobré vůle), P-1, on Lenovážné náměstí 2, Tel: 2421 6883; or the **Czech Association of People with Disabilities**, P-8, Karlínské náměstí 12, Tel: 2481 6997; or the **Union of Disabled People**, P-1, Konviktská 6, Tel: 2422 7203.

Electric Current

The current in the Czech Republic is usually 220 V. In more backward rural areas, you may encounter 120 V. If you travel with any appliances, you should definitely bring an adapter.

Embassies

Australia: P-6 Na Orechovce 38, Tel: 2431 0743, Fax:. 31 19 531. **Canada**, P-6, Mickieviczova 6, Tel: 2431 1108, Fax: 2431 0294. **Great Britain**, P-1, Thunovská 14, Tel: 5732 0355, Fax: 5732 1023. **New Zealand**: P-10, Dykova 19, Tel: 254 198, Fax: 254 198. **Republic of South Africa**, P-10, Ruská 65, Tel: 6731 1114, Fax: 6731 1395. **USA**, P-1, Tržiště 15, Tel: 5732 0663, Fax: 5732 0920.

Emergency

In an emergency, you can call one of the following Prague Telephone numbers. In public Telephone booths with Telephone cars, the first three of these numbers are always posted next to the card slot.

Fire 150
Ambulance 155
Police 158
Car Breakdown 154

Festivals and Holidays

Official holidays are January 1 (New Year's Day), Easter Monday, May 1

(Workers' Day), May 8 (Day of Liberation from Fascism), July 5 (Memorial Day for Slavic Missionaries), July 6 (anniversary of Jan Hus's death), October 28 (Republic Day), and three days at Christmas, December 24-26.

February: Dance events and balls at the beginning of the month. From the beginning of February to the beginning of April is the annual Matthias Fair on the Prague Exhibition Grounds.

March: Third Saturday in March: the Prague Spring March from the city center to Prčice.

Easter: Following an old fertility rite, young boys try to hit girls with sapling switches, and are doused with water by the girls in response. Women give men brightly-painted Easter eggs to restore peace within the home.

April: Start of boating season on the Moldau; on April 30, brooms are burned on the Prague Exhibition Grounds, to drive out evil spirits in accordance with an old tradition.

May: On May 8, the liberation from the German occupation is commemorated with a one-minute siren and with flowers. The second week of May sees the International Prague Book Fair in the Palace of Culture. And May 12 marks the beginning of the Prague Spring, a large music festival with performances in every hall and space in the city.

June: Rowboat and skull races on the Moldau below Vyšehrad on the first weekend of the month. In the last week of June, an international festival of contemporary dance is held in the National Theater.

August: A theater and puppet festival is held on Marksmen's Island.

September: At the beginning of the month the Prague Autumn, an international festival of classical music, is held in the Rudolfinum. There's an Autumn Trade Convention on the Exhibition Grounds. On the 3rd Sunday of the month there are kite-flying contests on

Letná. The last Sunday of the month is the date of a 10-km (7-mile) race that's been held since 1887; it starts in Běchovice and ends in Žižkov.

October: On the second Sunday of the month is the controversial steeplechase of Pardubice. The same day sees the *Velká Kunratická*, a cross-country race, in the forest of Kunratice. In early October the end of the swimming and boating season is marked with festivities on the Moldau. An International Jazz Festival is held in Lucerna Palace.

November: On November 17 there's a peaceful demonstration on Wenceslas Square to commemorate the end of Socialism and the Velvet Revolution.

December: Christmas markets are held throughout the country; in Prague, there are two on the pedestrian zone of the Old City Ring and on Na příkopě. On December 26, die-hards swim in the icy waters of the Moldau. And everyone throughout the country celebrates New Year's Eve on the 31st.

Lost & Found

If you either find or lose documents, apply to the Lost Property Office, P-3, Olšanská 3, Tel: 27 85 51-4. If you lose objects: Dopravní podnicky, P-2, Bojišti P-1, Tel: 9619 2173, or to P-1, Karolíny Světlé 5, Tel: 2423 5085.

Medical Assistance

Every Prague district has its own emergency medical services, one for adults and one for children.

For adults, from 4 pm to 7 am: **P-1**, Palackého 5, Tel: 2422 2521; **P-2**, Sokolská 27, Tel: 29 96 76 and 29 81 16; **P-3**, Koněvova 205, Tel: 684 86 85; **P-4**, Antala Staška 8o, Tel: 692 89 70; **P-5**, Kartourská 6, Tel: 53 92 69; **P-6**, Pod Marijánkow 12, Tel: 2051 3643; **P-7**, Dukelských hrdinů 1, Tel: 38 23 26; **P-8**, Mazurská 484, Tel: 854 35 08; **P-9**, Lovosická 40, Tel: 88 15 18; **P-10**, Nad Olšinami 4, Tel: 781 25 09.

For children after 4 pm until 7 am: **P-1**, Palackého 5, Tel: 2422 2520; **P-2**, Italská 3, Tel: 25 97 86; **P-3**, Koněvova 205, Tel: 684 75 36; **P-4**, Antala Staška 80, Tel: 692 89 70; **P-5**, Kartourská 6, Tel: 53 81 69; **P-6**, Pod Marijánkow 12, Tel: 2051 2199; **P-7**, Dukelských hrdinů 1, Tel: 38 23 26; **P-8**, Mazurská 484, Tel: 855 82 92; **P-9**, Lovosická 40, Tel: 88 15 15, **P-10**, Nad Olšinami 4, Tel: 781 09 90.

There are also emergency dental services in two districts of Prague:

P-1, Vladislavova 22, Tel: 2422 7663 (Mon-Fri 7 pm-7 am, Sat & Sun 24 hours); **P-4**, Antala Staška 80, Tel: 692 89 43 (Mon-Fri 4 pm-7 am, Sat & Sun 24 hours).

Medical Insurance

It's a good idea to check on your international medical coverage before you go. Make sure you are covered for emergency return flights.

Opening Hours

There are no general official opening hours in Prague. Stores are usually open Mon-Fri from 7 am-6 pm, Sat 8 am-noon. Some department stores are open Saturday until 4 pm. Some shops which cater to the tourist trade stay open on weekdays until 10 pm. Banks are open Mon-Fri from 8 am to 4 pm.

Orientation

When you realize that until 1782 there was no systematic system of numbering houses on streets in Prague, you'll understand why it is that residents had to use their imagination to help themselves, and others, get their bearings. You'll notice that every house has two numbers, one in red, one in blue. The red numbers, listed with the letters čp. (*číslo popisné* – the so-called conscriptions number), apply to houses within a given historic city district: numbering is separate in Staré Město, Nové Mesto, Malá Strana or Hradčany. This old system was sup-

plemented in 1868 with a new system, the more usual numbering according to a given street.

Prague's residents are particularly grateful to their Vltava, or Moldau, in that this river, of which the two springs are called the Cold Moldau and the Warm Moldau, is a valuable point of reference in finding one's way around the city. Streets which run parallel to the river are numbered from south to north; odd numbers are on the left, even ones on the right. For cross streets, the rule is as follows: on the left bank, numbers ascend toward the west; while they run toward the east on the right bank.

Sometimes, you'll run across the very first signs from the end of the 18th century, when streets were given names as well as their system of numbering. Welsche Gasse (Vlašská ulice) in the lesser City, for example, has been preserved in both German and Czech; while near the castle you can see the German name Georgi Gasse for Jiřská ulice (still written, in this case, with a U).

Since the Middle Ages, another characteristic aid to finding your way around in Prague were the symbols or nicknames attached to various houses. There are nearly two thousand house signs or symbols in the historic districts of Prague; most of them have been preserved, and many have been renovated or restored.

Through the centuries, the absolute top favorites among these signs have remained constant: angels, apples, bears, crowns, crosses, deer, eagles, grapes or vines, heads, horses of all breeds and sizes, keys, lambs, lions, figures of men and Moors, mermaids, oxen, pelicans, peacocks, roses, shoes in many forms, stars, storks, swans, and trees.

Pharmacies

Every district of Prague has at least one pharmacy with an emergency service: **P-1**, Palackého 5, Tel: 2422 2520; **P-2**, Belgická 37, Tel: 2423 7207; **P-3**, Koněvova

210, Tel: 6631 1369; **P-4**, Antala Staška 80, Tel: 42 44 87; **P-5**, Štefánikova 6, Tel: 5732 0918; **P-6**, Pod Marijánkow 12, Tel: 35 03 30; **P-7**, Milady Horákové 48, Tel: 37 54 92; **P-8**, náměstí Dr. V. Holého 15, Tel: 684 24 22; **P-9**, Sokolovská 304, Tel: 6631 0372; **P-10**, Olšinách 41, Tel: 781 10 68.

Photographing

You can easily find all of the major brands of film. There are also labs which develop prints of good quality in a matter of a few hours.

Post Offices

The Central Post Office in Prague 1, Jindrišská 14, Tel: 2422 8856, has a 24-hour service with a full range of postal services. It has fax facilities and a row of telephone booths where you can place international calls directly (the latter is open from 7 am-11 pm).

You can also send packages and letters around the clock at the post office in Prague 1, Hybernská 14, Tel: 2421 9701. You can send telegrams from any of Prague's 115 post offices or call them in by phone (Tel: 0127). For information about further postal services, call 2422 8588.

You can buy stamps (*známky*) at kiosks and tobacconists.

Letters sent *poste restante* go to the central post office (for address, see above). You can pick them up Mon-Fri 6:30 am-8 pm, Saturday 6:30 am-1 pm, upon showing your passport for identification. If you have an American Express Card, you can also have mail sent to their office on Václavské náměstí 56, Tel: 2422 4606; it's usually held there for about a month.

Cyber cafés are also popping up in case you need to e-mail!

Prague City Tours

As well as **PIS** (P-1, Na Příkopě 20, Tel: 26 40 22-3) and **ČEDOK** (P-1, Na Příkopě 18, Tel: 2419 7616, Fax: 232 16 56), a number of agencies organize city tours. A selection:

DCK Rekrea, P-1, Pařížská 28, Tel: 2481 0000, Fax: 232 29 37.

Sportturist, P-1, Národní 33, Tel: 2422 8341, Fax: 26 33 59.

IFB, P-1, Václavské náměstí 27, Tel: 2422 7253, Fax: 2422 7842.

If you'd like to ride through the city streets in a little train, contact **Ekoexpres**, P-2, Slezská 11, Tel: 25 31 59, Fax: 25 31 59. Trips begin about every hour on the Old City Ring behind the Hus Monument.

The Old City Ring is also the departure point for **carriage (fiacre) tours**. For information, contact the Czech Association of Fiacre Coachmen at the number 39 65 56. **Novum-tour** offers city tours in an observation bus: P-1, Vaclavské náměstí 21, Tel: 2423 5097, Fax: 2423 9065. As well as city tours, **Martin Tour** also offers **boat tours** and **panoramic flights**: P-1, Štěpánská 61, Tel/Fax: 2421 2473. If you'd like to see Prague from a **hot-air balloon**, you have two choices: **Emka tours**, P-6, V Luhu 716, Tel: and Fax: 43 44 34; or **Prague Tourist Ballooning Inc.**, P-3, Na Balkáně 812, Tel: and Fax: 684 53 87.

You can also get information about **boat tours** at the Palackého Bridge: P-2, Rašínovo nábřeží, Tel: 29 83 09 and 29 38 03, Fax: 2491 3862. In summer, the Prague Steamship Company runs excursions to Barrandov and Vyšehrad, the Zoo, Roztoky, or to Slapy Dam.

Sports in Prague

Bowling: Interhotel Forum, P-4, Kongresová 1, Tel: 6119 1326.

Golf: Hotel Golf, P-5, Tel: 52 32 51-7, open April 1-October 30, daily 9 am-sunset (Standard 72); Praha Karlštejn Golf Klub, Strahov Stadium, P-6, Tel: 35 78 03, App. 199 or 795 39 44.

Swimming: Swimming stadium Podolí, P-4, Podolská 74, Tel: 6121 4343, open Mon-Fri 6 am-10 pm, Sat and Sun 8 am-8 pm; SK Slavia Swimming stadium, P-10, Na Hroudě, Tel: 73 55 52, open Mon-Fri 6 -8 am, 6-8 pm, Sat and Sun 8 am-8 pm.

Tennis: Stadium Štvanice in Prague 7, Tel: 231 63 23 and 231 63 17.

Taxis

Taxis are cheap in Prague as long as you don't fall into the hands of one of the many swindlers who are driving around. Always check that there's a meter in the cab, or negotiate firmly to agree on a price that seems reasonable, and includes every kind of imaginable special supplement, rate, and tariff, before you start a trip.

If there is a meter, city trips are prices according to the lowest Rate 1, which should be displayed at the far right of the meter. Night trips will cost two to three times as much.

You can cut short a lot of the discussion about price if you demand a receipt, which is your right as a passenger. It has to list the distance and the price, which means you can also present it to the proper authorities if you need to lodge a complaint.

Here is a selection of taxi firms which operate around the clock:

AAA, Tel: 1080 and 2432 2432; **BM Taxi**, Tel: 8577 and 689 77 77; **Calling**, Tel: 700 42 55; **Taxi Arco**, Tel: 1088 or 6631 1254; **Radio taxi Trojická**, Tel: 2491 6666; **Profi Taxi**, Tel: 1035 or 6131 4111; **Rony**, Tel: 692 19 58; **Sedop**, Tel: 6731 4135 or 6731 4184; **Taxi Praha**, Tel: 2491 6666 or 2491 1559.

Telephones

The country code for the Czech Republic is 42; the city code for Prague is 02 within the Czech Republic, and 2 if you're calling from outside the country.

If you're placing an international call, just dial the country code for your own country. International country codes are listed in most Telephone booths.

For long-distance calls, it's a good idea to buy a telephone card in a kiosk, travel agency, or hotel. Phoning from hotels is expensive!

Tipping

In restaurants frequented by a local clientele, tipping is not expected. In more touristy areas, however, waiters and waitresses are beginning to expect tips of between 5 and 10%.

Tourist Information

Besides the host of travel agents to be found all over the place, the official tourist information office is the Prague Information Service (PIS), which has a number of branches in the city center: Na Příkopé 20, Tel/Fax: 26 40 23; Staroměstské náměstí 1, Tel. 2448 2018; Za Poříčskou branou 7, Tel: 231 11 16; Hlavní nádraží, Tel: 2423 9258.

Weights and Measures

The metric system is used throughout the Czech Republic.

GLOSSARY

Pronunciation

c like ts in its

č like ch in China

d' like j in jeans

e like a in fat

ě like ye in yellow

h is always aspirated

ch like ch in Loch Ness (ch follows h in the Czech alphabet)

j like y in yes

mě like *mnje* (see ň)

ň like gn in Cognac

ř is a rolled r followed by a French-sounding j (vaguely resembling rsh in the word harsh)

s like s in sick

š like sh

t' like ti in the Spanish word *angustia*

v like v in vase

v at the end of a word like f

y like i in sit
z like z in zip
z at the end of a word like s
ž like the French j in *journal*
ž at the end of a word like š

Stresses / Vowels

In Czech, the stress always falls on the first syllable of a word.

All Czech vowels, including y, are short. If they're written with an accent or a little circle over the u, they're drawn out; but the stress always remains on the first syllable.

Greetings and Stock Phrases

Good day	dobrý den
Good morning	dobré jitro
Good evening	dobrý večer
Welcome	srdečně vítam(e)
How are you?	jak se daří?
Goodbye	na shledanou
Thank you	děkuji
Please	prosím
Pardon me!	odpust'(te)!
Excuse me!	promiňte!

General Comprehension

Do you speak English?	mluvíte anglicky?
I don't understand	nerozumím
Yes	ano
No	ne
(Very) good	(velmi) dobře
Help!	pomoc!
Left	vlevo
Right	vpravo
Straight ahead	rovně
Over/above	nahoře
Under/below	dole
Here	zde
There	tam
Who?	Kdo?
Where?	Kde?
Where to?	Kam?
When?	Kdy?
Where is...?	Kde je...?
Do you have...?	Máte...?
I need...	Potřebuji...

Please give me	Dejte mi, prosím
How much does it cost?	Co to stojí?
Yesterday	Včera
Today	Dnes
Tomorrow	Zítra

Numbers

0	nula
1	jeden, jedna, jedno
2	dva, dvě
3	tři
4	čtyři
5	pět
6	šest
7	sedm
8	osm
9	devět
10	deset
11	jedenáct
12	dvanáct
13	třináct
14	čtrnáct
15	patnáct
16	sestnáct
17	šedmnáct
18	osmnáct
19	devatenáct
20	dvacet
21	jedenadvacet
22	dvaadvacet
23	třiadvacet
30	třicet
40	čtyřicet
50	padesát
60	šedesát
70	sedmdesát
80	osmdesát
90	devatdesát
100	sto
200	dvě stě
300	tři sta
400	čtyři sta
500	pět set
600	šest set
1000	tisíc
2000	dva tisíce
5000	pět tisíc
100 000	sto tisíc
1 000 000	milión

AUTHORS

Hana Černá has been working since the 1960s for Prague daily papers as well as international publications. Food writing is one of her specialties "Bohemian Cuisine."

Bernd F. Gruschwitz is a historian and English scholar. He has visited Prague often, both before and after the fall of the Iron Curtain. He works as a journalist and photographer, and did among others the *Nelles Guide Bali/Lombok.* "The Country of the Czechs," "Experiencing Prague," "The Outlying Districts," "Prague Secession."

Márton Rádkai, born in New York, is a freelance journalist for a number of renowned publishers. Previous publications include articles and photographs in the *Nelles Guides Hungary Paris, Bretagne, Greece* and *New York.* "Czech Music."

Hans-Horst Skupy was born in 1942 in Bratislava/Slovakia, but his preference has always been for Prague, Bohemia, and Czech culture, about which he's written numerous books, broadcasts and essays. A freelance journalist based in Ruhstorf/Rott in Lower Bavaria, he has contributed to a number of *Nelles Guides.* "Discovering Prague," "Central Bohemia," "Northern Bohemia," "Western Bohemia," "Southern Bohemia," "Eastern Bohemia," "Southern Moravia," "Northern Moravia," "The Family of Švejk," "All that Jazz," "Theater, Laterna Magika."

Zdeněk Zofka, Ph.D., is a historian specializing in Eastern European history. Since 1988, he has been the Director of Studies at the Bavarian Center for Political Education, where he's overseen numerous publications. "History," "Jewish Life in Prague," "The New Economy."

Dr. František Hudec, a Prague-based historian, updated this edition of the book.

PHOTOGRAPHERS

Archiv für Kunst and Geschichte,
Berlin   23l, 24l, 24r, 25, 26, 27l, 27r, 29, 30, 31, 32, 34, 35, 36r, 37, 224
Begsteiger, A. M.   208
Bondzio, Bodo   18r, 63, 70, 92/93 106, 120, 126, 167
Foto Mendrea   231
Goemann, Gerd Hesse   60, 80, 105, 222, 237r
Gruschwitz, Bernd F.   cover, 22, 40/41, 44, 51l, 52, 54, 59, 62, 64, 65, 76, 81 84, 94/95, 96, 101, 103, 108, 109l, 110, 112, 114, 118, 121, 122, 127, 128l, 131, 133, 138, 141l, 142, 143, 148, 149, 150, 160, 161l, 161r, 220, 234l, 234r, 236, 237l
Holzbach, R. / Bénet P.   14, 17, 39, 42/43, 51r, 55, 71, 73, 85l, 99, 102, 104, 117, 123, 124, 128r, 129, 130, 132,134, 147, 204, 206, 214/215, 221, 226, 228, 230, 232, 235, 238, 239
Janicke, Volkmar E.   20, 186l, 186r
Joerissen, Heinz   223
Müller, Ernst (Mainbild)   12/13, 50
Müller, Kai-Ulrich   66, 89
PHOTORED-ACTION, Ruhstorf (Helene Hartl and H.-H. Skupy)   18l, 19 33, 36l, 56, 109r, 119, 136/137, 141r, 146, 152/153, 156, 163, 164, 165,166, 168, 169, 170, 171, 172, 174, 176, 178, 180, 182, 183l, 183r, 185, 188, 190, 192, 193, 196, 200, 202/203, 210, 216/217, 218, 219, 229, back cover
Rex, Peter   38, 78, 88, 198, 225
Riethmüller, Robert   74, 227
Scheibner, Johann   68, 100
Schindler, Günter (Mainbild) 16, 23r, 48
Schmerheim, Sigrid   233
Schraml, Oskar (Archiv G. Amberg)   75, 154/155
Schwarz, Heiner   116
Seiffert, K.   87
Skupy-Pesek, Jitka   85r, 113
Stadler, Hubert   8/9, 10/11, 61
Stankiewicz, Thomas   162, 194

251

Explore the World

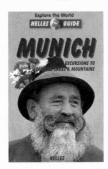

AVAILABLE TITLES

Australia
Bali / Lombok
Berlin and Potsdam
Brazil
Brittany
Burma → *Myanmar*
California
  Las Vegas, Reno,
  Baja California
Cambodia / Laos
Canada
  Ontario, Québec,
  Atlantic Provinces
Canada
  Pacific Coast, the Rockies,
  Prairie Provinces, and
  the Territories
Caribbean
  The Greater Antilles,
  Bermuda, Bahamas
Caribbean
  The Lesser Antilles
China – Hong Kong
Corsica
Crete
Croatia – *Adriatic Coast*
Cyprus
Egypt
Florida
Greece – *The Mainland*
Hawai'i

Hungary
India
  Northern, Northeastern
  and Central India
India – *Southern India*
Indonesia
  Sumatra, Java, Bali,
  Lombok, Sulawesi
Ireland
Israel - *with Excursions*
  to Jordan
Kenya
London, England and
  Wales
Malaysia
Mexico
Morocco
Moscow / St Petersburg
Munich
  Excursions to Castles,
  Lakes & Mountains
Myanmar (Burma)
Nepal
New York – *City and State*
New Zealand
Paris
Philippines
Portugal
Prague / Czech Republic
Provence
Rome

Scotland
South Africa
South Pacific Islands
Spain – *Pyrenees, Atlantic*
  Coast, Central Spain
Spain
  Mediterranean Coast,
  Southern Spain,
  Balearic Islands
Sri Lanka
Syria – *Lebanon*
Tanzania
Thailand
Turkey
Tuscany
U.S.A.
  The East, Midwest and South
U.S.A.
  The West, Rockies and Texas
Vietnam

FORTHCOMING

Canary Islands
Costa Rica
Greek Islands
Maldives
Norway
Poland
Sweden

Nelles Guides – authorative, informed and informative.
Always up-to-date, extensivley illustrated, and with first-rate relief maps.
256 pages, approx. 150 color photos, approx. 25 maps

Explore the World

AVAILABLE TITLES

Nelles Maps in European top quality!
Relief mapping, kilometer charts and tourist attractions.
Always up-to-date!